PROLEGOMENA TO ANY FUTURE MATERIALISM

Series Editors

Slavoj Žižek

Adrian Johnston

Todd McGowan

diaeresis

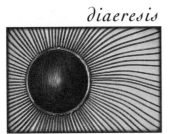

PROLEGOMENA TO ANY FUTURE MATERIALISM

Volume One: The Outcome of Contemporary French Philosophy

Adrian Johnston

Northwestern University Press
Evanston, Illinois

Northwestern University Press
www.nupress.northwestern.edu

Printed in the United States of America

10 9 8 7 6 5 4 3 2 1

Library of Congress Cataloging-in-Publication Data

Johnston, Adrian, 1974–
    Prolegomena to any future materialism. Volume one, The outcome of contemporary French philosophy / Adrian Johnston.
        p. cm. — (Diaeresis)
    "The present book is the first volume of a trilogy entitled Prolegomena to Any Future Materialism, to be followed by A Weak Nature Alone and Substance Also as Subject."
    Includes bibliographical references and index.
    ISBN 978-0-8101-2912-2 (pbk. : alk. paper)
    1. Materialism. 2. Philosophy, French—20th century. 3. Lacan, Jacques, 1901–1981. 4. Badiou, Alain. 5. Meillassoux, Quentin, 1967– I. Title. II. Title: Outcome of contemporary French philosophy. III. Series: Diaeresis.
B1809.M3J64 2013
146.3—dc23

                                                          2012049692

To Ezra, the gift of joyful beginnings

It has been rumored round the town that I have compared the stars to a rash on an organism where the skin erupts into a countless mass of red spots; or to an ant-heap in which, too, there is Understanding and necessity . . . In fact I do rate what is concrete higher than what is abstract, and an animality that develops into no more than a slime, higher than the starry host.

—G. W. F. Hegel

Contents

Preface

Clearing the Ground: The First Volume of
Prolegomena to Any Future Materialism

The present book is the first volume of a trilogy entitled *Prolegomena to Any Future Materialism,* to be followed by *A Weak Nature Alone* and *Substance Also as Subject.* As the title of the trilogy indicates, this project aims to establish the foundations for a new materialist theoretical apparatus. The splitting of this endeavor into three volumes reflects not only my need for a certain amount of textual space in order properly to execute this task—it also reflects a careful division of labor between the portions of this whole.

Volume 1, *The Outcome of Contemporary French Philosophy,* could be characterized as the "negative" introductory component of this project (with *A Weak Nature Alone* and *Substance Also as Subject* functioning as its complementary "positive" components). That is to say, this first volume focuses on critically clearing away an opening within contemporary philosophy/theory for the subsequent presentation, in the second and third volumes, of the specific variant of materialism I seek to spell out (what I call "transcendental materialism," to be defined preliminarily in this book and systematically delineated at length in its sequels). I found it both productive and urgent to engage closely with those figures and frameworks I feel are proximate to, although nonetheless significantly different from, my own approach and orientation to the same set of questions and problems.

To be more precise as regards the trilogy's overall organization, *The Outcome of Contemporary French Philosophy* lays out immanent critiques of three interrelated thinkers: Jacques Lacan, Alain Badiou, and Quentin Meillassoux. The critical assessments articulated herein foreground both what I draw from Lacan, Badiou, and Meillassoux as well as what exact difficulties and shortcomings plaguing their efforts I intend to overcome (in an *Aufhebung*-like manner) during the course of elaborating my variant of materialism in the second and third volumes of the trilogy. *A Weak Nature Alone* and *Substance Also as Subject* proceed to stipulate the necessary (at the level of metatranscendental substance) and sufficient (at the level of transcendental subjectivity) conditions respectively for a transcendental materialist theory of the subject, including this theory's accompanying ontology. The second volume unfolds via a historical narrative running from Hegel through Marxism and up to current Anglo-American analytic philosophy (especially the neo-Hegelianism of Pittsburgh and Chicago). The third volume employs resources appropriated from psychoanalysis, the sciences, and philosophy both historical and contemporary.

I consider the teachings of Lacan to be the most important and prescient source in the recent history of thought for the materialist ontologies advanced by those living thinkers I see myself as closest to in several manners: Badiou and Meillassoux, plus Slavoj Žižek. I have dwelt at length on Žižek's work in two previous books (*Žižek's Ontology: A Transcendental Materialist Theory of Subjectivity* [2008] and *Badiou, Žižek, and Political Transformations: The Cadence of Change* [2009]) as well as elsewhere.[1] In particular, at the conclusion of *Žižek's Ontology*, I outlined specific crucial contours of the materialism I intend to construct in detail over the course of this three-volume project (i.e., transcendental materialism as arising out of criticisms of the interlinked ontology and theory of the subject put forward by Žižekian philosophy).[2] Hence, extended treatments of Žižek's corpus in what follows would be unnecessary and, indeed, redundant.

However, fully acknowledging debts to and settling accounts with my other intellectual neighbors mentioned above (i.e., Lacan, Badiou, and Meillassoux) is mandatory labor that remains to be done. This is all the more obligatory given that I have arrived at the views underpinning my ongoing efforts through readings of and disagreements with these authors as key interlocutors. Specifically, what Lacan, Žižek, Badiou, Meillassoux, and I share in common, to varying degrees, is the pursuit of a materialism that is stringently atheistic (avoiding not only overtly religious, spiritualist, and/or theosophical notions, but also camouflaged versions of these resurfacing in apparently secular guises) and allied to the sciences (albeit with a number of marked divergences between us regarding both which sciences are identified as appropriate allies as well as even what constitutes a science as scientific strictly speaking). Particularly in relation to Lacan, Badiou, and Meillassoux, I am much less wedded to mathematical formalism, less inclined to hold up the formal sciences of mathematics as the alpha and omega of the very nature of scientificity. By sharp contrast, I am much more inclined to consider a substantial reckoning with the empirical, experimental sciences, especially biology with its sprawling branches (i.e., the life sciences), as absolutely indispensable for the formulation of a truly robust materialism uniquely capable of doing justice specifically to the structures and phenomena of subjectivity—structures and phenomena that, in the absence of such a reckoning, otherwise tempt one into entertaining ideas along dualistic and/or metaphysical lines, lines leading straight back to the old spiritualist ontologies of anti-immanentist idealism.

Arguably, the current sociocultural conjuncture involves the historically surprising strengthening of the hegemony of modes of religiosity that some, Marx and Freud quite notably, previously predicted would die a progress-driven death by this point. In terms of the specific textual grounds to be covered by this book, one among innumerable symptoms of this situation is the growing attention to and appreciation of Lacan's now renowned 1974 remarks regarding "the triumph of religion."[3] In stark opposition to the theses of 1927's *The Future of an Illusion*, Lacan predicts that religion will "triumph" not in spite of the thrusts and encroachments of modernizing science and technology, but precisely because of this relentless collective march forward. To be more exact, the Lacanian prophecy apropos this issue is that the more techno-scientific development intensifies and expands the meaninglessness of desacralization and disenchantment, all the more, to a parallel, proportional degree, will people turn to authorities appearing to guarantee the meaningfulness of life and the universe.[4] Lacan associates the attribution of meaning to the Real of being as the essence of religiosity per se. The growing "desert of the Real" is a harsh terrain within which subjects are prone to lapse into religious deliriums and hallucinations. Today's societies are living out the disastrous consequences of this toxic, potent inmixing of religion and science. Stuck between capitalist techno-manipulation and its irrationalist discontents, seesawing between the twin big Others of the Nature of scientism and the God of superstition within the constraining global space of a neo-liberal economy, humanity is stranded in the waking nightmare of a disgustingly reactionary and horrifically hopeless period of history.

As will be seen in the first chapter to follow here, Lacan's quite persuasive correction of Freud's glaringly falsified predictions of the withering away of religions in a world dominated by the Weltanschauung of the secular sciences is reinforced and supplemented by another line of argumentation. Lacan also contends, using such examples as eighteenth-century French materialism and Darwinian evolutionary theory, that the sciences of modernity, although ostensibly atheistic, actually are suffused with theological images and sensibilities. These disciplines and their practitioners tend to imagine material Nature in fashions revealing that this fantasized cosmic One-All, this totalizing big Other ruling the entirety of creation with its unbreakable laws, is a thinly veiled replacement for the presumably dead-and-buried God of monotheisms. This unambiguously indicates that, from a Lacanian perspective, the hegemony of the religious goes so far as not only to continue competing with the scientific long after early Enlightenment predictions bet on its demise, but even to encompass and shape the seemingly secular and atheistic positions of its self-deceived adversaries delusionally fighting it in vain.

Thus, for any materialism indebted to Lacan—this would include the materialisms advocated by Žižek, Badiou, Meillassoux, and me—it is far from enough simply to annex philosophically and speculatively embellish upon the resources and results of one, several, or all of the sciences, be they formal or empirical. In addition, a thoroughgoing theoretical critique of the residual vestiges of religiosity, its lingering ideational and ideological traces, hiding within these fields and their prevailing (self-)interpretations is requisite. Neglecting to carry out this philosophical exorcism dooms any aspiring materialist to remain haunted by ancient specters, to stay in the grip, whether knowingly or not, of stubbornly recalcitrant, resilient ghosts. In Lacan's eyes, an authentically atheistic materialism has yet to be forged (although, especially starting in 1845 with the criticisms of Feuerbachian materialism, Marx and the tradition that comes to bear his name take giant leaps in this direction—admittedly, Lacan tends to overlook most of the Marxist corpus). Žižek, Badiou, and Meillassoux, each in his own way, aspire to accomplish this challenge bequeathed by the French Freud. And yet, as perhaps another symptom of the current conjuncture, the "post-secular" turn in continental philosophy unfortunately has spread from its congenial loci of origin in phenomenology and certain strains of existentialism to infect Lacanian, Žižekian, and Badiouian circles (although Lacan, Žižek, and Badiou are avowed atheists, the fact that they indulge in sophisticated, sensitive treatments of, for instance, Christianity appears to be enough to encourage believers to latch onto them, perhaps attracted by the prospect of being able to dress up their dogmatic faith and rituals in the trendy, sexy attire of the latest avant-garde theoretical vocabularies imported from exotic Europe).

What is more, as will be maintained throughout *The Outcome of Contemporary French Philosophy*, Lacan, Badiou, and Meillassoux, judged by their own standards insofar as each purports to be both an atheist and a materialist, can be seen as failing successfully to forge an authentically atheistic materialism (on separate occasions, I have assessed Žižek along these same lines).[5] In other words, this book contains Hegelian-style immanent critiques of these three thinkers. Continuing in good dialectical fashion in the wake of extracting out of Lacan's, Badiou's, and Meillassoux's bodies of thought those concepts and claims invaluable for my own purposes, both *A Weak Nature Alone* as well as *Substance Also as Subject* will build, on this basis, a new materialism both profoundly influenced by these brilliant comrades of a shared cause as well as making up for the alleged shortcomings of their own attempts creatively to bring to realization the Lacanian vision of an Other-less, One-less ontology. Hopefully, this project will yield intellectual weapons suitable for deployment on multiple fronts simultaneously, able to be employed with equal effectiveness against the mutually entangled spiritualist and scientistic foes of today's post-Enlightenment, biopolitical era of nothing more than commodities and currencies.

Albuquerque, May 2012

Acknowledgments

I would like to begin by thanking all the friends and interlocutors with whom I have had the privilege and the pleasure of discussing the ideas that went into this book. Without them, this text would not exist. I am especially grateful to Alain Badiou, Richard Boothby, Bruno Bosteels, Nora Brank, Ray Brassier, Thomas Brockelman, Nathan Brown, Michael Burns, Lorenzo Chiesa, Tucker Dammin, Marc De Kesel, Paul Flaig, Martin Hägglund, Peter Hallward, Graham Harman, Reuben Hersh, Aaron Hodges, Dominiek Hoens, Tyler Innis, Thomas Johnston, Paul Livingston, Catherine Malabou, Tracy McNulty, Michael Olson, Knox Peden, Kenneth Reinhard, Jeremi Roth, Michael Shim, Gino Signoracci, Daniel Lord Smail, Brian Smith, Iain Thomson, Kathryn Wichelns, Jean Wyatt, Slavoj Žižek, and Alenka Zupančič. Additionally, the Theory Reading Group at Cornell University deserves special mention for having organized a series of outstanding annual gatherings that deeply shaped the content of this project; it was an honor and a joy to participate in those events. I also would like to thank both the Seminar in Experimental Critical Theory at the University of California, Los Angeles, and the Department of Philosophy at the University of Guelph for providing me, as a visiting speaker, with extremely useful critical feedback on this book's second and third chapters respectively. Finally, the excellent group of participants in my 2009 spring semester seminar on Badiou in the Department of Philosophy at the University of New Mexico helped inspire several of the ideas and arguments in this book.

I am delighted to be collaborating with Northwestern University Press on yet another project. They are an outstanding publisher with which to work. In particular, I profoundly appreciate the support and assistance of Anthony Steinbock, Henry Carrigan, and Anne Gendler.

As always, nothing would be possible for me without Kathryn Wichelns.

Modified portions of this volume have appeared, or are soon to appear, in several different venues: "Conflicted Matter: Jacques Lacan and the

Challenge of Secularizing Materialism," *Pli: The Warwick Journal of Philosophy*, no. 19 (Spring 2008): 166–88 (chapter 1); "Turning the Sciences Inside Out: Revisiting Lacan's 'Science and Truth,'" in *Concept and Form, Volume Two: Interviews and Essays on the Cahiers pour l'Analyse*, ed. Peter Hallward and Knox Peden (London: Verso, 2012) (chapter 2); "On Deep History and Lacan," *Journal of European Psychoanalysis*, no. 32, special issue: "Lacan and Philosophy: The New Generation," ed. Lorenzo Chiesa (2012): 91–121 (chapter 3); "What Matter(s) in Ontology: Alain Badiou, the Hebb-Event, and Materialism Split from Within," *Angelaki: Journal of the Theoretical Humanities* 13, no. 1 (April 2008): 27–49 (chapter 4); "Phantom of Consistency: Alain Badiou and Kantian Transcendental Idealism," *Continental Philosophy Review* 41, no. 3 (September 2008): 345–66 (chapter 5); "The World Before Worlds: Quentin Meillassoux and Alain Badiou's Anti-Kantian Transcendentalism," *Contemporary French Civilization* 33, no. 1 (Winter/Spring 2009): 73–99 (chapter 6); "Hume's Revenge: À Dieu, Meillassoux?," in *The Speculative Turn: Continental Materialism and Realism,* ed. Levi Bryant, Graham Harman, and Nick Srnicek (Melbourne: Re.press, 2010), 92–113 (chapter 7); "Pseudo-emergence: Against Meillassoux's Duotheism," *Umbr(a): A Journal of the Unconscious,* Buffalo: Center for the Study of Psychoanalysis and Culture, State University of New York at Buffalo (2013) (postface). I appreciate the editors allowing these portions to reappear here.

PROLEGOMENA TO ANY FUTURE MATERIALISM

"One Surely Will Be Found One Day to Make an Ontology with What I Am Telling You": The Road to a Post-Lacanian Materialism

In 1972, during a session of his nineteenth seminar (. . . *ou pire*), Lacan confidently predicts the eventual arrival of a novel brand of philosophy, a prediction that indeed now looks to have been amply vindicated. In the context of a discussion involving references to Plato's *Parmenides* and the theme of "the One"—the ears of connoisseurs of Badiou's philosophical writings cannot but prick up here[1]—he rather smugly prophesies that "one surely will be found one day to make an ontology with what I am telling you."[2] However off-putting Lacan's characteristic arrogance might be, one would be hard-pressed to deny that three of the most prominent figures on the contemporary French/French-inspired philosophical scene—these three are Žižek, Badiou, and Meillassoux—indeed set about constructing ontologies faithful to the later Lacan of the nonexistent big Other (*à la "le grand Autre n'existe pas"*), the psychoanalytic thinker of the not-All (*pas tout*) and a detotalized Real.

Of course, Žižek is adamant about being "a card-carrying Lacanian" (as he vehemently proclaims in a scene from Astra Taylor's 2005 documentary film *Žižek!: The Movie*) and is entirely explicit about his elevation of Lacan's declaration "the big Other does not exist" to the status of being an axiomatic tenet of his philosophical system.[3] Badiou initially might seem slightly less directly (self-)placed in a Lacanian lineage, at least in terms of his set-theoretic, post-Cantorian mathematical (meta-) ontology. But this first impression is utterly misleading. Although, in his 1989 *Manifesto for Philosophy*, Badiou appears to relegate Lacan's influence on his thought to merely one of his four extra-philosophical "conditions" as "generic procedures" of truth-production (i.e., art, love, politics, and science)—Lacan is credited with an evental rethinking specifically of love[4]—other Badiouian texts both before and after this first of his two succinct philosophical manifestos testify to a much deeper indebtedness to Lacanian analytic theory. Even within other of the pages of the first *Manifesto,* Lacan is crowned "the greatest of our dead";[5] also therein, Badiou likewise declares that "a philosophy is possible today, only if it is compossible with Lacan."[6] Maybe one should add to this by way of specifying that any cutting-edge materialist ontology and corresponding account of subjectivity nowadays must situate itself in Lacan's long shadow.

The slightly younger, pre-1988 (*Being and Event*) Badiou is at least as emphatic in this vein.[7] For this Maoist adherent of dialectical materialism, "Lacan . . . is our Hegel"[8] and "entirely like Hegel for Marx, Lacan is for us essential and divisible."[9] In a eulogy for *le maître absolu* written shortly after his death in 1981, Badiou reiterates these assertions—"For a French Marxist of today, Lacan functions as Hegel did for a German revolutionary of 1840."[10] *The Outcome of Contemporary French Philosophy* undertakes, among other things, a reinterpretation of Lacan very much along the lines indicated by Badiou (as will be evident in its first part). That is to say, this book, as a famous line from the first volume of *Das Kapital* has it, seeks "to discover the rational kernel within the mystical shell"[11] of Lacanianism. In particular, as does Badiou in his comparison of Lacan with Marx's "essential" Hegel, the project launched by this volume, while recognizing Lacan as crucial for the formulation of a lively, combative materialism for today, also takes seriously and renders quite precise his "divisibility" indicated by Badiou in conjunction with his essentiality ("essential and divisible"). To be more precise still, Lacan's thinking, despite its avowed allegiance to dialectics, materialism (of a somewhat strange sort),[12] and atheism (as the "barring" of all big Others), is nonetheless clouded by occasional bouts of backsliding into dangerous flirtations with Catholicism and a virulent hostility to the life sciences (albeit a hostility subtly qualified in thus-far underappreciated ways).[13] Ironically, notwithstanding his above-quoted remarks regarding Lacan, the same could be said of Badiou and Meillassoux too—or, at least, such will be one of the core contentions of the second and third parts of the book. In fact, all three of the authors of concern in the three parts of *The Outcome of Contemporary French Philosophy* (i.e., Lacan, Badiou, and Meillassoux) will be treated as divisible in Badiou's sense, namely, as treatable in the manner Marx treats Hegel. In each case, the task will be to extract from them crucial ingredients for a new materialism up to the challenging difficulties of the philosophical, political, scientific, and psychoanalytic present, all the while at the same time discarding certain rotten husks in which these ingredients sometimes remain encased. To put this in Hegelian phrasing, this will be a matter of raising Lacanian, Badiouian, and Meillassouxian materialisms to the dignity of their Notions, a process inseparable from an immanent critique of these thinkers' actually assumed stances.

As indicated, this book, the first volume of a trilogy, is itself organized into three parts. The first part, devoted to Lacan, consists of three chapters; the second and third parts, devoted to Badiou and then Meillassoux, each consist of two chapters. Badiou and Meillassoux are read as descendants (direct and indirect respectively) of the Lacan foretelling of future philosophers who will erect ontologies on the basis of his analytic teachings—hence their being placed after Lacan (with Badiou and Meillassoux being sequenced vis-à-vis each other as teacher and student). What follows in the rest of this introductory section is an outline of the seven chapters of the book explaining their individual contents and how they are related to compose the book as a whole.

The first chapter ("Conflicted Matter: The Challenge of Secularizing Materialism") pushes off from a succinct set of remarks made by Lacan during the course of his renowned seventeenth seminar of 1969–1970. Therein, he astutely observes how certain varieties of materialism, while being apparently atheistic, actually harbor hidden kernels of religiosity. In the context of ongoing discussions and debates regarding materialism today, these remarks now sound like a farseeing warning given that particular trajectories within post-Lacanian theory, supposedly materialist in orientation, openly conspire with elements of Christianity (not to mention the latent and blatant dogmas of various pseudosecular scientisms). Lacan's glosses on these issues can be heard as calling for further labor toward the elaboration of a completely secularized and genuinely atheistic materialism. The resources for this task, the initiation of which is attempted here, are drawn from a philosophically coordinated interfacing of psychoanalytic metapsychology, dialectical materialism, and cognitive neuroscience (with this interfacing itself taking guidance from Catherine Malabou's admirable, courageous efforts to bring together the neurosciences and select European theoretical traditions). Near the end of the chapter, a passage back through Lacan's discourse on the triumph of religion allows for the axiom of a Godless ontology of material being to be formulated as follows: There is just a weak nature (as conflict-ridden matrices of under-determination), and nothing more (an axiom later to serve as an anchor for the sequel volume *A Weak Nature Alone*).

The second and third chapters fundamentally are centered on isolating and criticizing two facets of Lacanianism: one, Lacan's anti-biologistic perspectives on the sciences (the second chapter) and, two, his intermittent reliance on sublimated and not-so-sublimated channelings of Christianity (the third chapter). The second chapter ("Turning the Sciences Inside Out: Revisiting 'Science and Truth'"), as its subtitle announces, orients itself through a careful parsing of Lacan's seminal *écrit* "*La science et la vérité*." During the course of this, it submits to trenchant scrutiny Lacan's and various Lacanians' excessive privileging of form (or formalism) over matter (and therefore, arguably, materialism) in their structuralist-inflected considerations of the sciences taken over straight from the philosopher and historian of science Alexandre Koyré. Koyré's Galileo-centric narrative of the history of the genesis of modern science, a genesis he ties to the Galilean view of mathematics as the language of nature, is equally authoritative for Badiou and Meillassoux as well. Whereas Lacan, Badiou, and Meillassoux favor an exclusively Galilean-Cartesian conception of scientificity, my project implicitly brings back into the picture the Baconian roots of the sciences. This amounts to an insistence that the "new method" of empirical experimentation (crucial to Galileo as well as Bacon) cannot be historically revised away at the behest of an agenda to reduce scientificity to nothing more than pure mathematical-style formalization alone. In this chapter, I return to the Freud of biology (i.e., the Freud Lacan questionably downplays and selectively bypasses in favor of the Freud of the signifier)[14] and couple this Freud with a range of current resources. On this basis, I put forward the thesis that a time both Freud and, once in a while, even Lacan permit themselves to anticipate finally has arrived and must now be recognized and declared: a moment when the life sciences are willing and able (even if not yet with widespread self-conscious transparency on their own) to vindicate some of the load-bearing speculative elements of the metapsychological edifice of psychoanalysis.[15]

The third chapter ("On Deep History and Psychoanalysis: Phylogenetic Time in Lacanian Theory") mounts an assault on a cherished article of faith in Lacanianism: the assertion that historical inquiries, whether ontogenetic individual histories or phylogenetic collective histories, extending beyond as before/behind the mediation of languages and symbolic orders are illegitimate and out of bounds. Of course, for different reasons, Badiou and Meillassoux similarly take issue with Lacanian-style linguistic idealism. Although tacitly agreeing with many of Badiou's objections to "*idéalinguisterie*" and Meillassoux's to "correlationism" (to be discussed in the second and third parts respectively), this chapter problematizes Lacan's prohibitions on queries into everything which precedes the symbolico-linguistic from an angle different from that of Badiou or Meillassoux. (Incidentally, Lacan's regressions back to Catholicism are at their worst and most flagrant around his recurrent pronouncements of a ban on asking the question of the origin of language, with the biblical line "In the beginning was the Word" and references to the Holy Spirit making repeated appearances in these contexts.) Drawing on historian Daniel Lord Smail's intriguing 2008 book *On Deep History and the Brain,* a book inventively blending the sciences of nature (especially the neurosciences) and culture, I level a series of arguments against Lacan's justifications for casting any and every being prior to the mysterious, impenetrable advent of *"le Verbe"* into the dark abyss of a noumenal, epistemologically inaccessible Real. This standard, orthodox Lacanian gesture bears witness to the lurking presence of a disguised, un-worked-through Judeo-Christian heritage persisting within Lacan's generally atheistic outlook. What is more, overcoming the Lacanian position challenged in this chapter is necessary for the genetic-emergentist model of subjectivity proposed as an essential component of the transcendental materialism of a weak nature advocated by my three-volume project. This is because the biologically informed picture of the temporally elongated dynamics of subject-formation painted in the first chapter of this book (as well as on numerous other occasions by me) is an ontogenetic narrative. As such, it presupposes the existence of a trans-subjective backdrop (in Lacanese, the sociosymbolic constellations of already-there big Others) into which the singular subject-to-be is thrown. Even if biomaterialist additions to the Freudian-Lacanian account of ontogenetic subject-formation are granted, analytic opponents of this sort of science-informed enterprise ultimately could counter that, in the absence of a purportedly impossible and unfeasible phylogenetic narrative of the very emergence of the sociolinguistic dimension of culture out of nature, an antinaturalist creed is preferable and superior to naturalist dabblings. For the cause motivating this entire project, putting to rest such resistances—these resistances also operate as rationalizations for those who wish to bury their heads in stale sand, thereby complacently and comfortably ignoring momentous intellectual upheavals going on all around them outside their scholarly comfort zones of specialization—is a requisite, integral step in the direction of a defensible materialism drawing strength from so much of what is insightful and groundbreaking in Lacan's sublimely rich oeuvre.

The second part of the book advances a two-pronged attack on Badiouian materialism as one of its most formidable and worthy adversaries. The fourth chapter ("What Matter(s) in Ontology: The Hebb-Event and Materialism Split from Within") casts Badiou's materialist credentials directly into doubt and the fifth chapter ("Phantom of Consistency: Kant Troubles"), dovetailing with the fourth, undermines Badiou's attempts to distance himself as far as possible from Kantian transcendental idealism (as perhaps the strongest and most plausible of the philosophies opposed to materialism). To go into more detail, the fourth chapter juxtaposes Badiou's professions of being a materialist with his musings on scientificity (an assumption behind this project is that no materialism deserving of the title can avoid an intimate alliance with the modern, post-Baconian/Galilean sciences). Badiou presents his philosophy as thoroughly and consistently materialist in ways that follow in the footsteps of thinkers ranging from Lucretius to Mao. However, considering Badiou's decision to restrict ontology to the formal science of mathematics, there are numerous reasons for suspecting that his philosophical framework, at least in the wake of *Being and Event,* fails to remain faithful to some of the most basic and foundational principles of materialism. In particular, his problematic antinaturalism, entailing a wholesale rejection of the life sciences as relevant to forging a materialist theory of subjectivities, is at risk of legitimating varieties of religious and spiritualist metaphysics. Moreover, Badiou's presumptions regarding the notions of nature at stake in the natural sciences are, at this point in time, both theoretically and empirically indefensible. Again following the lead of Malabou, there is an alternative to be explored here: expressed in Badiouian terms, the metaontological choice to recognize the discovery of the brain's plasticity as an event (i.e., the neuroscientific Hebb-Event, named after Donald O. Hebb) with numerous crucial ramifications for ontology promises to provide a crucial component for the articulation of a truly materialist account of subjectivity—an account without which, as Marxist materialism from 1845 and after warns, one is unpalatably left with either dualistic idealism or the reductive/eliminative monism of mechanistic materialism (whether eighteenth- or twenty-first-century versions), the latter replacing the God of monotheistic theologies with the stand-in of a taken-on-faith Nature to which the powers of the old divinity are transferred.

The fifth chapter departs from a focus on Badiou's identification of Kant as one of his principal philosophical enemies. Kant's critical philosophy is anathema to Badiou not only because of the latter's openly aired hatred of the motif of finitude so omnipresent in post-Kantian European intellectual traditions—Badiou blames Kant for inventing this motif—but also because of its idealism. For Badiou-the-materialist, as for any serious philosophical materialist writing in Kant's aftermath, transcendental idealism must be dismantled and surpassed. In his recent works (especially 2006's *Logics of Worlds: Being and Event, 2*), Badiou attempts to invent a non-Kantian notion of the transcendental, a notion compatible with the basic propositions of materialism. However, from *Being and Event* up through the present, Badiou's oeuvre contains indications that he has not managed fully to purge the traces of

Kantian transcendental idealism that arguably continue to haunt his system—with these traces clustering around a concept Badiou christens "counting-for-one" (*compter-pour-un*). The result is that, when all is said and done, Kant's shadow still falls over Badiouian philosophy—this is despite Badiou's admirable, sophisticated, and instructive attempts to step out from under it—thus calling into question this philosophy's self-proclaimed status as materialist through and through. To be clear, I am in fundamental solidarity with Badiou (and Meillassoux) in his critiques of Kantian transcendental idealism and post-Kantian philosophies of the fetishized finite. However, I think that Badiou's non-Hegelian assaults on Kantianism and its offspring ultimately fail.

The transition from the second to the third parts of the book follows Badiou's own appeals—these appeals are made in his struggles to separate himself from Kant investigated in the preceding fifth chapter—to the work of his student Meillassoux. In his ostensibly materialist efforts to delineate a new conception of the transcendental distinct from that of Kantian transcendental idealism, efforts at the heart of *Logics of Worlds,* Badiou partially relies upon the arguments of his protégé. Éditions du Seuil released Meillassoux's debut book, *After Finitude: An Essay on the Necessity of Contingency,* just a couple of months before Badiou's sequel to *Being and Event;* and the latter (*Logics of Worlds*) makes explicit references to the former (*After Finitude*). And yet, although Meillassoux is a student of Badiou, there are significant differences between them which the sixth chapter ("The World Before Worlds: The Ancestral and Badiou's Anti-Kantian Transcendentalism") seeks to clarify and sharpen. In this chapter, I make the argument that *After Finitude* fails to provide *Logics of Worlds* with what this key component of Badiou's philosophical system needs in order to advance a transcendentalism purified of all Kantian and/or idealist traces of an invariably accompanying subjectivity (i.e., a transcendental without a transcendental subject). But, going even further, I maintain that Meillassoux's brand of realist "speculative materialism" implicitly contests Badiou's claims to be an uncompromising, full-fledged materialist. Placed side by side with Meillassoux, who embraces the natural sciences as integral to any realist materialism worthy of the name, Badiou, with his antinaturalism (inherited straight from mid-century Sartrean phenomenological existentialism and fueled by Badiou's understandable polemical opposition to the capitalist biopolitics of what he calls "democratic materialism"), ends up appearing to be far from loyal to materialism as developed from Lucretius onwards. Here, the master must become the student of his student if he wishes to make his "materialist dialectic," as presented in *Logics of Worlds,* truly materialist in more than name alone.[16]

But, as foreshadowed in the later portions of the sixth chapter and articulated at length throughout the seventh chapter ("Hume's Revenge: À *Dieu*, Meillassoux?"), the case is made that any living materialist preserving a fidelity to the dual legacies of Marxism and psychoanalysis (not to mention to the sciences of modernity) ought to be profoundly ambivalent toward Meillassoux's speculative materialism. On the one hand, *After Finitude* takes significant strides in rendering increasingly implausible antirealist tendencies prominent (although not uniformally dominant) across the two-century span of post-Kantian European philosophy.[17] Meillassoux is adept at revealing the absurd conclusions adherents of these antirealist doctrines would be led to if they were to be logically consequent about their convictions. Moreover, he is quite right to maintain that the sciences and some of their spontaneous philosophies (as Louis Althusser would put it) are an indigestible bone in the throat for much of continental antirealism. However, on the other hand, the ontology Meillassoux opts to posit on the basis of his realist anticorrelationism not only immediately poisons fatally his attempted rapprochement between the long-estranged couple of European philosophy and the sciences—this incipient system, centered on Meillassoux's concept of a "hyper-Chaos" arrived at through a hasty ontologization of Hume's epistemological problem of induction, ends up preaching an odd gospel: what Meillassoux christens his "divinology" of a God who does not yet exist, but might at any moment. The rightfully dismissive scorn for postsecular "fideism" expressed in *After Finitude* distracts from what must strike the minimally discerning eye as, in several fashions, a reenactment of pre-Kantian theosophies that were deservedly and decisively demolished by Kant's critical turn. The *Critique of Pure Reason* marks a pivotal historical point of no return, even for materialism as incompatible with Kantian transcendental idealism.

The postface outlines exactly how the two sequel volumes of *Prolegomena to Any Future Materialism* (*A Weak Nature Alone* and *Substance Also as Subject*) go on to advance a realist materialism that avoids the problems and pitfalls plaguing Lacan, Badiou, and Meillassoux as portrayed herein while simultaneously retaining the laudable merits of their substantial contributions to thought. Each faux pas by them, as taken up in what ensues below, should be considered in a Hegelian light as a *felix culpa*, a fortunate misstep mapping out paths leading to truths that come into view precisely thanks to these very falsehoods and errors. Such is the trajectory ahead.

Part 1

Jacques Lacan: Between the Sacred and the Secular

1

Conflicted Matter: The Challenge of Secularizing Materialism

§1 Emerging Cracks: The Birth of a Truly Atheistic Materialism

Materialism, the brute insistence that there is nothing alien to matter, appears to offer no place whatsoever to anything even vaguely intangible or spiritual. It denies that there are ineffable entities or forms set apart from the immanence of incarnate beings. Badiou characterizes this basic position of vehement opposition vis-à-vis all varieties of idealism as "a philosophy of assault."[1] More specifically, materialist philosophies throughout history exhibit a common hostility toward religiosity insofar as the latter appeals to the supposed existence of some sort of extraphysical, immaterial dimension of transcendent (ultra-)being. From Lucretius to La Mettrie and beyond, the natural world of the material universe is celebrated, in an anti-Platonic vein, as a self-sufficient sphere independent of ideas or gods.[2] A properly materialist ontology posits matter alone— nothing more, nothing less.

And yet, despite the clarity and simplicity of this rejection of spirituality in all its guises, a rejection functioning as an essential defining feature of any and every species of materialism, periodic critical reminders seemingly are necessary in order to ward off the recurrent tendency to backslide into idealism through blurring the lines of demarcation between materialism and what it rejects. A century ago, V. I. Lenin, in his 1908 text *Materialism and Empirio-Criticism,* issues just such a reminder (a reminder drawing heavily upon Friedrich Engels's insistence, in his 1888 *Ludwig Feuerbach and the Outcome of Classical German Philosophy,* on the centrality of this elementary, insurmountable "split . . . into two great camps,"[3] that is, materialism and idealism). Regardless of the many philosophical shortcomings of this hundred-year-old book (as well as its sheer monotony and mind-numbing repetitiveness), one of its priceless virtues is Lenin's unflinching insistence on the indissoluble, black-and-white border strictly separating materialism from idealism. Lenin tirelessly uncovers, exposes, and critiques a number of subtle and not-so-subtle efforts to disguise and pass off idealist notions as materialist concepts, efforts to soften the stinging antispiritualist, irreligious virulence of this ruthlessly combative philosophical stance. Just as Søren Kierkegaard maintains that agnosticism ultimately cannot distinguish itself from atheism[4]—for Kierkegaard, as for Blaise Pascal,[5] not choosing to believe (i.e., agnosticism) is still tantamount to choosing not to believe (i.e., atheism)—so too does Lenin contend that there is no genuine middle ground between materialism and idealism, with any compromise or negotiation between the two amounting, in the de facto end, to a disingenuous, obfuscating betrayal of the materialist position in favor of idealist tendencies.[6]

To resuscitate the heart of materialism today, another such Leninist gesture is urgently called for in light of recent philosophical trends seeking to render materialist thinking compatible with such orientations as Platonism and Judeo-Christianity. Materialism is at risk of, as it were, losing its soul in these confused current circumstances, since it is nothing without its denial of the existence of deities or any other ephemeral pseudothings utterly unrelated to the realness of the beings of matter. Succinctly stated, a nonatheistic materialism is a contradiction in terms. When, for instance, the objects/referents of theology, mathematics, and structuralism are spoken of as though they are equally as "material" as the entities and phenomena addressed by the natural sciences, something is terribly wrong. At a minimum, this muddle-headed situation raises a red flag signaling that the word "matter" has become practically meaningless. Dangerous dilutions of materialism, dilutions resembling the then contemporary trends of Machism and empirio-monism denounced by Lenin in 1908 as means for weakening and subverting materialism, are part of the contemporary scene in the theoretical humanities. Another materialist effort at assault is required once more, a stubborn, unsubtle effort that single-mindedly refuses to be distracted and derailed from its task by engaging with the seductive nuances and intricacies of elaborate systems of spiritualism however honestly displayed or deceptively hidden. In light of Lacan's insistence that the truth is sometimes stupid[7]— one easily can miss it and veer off into errors and illusions under the influence of the assumption that it must be profoundly elaborate and obscure—a tactical, healthy dose of pig-headed, close-minded stupidity on behalf of materialism might be warranted nowadays.

Strangely enough, in a session of his famous seventeenth seminar on *The Other Side of Psychoanalysis* given during the academic year 1969–1970, Lacan utters some rather cryptic remarks that predict a resurfacing of the need for a new purifying purge of the ranks of materialism, enabling the line separating it from idealism to be drawn yet again in a bold, unambiguous fashion. Therein, he advances a surprising thesis—"materialists are the only authentic believers"[8] (this thesis is later echoed in the twentieth seminar of 1972–1973[9] as well as foreshadowed by discussions in the seventh seminar of 1959–1960 about the concealed presence of God in evolutionism).[10] Of course, what renders this quite counterintuitive claim initially so odd is the deeply ingrained association between materialism and atheism. At its very core, does not material-ism constitute a rude, violent attack upon the conceptual foundations of all religions? Do not the diverse manifestations of this philosophical discipline—in 1970, Lacan clarifies that the materialism he has in mind here is that of the eighteenth century in particular (i.e., that elaborated by Julien Offray de La Mettrie, Denis Diderot, and the Marquis de Sade, among others)—share an antipathy toward faith in anything above and beyond the de-spiritualized immanence of the material universe? This very last word ("universe"), insofar as it implies a vision of material being as the integrated organic totality of a cosmic One-All, contains the key to decoding productively Lacan's startling assertion that the material-ism usually hovering around and informing the natural sciences—the naturalism espoused during the eighteenth century arguably continues to serve, more often than not, as (to quote Althusser) the spontaneous philosophy of the scientists—represents a disguised body of religious belief despite itself.

Through the example of Sade (in particular, select passages to be found in his *Juliette*),[11] Lacan explains that the materialists of the eighteenth century end up making matter into God[12] (and doing so, it might be noted, in certain ways resonating with the ancient atomism of Lucretius).[13] Material being becomes something eternal, indestructible, and omnipotent (the first two of these three features allegedly being embodied, in Sade's writings, by the immortal body of the torturer's vic-tim, a fantasized flesh able to endure indefinitely an infinite amount of pain).[14] Lacan views the Sadian flux of nature, with its intense processes of becoming, as the basis for a monotheism-in-bad-faith resting on foun-dations not so different from those of the enshrined religions spurned by the ostensibly atheist libertine. Apart from Sade's views on nature, Lacan also emphasizes again and again how Sade's practical philosophy (specifically his ethics) involves the pseudotransgressions of a perverse subject; this subject's vain, petty pleasures either secretly strive to sustain the existence of a God-like big Other serving as a locus of moral judg-ment in relation to his or her perverse activities or pretend to be placed at the service of this Other's enjoyment.[15] In the case of Sade *avec* Lacan, the supposedly vanquished divinity of monotheistic religion returns with a vengeance in the guise of a system of nature at one with itself, a cos-mos harmoniously constituting the sum total of reality (much like the murdered primal father of Freud's *Totem and Taboo*, who is endowed with even greater potency when reincarnated in the form of a body of pro-hibitory laws).[16] God is far from dead so long as nature is reduced to being the receptacle for and receiver of his attributes and powers. It is not much of a leap to propose that the scientism accompanying modern natural science as a whole, up through the present, tends to be inclined to embrace the nonempirical supposition of the ultimate cohesion of the material universe as a self-consistent One-All (hence, in the twenty-fourth seminar, Lacan's assertion that science, even in the current era, relies upon "the idea of God").[17] In this resides its hidden theosophical nucleus. Lacan's claims regarding Sade and eighteenth-century materi-alisms, materialisms still alive and well today, imply a challenge to which a novel contemporary constellation involving alliances between fac-tions within philosophy, science, and psychoanalysis can and must rise: the challenge of formulating a fully secularized materialism, a Godless ontology of material being nonetheless able to account for those things whose (apparent) existence repeatedly lures thinkers onto the terrain of idealist metaphysics.

§2 "You've Got to Break Some Eggs to Make an *Hommelette*": Lacan and the Materialist Legacies of Eighteenth-Century France

Sade isn't the only example of the disavowed or repressed religiosity Lacan imputes to the materialism of eighteenth-century France. The contemporaries La Mettrie and Diderot are, in peculiar manners, more productive to examine here. The Lacan of the 1950s is understandably rather critical of La Mettrie's mechanical materialism, despite sympathet-ically viewing La Mettrie as a precursor of cybernetics[18] (of course, cyber-netics is the parent discipline of what comes to be cognitive science[19]— and, at the time, Lacan sees cybernetics as moving along lines similar to his antihumanist accounts of the symbolic-linguistic structuring of the unconscious and subjectivity).[20] In particular, he is wary of La Mettrie's grounding of the human creature's machine-like being in the physical stuff of the natural, organic body.[21] For Lacan, psychoanalysis, starting with Freud himself and continuing through ego psychology and object-relations theory, recurrently expresses the craving for the reassurance that there's a solid biological foundation (as bodily energy, instinctual forces, etc.) underpinning the conceptual scaffolding of metapsychol-ogy. Due to this craving, something akin to the mechanistic materialism of La Mettrie allegedly exerts an attractive pull on the imaginations of analysts.[22] Lacan is opposed here not so much to the mechanistic depiction of humanity—during this early period of *le Séminaire*, he often portrays his quasi-structuralist antihumanism as likewise, so to speak, in-humanizing human beings such that they come to resemble machines run by the programs of impersonal symbol systems—but to the naturalizing materialism of La Mettrie (and, by extension, the Diderot who unreservedly tethers the soul [*l'âme*] to the body).[23] He contends that analysts who surrender to the temptation to hypothesize biological grounds for the phenomena addressed by analysis succumb to an illusion, misrecognizing the Symbolic dimension of the non-biological, structural dynamics of signifiers as the Real dimension of the natural flesh of the human animal.[24] From a perspective concerned with the distinction between materialism and idealism, it seems that Badiou is not without a certain amount of justification for accusing this Lacan of "*idéalinguisterie*," an antimaterialist, macro-level idealism of the symbolic order in which a transindividual, semidematerialized formal network autonomously dictates the functioning of its subjected subjects.[25]

However, La Mettrie's materialism merits closer examination in light of my agenda to forge a thoroughly atheistic materialism using select resources from philosophy, psychoanalysis, and the natural sciences. On the one hand, La Mettrie cannot be exculpated in the face of charges (leveled by Lacan, among others) that he promotes a vulgar naturalism according to which the only real reality is that of physical bodies. He is indeed largely guilty of striking such a stance. And yet, on the other hand, despite his endorsement of a reductive monism of unified, conflict-free corporeal substance—La Mettrie speaks of everything as having been shaped out of "but one dough"[26] and of "the material unity of man"[27]—he subsequently veers, somewhat inconsistently, in the direction of a Spinozistic dual-aspect monism (the inconsistency being the fact that Baruch Spinoza's monistic God-substance is neither thinking nor extended substance, with both the ideas of minds and the parts of bodies being two aspects [i.e., "attributes"] of this one neither-mental-nor-physical substance).[28] La Mettrie admits that, despite his insistence on the dependence of the spiritual mind/soul upon the stuff of the body (with its material brain), the details of the rapport binding the former to the latter remain mysterious—"we come to connect the admirable power of thought with matter, without being able to see the links, because the subject of this attribute is essentially unknown to us."[29] He goes on to declare that "man is a machine, and . . . in the whole universe there is but a single substance differently modified."[30] It is somewhat unclear whether this "single substance" is still strictly corporeal in nature, especially if, as in Spinoza's rationalist metaphysics, "thought" and "matter" are two different modifications of a single, universal substance. Perhaps

La Mettrie's 1747 assertions, whether intentionally or unintentionally, open onto the enigma/problem of constructing a materialism that can affirm, at the same time, both a monism of matter as well as a distinction between matter and mind without invoking a God-substance as a medium inexplicably sustaining an all-encompassing unity-in-difference. In this vein, Lenin insists, "That both thought and matter are 'real,' *i.e.,* exist, is true. But to say that thought is material is to make a false step, a step towards confusing materialism and idealism."[31] The difficulty would be to formulate a materialist distinction between the physical and the mental without simply reducing the latter to the former,[32] a difficulty Badiou too identifies when, in his 1982 *Theory of the Subject,* he depicts materialism as resting on two axioms in tension with each other: first, the monist thesis "There is the One" (i.e., the "thesis of identity"), meaning that, ontologically speaking, there is only matter as the "the primitive unity of being"; and, second, the posited hegemony of matter over mind (i.e., the "thesis of primacy"), a posited hegemony that seems to contradict the first monist thesis by maintaining that "There is the Two" (i.e., the dualist thesis that there is a distinction between that which is material and that which is not).[33] Or, as the cognitive scientist Douglas Hofstadter admits, neither monism nor dualism is an unproblematic ontological option.[34] Anyhow, apropos La Mettrie, Lacan would point out that what still remains religious in his thinking is the insistence on the fundamental self-consistency of nature as an undivided cosmic totality.

Diderot's 1769 *D'Alembert's Dream* contains an explicit affirmation of the unified oneness of a natural All as the sole real being to be hypothesized by a defensible ontology. Through the mouth of d'Alembert, Diderot proclaims:

> You talk of individuals, you poor philosophers! Stop thinking about your individuals and answer me this: Is there in nature any one atom exactly similar to another? No . . . Don't you agree that in nature everything is bound up with everything else, and that there cannot be a gap in the chain? Then what are you talking about with your individuals? There is no such thing; no, no such thing. There is but one great individual, and that is the whole. In this whole, as in any machine or animal, there is a part which you may call such and such, but when you apply the term individual to this part of a whole you are employing as false a concept as though you applied the term individual to a bird's wing or to a single feather of that wing. You poor philosophers, and you talk about essences! Drop your idea of essences. Consider the general mass.[35]

From the perspective of a Lacanian consideration of the division between religious and atheistic materialisms, the latter entails insisting that there indeed are "gaps" subsisting within the natural world of the material universe, that it is not the case that "everything is bound up with everything else" in the form of some sort of homogenous continuum. La Mettrie and Diderot (as well as Sade) follow in the footsteps of Spinoza insofar as they subscribe to the philosophical fantasy of substantial being as an exhaustively integrated and entirely self-cohering field devoid of real ruptures or splits. Nature is here imagined to be a clockwork machine whose gears and mechanisms hum away as components smoothly synched up with each other in a seamless system of grand-scale organization, a symphonic part-whole harmony or perfect symbiosis between microcosm and macrocosm. Later in *D'Alembert's Dream,* the character Bordeu asserts, "Nothing that exists can be against nature or outside nature."[36] On a particular reading, this assertion regarding the uninterrupted internal consistency of the natural world might sound slightly dissonant with some observations made by this same character at a previous moment in the dialogue. Earlier, Bordeu states: "There may be only one center of consciousness in an animal, but there are countless impulses, for each organ has its own."[37] He continues:

> The stomach wants some food, but the palate doesn't, and the difference between the palate and the stomach on the one hand and the complete animal on the other is that the animal knows that it wants something whereas the stomach or palate want something without knowing it. Stomach or palate is to the complete being much as the brute beast is to man. Bees lose their individual consciousness but keep their appetites or impulses. An animal fibre is a simple animal, man is a composite one.[38]

The human being is "composite" to the extent that he or she is a hodge-podge of opposed desires driven by a disparate jumble of incompletely organized organs. Bordeu's remarks suggest that human nature, as built up out of multiple components, is shot through with inconsistencies and tensions right down to the material bedrock of the organic body, a body therefore containing nonorganic dimensions that themselves are not simply inorganic (something that the sciences of the twenty-first century make much more glaringly evident than those available to the thinkers of the eighteenth century). This can be interpreted so as to indicate, apropos Bordeu's later assertion quoted above ("Nothing that exists can be against nature or outside nature"), that naturalizing human being (i.e., not allowing humans to stand above-and-beyond the natural world in some immaterial, metaphysical zone) correlatively entails envisioning nature as, at least in certain instances, being divided against itself. An unreserved naturalization of humanity must result in a defamiliarization and reworking of those most foundational and rudimentary proto-philosophical images contributing to any picture of material nature.[39] The new, fully secularized materialism (inspired in part by Freudian-Lacanian psychoanalysis) to be developed and defended in *Prolegomena to Any Future Materialism* is directly linked to this notion of nature as the self-shattering, internally conflicted existence of a detotalized material immanence.

In the context of a discussion of philosophy and religion apropos eighteenth-century French materialism, one cannot pass over in silence the figure of the egg forcefully invoked by Diderot in *D'Alembert's Dream*. After discussing with d'Alembert an imagined thinking clavichord, a "philosopher-instrument" akin to La Mettrie's machine-man,[40] Diderot cries out, "Look at this egg: with it you can overthrow all the schools of theology and all the churches in the world."[41] Given Lacan's contention regarding the displaced religious beliefs allegedly harbored by the superficially irreligious rhetoric of these eighteenth-century discourses drawing on the sciences of their time, one might take Diderot's exclamation with a grain or two of salt. Furthermore, the fact that this same egg-example features in the entry for "Spinozist" in the *Encyclopédie* adds to such Lacanian suspicions[42] (despite, admittedly, the many philosophical and historical complications associated with classifying Spinoza as a religious thinker and his omnipresent God as at all related to the deities of the mainstream monotheistic religions). Nonetheless, Diderot is not entirely incorrect to see in his egg a vision of an explosive materialism with devastating implications for theosophical doctrines resting upon any God as an enveloping, self-consistent One-All, be these beliefs avowed (as in religion) or disavowed (as in eighteenth-century mechanistic materialism).

For Diderot, the significance of an egg is that it purportedly embodies a point of transition from what seems to be inanimate and insensate (i.e., the egg itself) to what is readily acknowledged as animate and sentient (i.e., the creature born out of the egg). He concludes that, in order to explain this apparently miraculous genesis of perceiving and feeling life out of what looks to be lifeless, inert matter, one must "entertain a simple hypothesis that explains everything—sensitivity as a property common to all matter or as a result of the organization of matter."[43] The two prongs of this hypothesis are not the same or equivalent claims: the former careens in the direction of a sort of pan-psychism positing sentience as an element ubiquitously distributed across the entire material universe, whereas the latter (as will be seen later) points in the direction of secular(izing) paths subsequently traversed by the life sciences in general and the neurosciences in particular. From a Lacanian standpoint, the religious impulse still operative in Diderot's supposedly anti-religious gloss on the example of the egg is manifested by the insistence upon a smooth continuity between different types and states of matter, an imagined continuity behind which lurks the specter of being as one vast cosmic wholeness (and, obviously, this religious-spiritualist impulse is further revealed by the flirtation with pan-psychism).

The atheistic potentials of Diderot's egg reside in two features of this object: one, eggs create the appearance of a sudden emergence (or, apropos the egg as a metaphor for the rapport between matter and mind, this also involves the emergence of appearance itself); two, emergences from eggs require cracks (i.e., the splitting open and shattering of eggshells). Regardless of the authorial intentions of Diderot circa 1769—Diderot's pseudoemergentism ultimately posits a supposed continuity (rather than discontinuity) underlying the transformative dynamics of life—this image-example of the egg thus shelters within itself a picture of processes in which antagonisms, fissures, and tensions within the Real of material being provide openings through and out of which explode phenomena and structures whose genesis marks an abrupt rupture with what came before (i.e., the prior movements and substances, with their laws and logics, preceding this discontinuous emergence). And, like Diderot, Lacan too has an egg in hand, namely, his "*hommelette*" starring in the well-known myth of the lamella.[44] In line with the broader psychoanalytic motif of subjectivity as fractured and split, this broken man-egg (or, more accurately, man-omelet) can be construed, among other things and specifically with reference to the egg of Diderot, as a metaphor for the rough edges of natural discontinuities that allow for and enable the materially emergent subject's denaturalizing of its own nature.

On several occasions, Lacan proposes that, whereas the smooth material-temporal continuum of evolutionary theory (like the Spinoza-inspired materialisms of Sade, La Mettrie, and Diderot) is a fundamentally theological notion despite its outwardly atheistic appearance (i.e., nature takes on the features and qualities of God),[45] only the originally Christian notion of creation ex nihilo, of abrupt emergences that cannot be reduced to or predicted by a prior substantial ground, is appropriate to a thinking that really is done with all things religious. He maintains that "the creationist perspective is the only one that allows one to glimpse the possibility of the radical elimination of God,"[46] and that "a strictly atheist thought adopts no other perspective than that of 'creationism.'"[47] At this point, the obvious question to be asked and answered is: What does Lacan see as the essence of atheism proper?

On three particular occasions during the course of his teaching,

Lacan provides exemplary explanations for what he, as a psychoanalyst, understands to be the true core of an atheistic stance. In a 1963 session of the tenth seminar, he raises the questions of whether practicing analysts should themselves be atheists and whether patients who still believe in God at the end of their analyses can be considered adequately analyzed for the purposes of determining when to terminate treatment.[48] Referring to obsessional neurotics, with their unconscious fantasies of an omniscient Other observing each and every one of their little thoughts and actions, Lacan implies that such analysands would need to move in the direction of atheism in order to be relieved of those symptoms tied to this belief in the "universal eye" ("*oeil universel*") of a virtual, godlike observer of their existences.[49] He then immediately goes on to assert that "such is the true dimension of atheism. An atheist would be someone who has succeeded at eliminating the fantasy of the All-Powerful."[50] Interestingly, right after this remark, he mentions Diderot and casts into doubt whether this exemplary French materialist really can be considered a true atheist.[51] Insofar as Diderot, along with his fellow materialists of the period, replaces an all-powerful God with an all-powerful Nature—this Nature is also all-knowing to the extent that it is made into the repository of every possible answer to any query capable of satisfactory "scientific" formulation—he cannot be said to be authentically atheist in the eyes of Lacan. Lacan's version of the experience of analysis involves a "psychoanalytic ascesis"[52] entailing "atheism conceived of as the negation of the dimension of a presence of the all-powerful at the base of the world."[53] That is to say, traversing the fantasy of an omnipotent and omniscient big Other, whether this Other be conceived of as God, Nature, the analyst, or whatever, is an unavoidable rite of passage in the concluding moments of an analysis seen through to a fitting end.

Lacan rearticulates these indications regarding atheism even more decisively and forcefully in the sixteenth and seventeenth seminars. In the sixteenth seminar, Lacan alleges that being an atheist requires putting into question the category of the *sujet supposé savoir* (not only as incarnated in the transference-laden figure of the analyst, but also as any Other presumed to vouch for the maintenance of an overarching horizon of final, consistent meaning). Without letting fall and enduring the dissipation of the position of the subject supposed to know, one remains, according to Lacan, mired in idealism and theology; he equates belief in such an Other-subject with belief in God.[54] As Lacan succinctly states, "A true atheism, the only one that would merit the name, is that which would result from the putting in question of the subject supposed to know."[55] The following academic year, in the seventeenth seminar, he bluntly asserts that "the pinnacle of psychoanalysis is well and truly atheism."[56] Whereas the Lacan of the tenth seminar indirectly insinuates that undergoing the end of analysis (including traversing those fantasies linked to the transferential status of the analyst as an instantiation of an Other supposedly "in the know") results in an atheistic loss of faith in any kind of Almighty, here, in 1970, he directly declares this outcome to mark the apex of the analytic experience.[57]

§3 Toward a Conflict Ontology: Freud, Mao, and the Ubiquity of Antagonism

Apart from clinical practice, what makes psychoanalysis, at the most foundational theoretical level, a Godless discipline? More specifically, how might psychoanalytic theory make a crucial contribution to the formulation of a scientifically informed materialism that doesn't rest upon an either implicit or explicit set of theosophical-ontological suppositions regarding some sort of internally integrated One-All? The key Lacanian slogan for an atheistic materialism might appear to be his declaration that *"le grand Autre n'existe pas."*[58] The nonexistence of the big Other is indeed a tenet central to Lacan's above-delineated characterizations of genuine atheism. However, this tenet by itself doesn't guarantee a materialism that would be fully secularized according to Lacan's own criteria for what would count as a thoroughly God-forsaking ontology. Although the absence of the big Other precludes imagining an ordering of reality from above, it doesn't foreclose the possibility of hypothesizing the return of a mellifluously orchestrated material universe, a unified natural world, through bottom-up dynamics and processes. A mechanistic materialism akin to that of La Mettrie or Diderot readily could resurface via such hypotheses (as Lacan would remind readers at this juncture, evolutionism is not shy about positing a continuity from below causally enchaining together vast, web-like networks of organisms and environments—God lives on, even if not in a traditional, top-down embodiment). To support an atheistic materialism, the declaration "The big Other does not exist" requires supplementation by another thesis: in the absence of every version of this Other, what remains lacks any guarantee of consistency right down to the bedrock of ontological fundaments. Strife, potential or actual, reigns supreme as a negativity permeating the layers and strata of material being.

The positing of conflict as ubiquitous and primary is precisely what makes psychoanalysis a Godless discipline. In, for instance, both *The Future of an Illusion* and his *New Introductory Lectures on Psycho-Analysis,*

Freud depicts the antireligious thrust of analysis as merely of a piece with a larger demystifying scientific worldview.[59] Apart from Lacan's arguments to the contrary sketched above (i.e., the materialisms of the natural sciences are not automatically atheist, even when presented as such), the subsequent course of sociocultural history also contains ample evidence that the advancement and coming-to-power of the Weltanschauung of the sciences is far from having succeeded at shunting religions to the marginalized fringes of collective life. If anything, rather than the religion-science relationship being a zero-sum balance in which the waxing of one entails the proportional waning of the other, the aggressive incursions of the sciences routinely have met with a correspondingly robust counter-aggression from religious quarters.

Lacan's contentions that religion is anything but finished are based upon this observed persistence of religiosity in a scientific world. He often discusses religion in the context of its relations to both science and psychoanalysis (and he at least agrees with Freud that analysis invariably results in a demystification effect in relation to religion).[60] According to Lacan, the religious provides a shock absorber of meaning (*sens*) cushioning the blows issuing forth from the inroads made into the meaningless material Real by the scientific[61]—with this being necessary when neither of the fetishes furnished by science, neither its imagined hypothetical God's-eye view as the regulative ideal of exhaustive explanation nor its numerous by-products in the form of technogadget toys, proves to be satisfactory enough.[62] Incidentally, especially given the seemingly unstoppable, death-drive-like march of science[63] coupled with religion's role as the provider of sufficient sense to sustain those caught up in this march, psychoanalysis is unlikely to have much luck gaining a hearing amidst the breathless hustle-and-bustle of this ever-accelerating frenzy. Like science, psychoanalysis divests reality of meaning through revealing the nonsensical Real composing and shaping this reality.[64] But, unlike science, it refuses to offer the compensations of either the promise of total knowledge or objects of pleasurable consumption. In this situation, analysis cannot hope to compete with the mass appeal of religion, particularly under the conditions of late capitalism and the ways in which science and religion interact within it.[65] Nonetheless, what makes psychoanalysis, this theoretical-practical configuration quietly limping alongside the interlinked movements conjoining science and religion, utterly atheistic is not, as per Freud, its allegiance to the Enlightenment worldview of scientific-style ideologies. Rather, its placement of antagonisms and oppositions at the very heart of material being, its depiction of nature itself as divided by conflicts rendering it a fragmented, not-whole non-One, is what constitutes the truly irreligious core of psychoanalytic metapsychology as a force for merciless desacralization.

Conflict is an omnipresent motif/structure in Freud's corpus. However, in some of his later, post-1920 texts, what becomes much clearer and more apparent is that, from a Freudian perspective, irreconcilable discord and clashes arise from antagonistic splits embedded in the material foundations of human being. Although there are numerous problems with the fashions in which Freud biologizes psychical life, there is also something invaluable in his naturalization of conflict in terms of the war between *Eros* and the *Todestrieb* raging within the bodily id,[66] namely, a germinal ontological insight that shouldn't suffer the fate of the proverbial baby thrown out with the bathwater of Freud's scientistic biological reductionism.[67] Freudian psychoanalytic metapsychology here contains the nascent potentials for the formulation, in conjunction with select resources extracted from today's natural sciences, of a conflict ontology, a theory of the immanent-monistic emergence of a disharmonious ontological-material multitude or plurality. Perhaps, as Eric Kandel indicates, the time Freud anticipates as yet-to-come, a time which indeed is finally ripe to draw psychoanalysis back into the orbit of the sciences, has arrived at last.[68]

The basic ingredients for creating a new, entirely atheistic materialism are to be drawn not only from Freud's tacit indications pointing in the direction of a possible conflict ontology—Mao Tse-Tung's version of the distinction between mechanistic and dialectical materialisms is of great importance in this task too. For Engels, the mechanistic materialism of eighteenth-century France is limited by two interrelated flaws: a reductionist neglect of various logics other than those depicted in the laws of mechanics proposed by the physical sciences of the time, as well as a resulting inability to grasp the dynamics of processes of historical becoming in an ever-changing universe (these flaws, as Engels concedes, are necessary features of a materialism grounded in a historical context in which Newtonian mechanical physics is the cutting edge of the natural sciences).[69] In his 1937 essay "On Contradiction," Mao further illuminates the nature of the distinction between these two materialist orientations:

> While we recognize that in the general development of history the material determines the mental and social being determines social consciousness, we also—and indeed must—recognize the reaction of the mental on material things, of social consciousness on social being and of the superstructure on the economic base. This does not go against materialism; on the contrary, it avoids mechanical materialism and firmly upholds dialectical materialism.[70]

Mechanistic materialism is nondialectical to the extent that it admits solely a unidirectional flow of causal influence from matter to mind. For a materialist such as La Mettrie or Diderot, mental life and every socio-cultural thing collectively connected with it can be only impotent, inef-fective epiphenomena, residual illusions discharged by biophysical sub-stances seamlessly and inextricably bound up with the world of nature and the englobing universe of matter. That is to say, matter dictates its laws to mind, and never the other way around. As Engels observes, this "old materialism," in its ahistoricism,[71] fails even to ask, let alone answer, questions as to how human brains are shaped and transformed by forces and factors operative within historical dimensions.[72] And, as Mao indicates, dialectical materialism, unlike its mechanistic philo-sophical predecessor, admits a bidirectional flow of causal influences between matter and mind (i.e., a dialectic, albeit one in which the two poles involved are not perfectly equal or evenly balanced). In particular, Mao's version of dialectical materialism allows for exceptional circum-stances when the mental tail can and does start reciprocally wagging the physical dog, when the determined starts affecting the determinant.[73] The young Maoist Badiou, in his 1975 text *Theory of Contradiction,* stipu-lates that one must adhere to two principles in order to be a dialectical materialist: materialism requires granting that material things usually occupy the determining position in most situations; and dialectics (as nonmechanistic) requires granting that this default position of material dominance is vulnerable to disruption, negation, or suspension.[74] A key aspect of the Badiouian Mao's ontology is its axiomatic proposition that there is only a conflict-plagued One-that-is-not-One as a plane of mate-rial immanence, both natural and historical, fragmented from within by the pervasive negativity of scissions and struggles.[75] Additionally, by contrast with accepted (but erroneous) notions regarding the Hegelian dialectic, Maoist dialectics treats any instance of cohesion, stability, or unity, any resting point, as a temporary, transitory moment, an ephem-eral outcome, in a process of interminable, opposition-driven historical becoming, a trajectory of perpetually renewed division and fissuring.[76] The kinesis of struggle is primary; the stasis of peace is secondary, excep-tional, and fleeting.[77]

What makes Maoist dialectical materialism particularly useful in the present context is its emphasis on the pervasiveness of dynamic con-tradiction, even down to the raw flesh and bare bones of nature itself.[78] More specifically, Mao's account of causality in the context of elaborat-ing his form of dialectical materialism can be interpreted as putting in place a foundational requirement to be met by any materialism acknowl-edging some sort of distinction between matter and mind (i.e., any non-mechanistic, noneliminative materialism). In *Theory of the Subject,* Badiou demands a materialism that includes, as per the title of this book, "a theory of the subject."[79] Such a materialism would have to be quite distinct from mechanistic or eliminative materialisms, insofar as neither of the latter two leave any space open, the clearing of some breathing room, for subjectivity as something distinguishable from the fleshly stuff of the natural world. However, a materialist theory of the subject, in order to adhere to one of the principal tenets of any truly materialist materialism (i.e., the ontological axiom according to which matter is the sole ground), must be able to explain how subjectivity emerges out of materiality—and, correlative to this, how materiality must be configured in and of itself so that such an emergence is a real possibility.

This explanatory requirement is precisely one of the issues at stake in Mao's discussions of internal and external causes. After stating that "materialist dialectics . . . holds that development arises from the contradictions inside a thing"[80] (i.e., beings are split from within by antagonisms and tensions enabling them to undergo becomings), Mao proceeds to state:

> As opposed to the metaphysical world outlook, the world outlook of materialist dialectics holds that in order to understand the development of a thing we should study it internally and in its relations with other things; in other words, the development of things should be seen as their internal and necessary self-movement, while each thing in its movement is interrelated to and interacts on the things around it. The fundamental cause of the development of a thing is not external but internal; it lies in the contradictoriness within the thing. There is internal contradiction in every single thing, hence its motion and development. Contradictoriness within a thing is the fundamental cause of its development, while its interrelations and interactions with other things are secondary causes. Thus materialist dialectics effectively combats the theory of external causes, or of an external motive force, advanced by metaphysical mechanical materialism and vulgar evolutionism. It is evident that purely external causes can only give rise to mechanical motion, that is, to changes in scale or quantity, but cannot explain why things differ qualitatively in thousands of ways and why one thing changes into another.[81]

Soon after this statement, he further elaborates:

> According to materialist dialectics, changes in nature are due chiefly to the development of the internal contradictions in nature. Changes in society are due chiefly to the development of the internal contradictions in society . . . Does materialist dialectics exclude external causes?

> Not at all. It holds that external causes are the condition of change
> and internal causes are the basis of change, and that external causes
> become operative through internal causes.[82]

This last claim is then immediately repeated for the sake of emphasis: "It
is through internal causes that external causes become operative."[83] The
early Badiou of *Theory of Contradiction* endorses these assertions made by
Mao.[84] And, in resonance with Lacan's above-glossed remarks apropos
the religiosity nascent within the linear continuity of evolutionary theory,
Badiou highlights, in this same 1975 treatise, the nonevolutionary character of the models of historical-material change offered by Leninist-
Maoist dialectical materialism, models centered on discontinuous,
sudden "ruptures," leap-like transitions from quantity to quality[85] (interestingly, the neuroscientist Jean-Pierre Changeux uses similar language
when talking about the genesis of mind from matter).[86]

Along Maoist lines, constructing a theory of subjectivity entirely
compatible with the strictures of a thoroughly materialist ontology (a
project called for by Badiou himself)[87] necessitates, in the combined
lights of psychoanalytic metapsychology and dialectical materialism, two
endeavors: first, delineating the materiality of human being as conflicted
from within, as a point of condensing intersection for a plethora of
incompletely harmonized fragments; second, exploring how the endogenous causes of these conflicts immanent to the materiality of human
being can and do interact with exogenous causal influences.[88] As Mao
rightly underscores, the latter by themselves (i.e., purely external variables) are ineffective. What makes the kinetics of dialectical materialism
possible is an external activation of potentials intrinsic to the internal
configurations of certain beings.

§4 From Dialectical to Transcendental Materialism:
Malabou, Neuroscience, and Images of Matter Transformed

The groundbreaking work of Catherine Malabou brilliantly brings to the
fore these very issues through a simultaneous engagement with both dialectical materialism and cognitive neuroscience. Echoes of those aspects
of Maoist thought mentioned above can be heard in her insistence, in
the context of discussing Hegel's dialectic, Heidegger's destruction, and
Derrida's deconstruction, that externally overriding something requires
this thing's complicity in terms of its "plastic" inner structure,[89] a structure embodying the "schizoid consistency of the ultra-metaphysical

real"[90] as the nondialectical ontological origin/ground of dialectics[91] (i.e., being itself as inconsistent and conflict-ridden). Entities must possess the proper "ontological metabolism" in order to be open to and affected by encounters with alterities.[92] Malabou's 1996 doctoral thesis on Hegel, *The Future of Hegel*, concludes with a reference to the life sciences as offering the resources for the development of an ontology ready to meet the explanatory-theoretical demands pronounced by the dialectical materialist tradition in ways that this tradition itself thus far hasn't been able to accomplish on its own.[93]

These 1996 gestures in the direction of natural science come to full fruition in Malabou's revolutionary 2004 book *What Should We Do with Our Brain?*—this title echoes the French translation of Lenin's *What Is to Be Done? (Que faire?)*—a book centered on a reading of today's cognitive neurosciences as spontaneously generating and substantiating a dialectical materialist ontology[94] (and this whether they realize it or not).[95] Without the space presently to do adequate justice to the entire range of complex, convincing arguments advanced in this text, several points made by Malabou deserve to be noted here as stipulations for a thoroughly secularized materialism sensitive to the breakthroughs and insights achieved by the sciences of nature. Focusing on the biological level of human being, she correctly notes that the widespread notion of genetic determinism, according to which the physical body is entirely shaped and controlled by genes, is simply inaccurate, a falsifying distortion of the facts. The truth, rather, is that a "genetic indetermination" (i.e., genes determine human beings not to be entirely determined by genes)[96] and the neural plasticity linked to this indetermination ensure the openness of vectors and logics not anticipated or dictated by the bump-and-grind efficient causality of physical particles alone.[97] In other words, one need not fear that bringing biology into the picture of a materialist theory of the subject leads inexorably to a reductive materialism of a mechanistic and/or eliminative sort; such worries are utterly unwarranted, based exclusively on an unpardonable ignorance of several decades of paradigm-shifting discoveries in the life sciences.[98] No intellectually responsible philosophical materialism can justify ignoring the evidence unearthed in these highly productive fields of adjacent research—unless, of course, what is secretly or unconsciously desired is a spiritualist ideology disguising itself in the faded-fashion garb of a now awfully dated antinaturalism.

A chorus of voices on the empirical side of discussions of the brain (i.e., neuroscientists and cognitive scientists) speak as one in support of the basic, fundamental premises underlying the effort underway here to appropriate the resources of the neurosciences for the delineation of a reinvigorated materialist ontology (an appropriation informed and guided by a combination of Freudian-Lacanian psychoanalytic metapsychology and the resources of European philosophy from the end of the eighteenth century through the present). To begin with, not only do some researchers in the neurosciences see the notorious nature-nurture distinction as dialectical[99]—it has even been suggested that the very distinction itself is invalid due to the utter inextricability of what is referred to by these two inadequate terms and the irresolvable undecidability that thereby results[100] (in the area of psychopathology, Kandel, a vocal neuroscientific advocate on behalf of a new rapprochement between psychodynamics and the life sciences, suggests scrapping the old distinction between biological and nonbiological mental disorders).[101] Most of the resistance to having anything to do with the life sciences, a resistance widespread within the worlds of Lacanianism and continental philosophy, is due to the misperception that embracing these sciences inevitably leads to the crudest forms of reductionism (i.e., genetic determinism, epiphenomenalism, etc.).[102] But, as Benjamin Libet observes, vulgar reductive materialism is scientism (as pseudoscientific ideology), not science.[103]

In fact, these scientists are at pains to stress that their disciplines are not rigid frameworks within which the natural, on the one hand, and the cultural-historical-social, on the other hand, are to be strictly opposed, with the fixed, frozen essences of the former always trumping the subservient (epi)phenomena of the latter.[104] As Lesley Rogers puts it, "the idea of biology as immutable is largely incorrect."[105] And, as Joseph LeDoux explains, a material-neuronal conception of the subject neither is opposed to nor demands the elimination of theories of nonbiological subjectivity.[106] There are numerous arguments for why the neurosciences and the biology on which they rest are not reductive, only some of which can be outlined briefly in the context of the current discussion. The dialectic between innate nature and acquired nurture, if one still can use these terms, permeates even the level of genetics (and, much reductionism and the opposition it generates lean on a fatally flawed picture of genetics).[107] LeDoux helpfully points out that nature-nurture interaction is operative from the very beginnings of life, given that the developing embryo takes shape in a womb connected to a maternal body that itself is entangled in vast mediating networks of more-than-biological configurations and interactions[108] (not to mention the Lacanian analytic caveat that both conception and what leads up to it are woven into elaborate, knotted webs of influential factors conscious and unconscious). Although the genotype sets in place certain loose, broad parameters establishing a wide bandwidth of possibilities and permutations for what the phenotype can actualize/express (what Changeux calls a "genetic envelope"),[109] in no way could it be said in any straightforward manner that anatomy is destiny (to invoke an oft-misinterpreted Freudian one-liner).[110] Especially within the brain, the genetic is significantly modulated by the epigenetic (i.e., experience, learning, socialization, etc.).[111] Furthermore, such complications are not confined exclusively to the "nature" half of the nature-nurture distinction—the life sciences are also in the process of calling into question the "nurture" half, a process prompted by a realization that the notion of "environment" is incredibly hazy, insufficiently precise to serve as a concept for rigorous reflection.[112] Considering these rudimentary, ground-zero truths in the life sciences, no sort of standard reductionism is in the least bit tenable insofar as the mind-bogglingly complex number of variables converging on a multi-determined brain and body render in advance any one-sided depiction of these matters intellectually bankrupt.[113]

Furthermore, certain aspects of genetics properly conceived are crucial for an adequate appreciation of the neurosciences. The link Malabou mobilizes, in her discussions of the philosophical implications of brain studies, between what she accurately describes as "genetic indetermination" and neural plasticity is indeed empirically well-established. The brain is genetically programmed to be open and receptive to reprogramming (which includes alterations of gene expression at the phenotypic level) through learning experiences in relation to the contextual vicissitudes of exogenous contingencies.[114] This determined lack of determination, this preprogramming for reprogramming, is an important aspect of what is meant by characterizing the brain as "plastic." Neuroplasticity is considered by those working in the life sciences to be an incredibly significant feature in the development and functioning of human brains.[115] LeDoux identifies the plastic synaptic connections of neurons, hardwired for rewiring, to be the precise material points where nature and nurture collide, the crossroads at which genetics and epigenetics are folded into assemblages that are theoretically unsliceable tangles of hyperdense complexity.[116] He even goes so far as to conjecture that neuroplasticity in humans is an "exaptation," namely, something that starts out as an evolutionarily advantageous adaptation in response to certain environmental pressures and problems but eventually becomes, so to speak, transfunctionalized, derailed from its initial means-ends pathways and expropriated for other projects that are nonnatural vis-à-vis strict evolutionary considerations.[117] (However, LeDoux's use of the term "exaptation" deviates from its meaning as initially defined by Stephen Jay Gould and Elisabeth S. Vrba.)[118]

At a more general level (and in line with the previously enumerated requirements of a Lacan-inspired atheistic materialism), Malabou describes the "ontological explosion" of the mental out of the neuronal[119]—"out of" is intended in two senses, both as immanently arising from and as autonomously exceeding through escape from—as event-like,[120] a sharp break requiring (as Mao would put it) the "internal causes" of the ontological-material plasticity of the human biological body. More-than-biological "external causes" (again in the Maoist sense) are able to have their mediating effects on individuals thanks not only to bodily plasticity in Malabou's precise sense—for her, the plastic designates, at the same time, both the receptivity of the malleable and the resistance of the congealed,[121] namely, a literal contradiction in the fragmented flesh[122]—but also because of the antagonisms and discordances materialized in the embodied being of humans. She maintains that "the historico-cultural shaping of the self is not possible except starting from this natural and primary economy of contradiction."[123] She proceeds to claim that "there is a *cerebral conflictuality,* there is a tension between the neuronal and the mental"[124] (i.e., although the mental emerges out of the neuronal, the former comes to be at odds with the latter—this immanent genesis of the thereafter-transcendent-as-separate is the core concern of transcendental materialism).[125] Malabou pleads for a "new materialism,"[126] a "reasonable materialism"[127] that neither indefensibly ignores the sciences of material being (especially the neurosciences as relevant to a materialist theory of subjectivity unafraid of—God forbid—dirtying its hands with actual, factual matter) nor uncritically accepts the ideological distortions of these sciences by those seeking to exaggerate one side of plasticity at the expense of the other (i.e., to promote pseudoscientific visions of humanity either as rigidly fixed in place by an evolutionary-genetic-neural determinism or as infinitely flexible according to the insistence of the social constructionism arising from late-capitalist economic-political machinations). For Malabou, as for me, "a reasonable materialism seems to us to be one which poses that the natural contradicts itself and that thought is the fruit of this contradiction."[128]

§5 A Weak Nature, and Nothing More: The True Formula of a Fully Atheistic Materialism

At this juncture, closely examining Lacan's 1975 interview entitled (by Jacques-Alain Miller) "The Triumph of Religion" ("Le triomphe de la religion") in light of the preceding discussions concerning the philosophical establishment of an atheistic materialism shaped around the conjunction of metapsychology and the neurosciences will be especially fruitful. Early on in this text, Lacan speaks of a difference between "that which goes" (*"ce qui marche"*) and "that which does not go" (*"ce qui ne marche pas"*), the former being the "world" (as the normal run of things in familiar Imaginary-Symbolic reality) and the latter being the Real (as excluded from and disruptive of the running of this reality). He notes that psychoanalysts concern themselves with this Real as what does not fit into the smooth movements of quotidian reality.[129] The analyst's presence testifies to this Real-that-does-not-go, quietly witnessing and marking those occurrences in which it surfaces (such as, during an analysis, in unintended double-entendres, slips of the tongue, bungled actions, acting out, and so on). He or she occupies this position and remains there as a "symptom" of that which resists going with the flow of the everyday world. However, a cultural "cure" for psychoanalysis, as itself a symptom of the "discontent of civilization of which Freud has spoken,"[130] is readily available: religion as a means of repressing the symptoms (including analysis itself) of the unworldly Real that disrupts worldly reality.[131]

Lacan goes on to warn against equivocating between the symptom and the Real. He argues thus:

> The symptom is not yet truly the real. It is the manifestation of the real at the level of living beings. As living beings, we are settled, bitten by the symptom. We are sick, that is all. The speaking being is a sick animal. "In the beginning was the Word" says the same thing.[132]

By virtue of the human being's irreparable transubstantiation into a speaking being (i.e., a *parlêtre*), this "living being" becomes a "sick animal." What begins with the genesis of "the Word"—throughout "The Triumph of Religion," Lacan plays with this Christian notion/motif[133]— are illnesses constitutive of the human condition. Additionally, Lacan's distinction between symptom and Real involves a few nuances worthy of attention. To begin with, the living being's animality is associated with the Real itself. And this Real not only introduces dysfunctions into the world of Imaginary-Symbolic reality—it comes to be worked and reworked, written and overwritten, by its own manifestations (in the form of symptoms) within this logos-inaugurated reality. A Real beyond, beneath, or behind its own symptomatic manifestations is caught up in a dialectical entanglement with these same manifestations. In view of this, Lacan continues:

> But the real real, if I can speak thusly, the true real, is that which we are able to accede to via an absolutely precise way, which is the scientific way. It is the way of little equations. This real there is the exact one which eludes us completely.[134]

The Real underlying and making possible both the emergence of speaking beings out of living beings as well as the symptoms (as *sinthomes*)[135] of these thus-afflicted animals is not some ineffable *je ne sais quoi*, some mysterious noumenal "x." For Lacan, "the real real," this "true real," is precisely what the ways of the sciences enable to be accessed lucidly and rigorously in its truth. Of course, Lacan's mention of "little equations" in the quotation above hints at a conception of science according to which the hallmark of scientificity is mathematical-style formalization— the greater the degree of mathematical-style formalization, the greater the degree of scientificity (for more on this, see the second chapter to follow). But, in addition to the ample evidence scattered throughout his teachings that Lacan sometimes associates the Real with things fleshly and corporeal (and not just mathematical/formal), the block quotation just prior to the one above associates the Real with the living animality of the human organism, an animality that gets hopelessly entangled with the mediating matrices of symbolic orders (these two quotations are situated one immediately after the other on the same page of "The Triumph of Religion"). Hence, perhaps the science Lacan is thinking of here is not just the mathematized physics of quantum mechanics, but an adequately formalized science of life. If so, then one of the important consequences entailed by this is that there could be a scientifically shaped treatment of a genuine Real-in-the-flesh as a precondition for the immanent surfacing out of this animal materiality of something different, other, or more than this materiality (i.e., the *parlêtre* as a denaturalized, but never quite completely and successfully denaturalized, living being).[136]

Toward the end of "The Triumph of Religion," Lacan pronounces a couple of additional utterances regarding the Real. After denying that he is a philosopher proposing an ontology[137]—my philosophically guided ontologization of the version of the Real presently under discussion thereby deviates from Lacan's position in this respect—he emphatically rejects the suggestion, made by the interviewer, that his register of the Real is akin to Kant's sphere of noumena. Lacan protests:

> But this is not at all Kantian. It is even on this that I insist. If there is
> a notion of the real, it is extremely complex, and on this account it is
> not perceivable in a manner that would make a totality. It would be an
> unbelievably presumptuous notion to think that there would be an all
> of the real.[138]

Badiou, appealing to a combination of the Galilean modern scientific mathematization of natural matter and the mathematical infinitization of infinity itself in Cantorian trans-finite set theory, insists that there is no cosmic wholeness of Nature since there is no grand unifying One.[139] Lacan likewise rejects the idea that it would be possible to make an "All" of the Real, to encompass it in the enveloping form of an integrated totality. Presumably, one of Lacan's reasonable assumptions underpinning this denial of Kantianism is that Kant's noumenal realm of things-in-themselves is fantasized by Kant as an ontological domain of entirely consistent being subsisting outside the contradiction-plagued epistemological domain of subjective cognition.[140] What is more, insofar as Lacan contends that scientific thought provides a direct path of entry into the inconsistent, detotalized, and not-All Real, he, unlike Kant, maintains that one can transgress the ostensible "limits of possible experience" so as to lay one's hands on material being *an sich*. Interestingly, Lacan proceeds to speculate that the inconsistency of the Real might involve its "laws"—the sciences are responsible for delineating these structuring principles—evolving, that the ordering framework of this register might be fundamentally unstable, moving about and drifting.[141] Not only is this speculation now a part of astrophysical thinking about the rapid evolutionary congealing of the laws of physics out of the Big Bang—in his 2006 book *After Finitude*, Meillassoux, partially through both a break with Kantian and post-Kantian idealist "correlationism" as well as an ensuing ontologization of Hume's epistemology (with its recasting of conceptualizations of causality), argues for envisioning brute being in and of itself as absolutely contingent and lawless, its law-like patterns and regularities always potentially capable of change.[142] (Meillassoux's "speculative materialism" is examined and critiqued in the sixth and seventh chapters as well as the postface below.)

In two coauthored articles, Lorenzo Chiesa and Alberto Toscano provide exemplary, superlative readings of some of the crucial subtleties contained in "The Triumph of Religion." In that text, Lacan, despite his openly avowed atheism, perplexingly declares Christianity to be "the one true religion."[143] Chiesa and Toscano helpfully clarify that what this actually means is that, from a Lacanian perspective, the Christian religion is the least false of the various religions.[144] The reason for this has to do with Lacan's earlier assertions to the effect that whereas evolutionary theory unwittingly continues to be theosophical by virtue of its reliance upon an omnipotent, all-embracing material-historical continuum (i.e., a seamless, uninterrupted One-All of Nature),[145] creationism, especially the Christian notion of creation ex nihilo, inadvertently opens the door to the founding of a materialism without God:

> Lacan, a self-professed atheist, repeatedly refers to Christianity as "*la vraie religion*." To cut a long story short, according to Lacan, Christianity

is the "true religion" insofar as, more than any other religion, it comes nearest to the materialistic truth of the creation *ex nihilo* of the signifier: "In the beginning was the Word." The *ex nihilo* of the *logos,* or better, the *logos* itself *as* the *ex nihilo,* is the specific feature that, for Lacan, differentiates Christianity from other monotheistic religions that are also creationist.[146]

Just as a kernel of religiosity resides in the heart of supposedly atheistic evolutionary theory, so too does a kernel of atheism reside within the heart of supposedly religious Christianity. But, one might ask: given the counterintuitive ring to this series of propositions, what qualifies the Christian doctrine of creation ex nihilo as both atheist and materialist? And what antireligious advantages does this concept drawn from the inner sanctum of a particular religion have over the desacralizing ontology of transcendence-stifling immanence implicit in evolutionism? Chiesa and Toscano offer the following elucidating explanations:

> Why would Christian creationism, based as it is on the *logos* as the *ex nihilo,* contain *in nuce* a form of atheistic materialism? Lacan's theory of the emergence of the signifier *ex nihilo* is both materialistic and atheistic since it is grounded on the assumption that language, and the symbolic order, is unnatural rather than supernatural, the contingent product of man's successful *dis*-adaptation to nature. Such an unnatural dis-adaptation, which obviously dominates and perverts nature, can nevertheless only originate immanently from what we name "nature" and thus contradicts the alleged continuity of any (transcendentally) "natural" process of evolution.[147]

Elsewhere, they repeat the above almost verbatim,[148] to which is appended the declaration that "nature is *per se* not-One"[149]—a declaration rooted in various statements regarding the notion of nature made by Lacan, including ones contemporaneous with "The Triumph of Religion."[150] (Joan Copjec similarly refers to Lacan's "proposal that being is not-all or there is no whole of being,"[151] invoking the Lacanian theme of the "deficit of the world," its "incompleteness").[152] Chiesa and Toscano, while illuminating how Lacan extracts an atheistic materialism from the ex nihilo of Christianity, even describe "the (supposed) primitive 'synthesis' of the primordial real" as having "been broken due to a contingent 'material' change that is immanent to it."[153] The twist the reworked materialism of this project adds to these very insightful comments is the assertion that the "primordial real" of natural matter is not synthesized, that, insofar as subjects exist in the first place, it is always-already "broken"—with this brokenness, this self-shattered status of a disharmonious nature devoid of any One-All, being a material condition of possibility for the immanent genesis of subjectivity out of the conflict-ridden groundless ground of materiality.

In "The Triumph of Religion," Lacan speaks of various cures for anxiety. Specifically, he suggests that a range of conceptions of humanity function in this capacity: "Against anxiety, there are heaps of remedies, in particular a certain number of 'conceptions of man,' of what man is."[154] This applies not only to religion, which Lacan has in mind in this context—it is also relevant to a speciously scientific scientism that genuine science is in the process of demolishing. More specifically, misrepresentations of the "man of science" as either inflexibly determined by the efficient mechanical causes of evolution and genetics or flexibly malleable as an infinitely constructible and reconstructible social, cultural, and linguistic being are often promoted by the biopolitical ideologies of "democratic materialism" described so well by Badiou.[155] A materialism based on science as opposed to scientism and faithful to the furthest-reaching consequences of Lacan's dictum according to which no big Other of any sort exists (including almighty Nature as well as God) has no place in it for the different pseudoscientific images of humanity advertised by today's reigning biopowers.

The time has come to pronounce the true formula of atheistic materialism: there is just a weak nature, and nothing more. All that exists are heterogeneous ensembles of less-than-fully synthesized material beings, internally conflicted, hodgepodge jumbles of elements-in-tension—and that is it. What appears to be more-than-material (especially subjectivity and everything associated with it) is, ultimately, an index or symptom of the weakness of nature, this Other-less, un-unified ground of being. The apparently more-than-material consists of phenomena flourishing in the nooks and crannies of the strife-saturated, underdetermined matrices of materiality, in the cracks, gaps, and splits of these discrepant material strata.

Fear-driven antinaturalism, responsible for much of the resistance in continental philosophy and European psychoanalysis to a sustained engagement with the life sciences, tacitly accepts the notion of a strong nature as Almighty, as an overdetermining, omnipotent cosmic Substance. If Lacan is indeed correct that the ostensibly atheistic materialists of eighteenth-century France remain, in reality, religious believers despite themselves, then continental European antinaturalists and their followers are also, regardless of whatever they might say, adherents of fideism—they have faith in a natural big Other, even if this faith manifests itself through perverse rejections of and rebellions against this Other. Moreover, such antinaturalists, in accepting the image of a strong nature while simultaneously wanting to preserve the affirmation that there is something in excess of this same nature, are forced to rely upon a spiritualist metaphysics of one sort or another in the form of strict, rigid ontological dualisms (however avowed or disavowed). If an atheist, as Lacan claims, is he or she who acknowledges the nonexistence of the big Other and the absence of anything all-powerful at the foundation of existence, then anyone accepting an image of natural being as an ultra-powerful One, whether reductionist materialists or their reactive and reactionary opponents, is, in the end, no different in kind than the most fervent of the faithful.

2

Turning the Sciences Inside Out: Revisiting "Science and Truth"

§1 Formalism and Antihumanism: The Scientific Subject of Lacan

Nobody could accuse Lacan of modesty. The title of his contribution to the inaugural January 1966 issue of the now-legendary journal *Cahiers pour l'Analyse* promises to address not one, but two mammoth matters in the space of a single article-length intervention. "Science and Truth," originally delivered on December 1, 1965 as the opening session of his thirteenth annual seminar on "The Object of Psychoanalysis," eventually appears as the final essay in the *Écrits* (apart from this book's two appendixes), published later in 1966. The topics of *science* and *vérité* are discussed by Lacan repeatedly throughout the twenty-seven years of *le Séminaire* and in various other texts.

In order to set the stage properly for an examination of "Science and Truth," a bit of foreshadowing is requisite. The title of this specific *écrit* likely would lead a psychoanalytically inclined reader approaching it for the first time to expect yet another disquisition rehashing the recurrent debates about whether or not psychoanalysis can and should be qualified as somehow scientific. Both the brief write-up of the eleventh seminar as well as the back cover of the 1973 French edition of this seminar (the first of Lacan's seminars to be published in book form under the editorial care of Jacques-Alain Miller) succinctly announce a "radical" reframing of these debates, shifting emphasis away from the question "Is psychoanalysis a science?" and toward the question "What would a science be that included psychoanalysis?"[1] Of course, Lacan doesn't hesitate on a number of occasions to air his views in response to the former query. But, his most interesting and important speculations regarding the sciences and scientificity, speculations arguably still of great interest and import today after the passage of over forty years, do not hint at how psychoanalysis must change in adapting itself to the methods and results of the extant versions of the experimental physical sciences; this standard angle of approach frequently is adopted by those in the analytic field anxiously concerned to gain whatever amount possible of legitimizing recognition and acceptance from the established empirical sciences.

Rather, as his substitution of a different question asking about the science-psychoanalysis rapport indicates, Lacan turns the tables, reversing the standard angle of approach: How must the sciences change in order to take account of everything that is revealed in the theory and practice of analysis?[2] Similarly, in the opening session of the eleventh seminar, he muses that "psycho-analysis ... may even enlighten us as to what we should understand by science, and even by religion."[3] Analysts shouldn't reduce themselves to being mere suppliants with respect to the scientists and their institutionally supported (and well-funded) authority. What is more, debates about the relationship between psychoanalysis and science should not revolve around intellectual dominance-submission games in which two disciplines face off in a contest to decide which will have grounding priority over the other.

"Science and Truth" can be interpreted as a strange transitional text moving back and forth between the two questions raised for Lacanian psychoanalysis apropos science (i.e., "Is psychoanalysis a science?" and "What would a science be that included psychoanalysis?"). On the one hand, this essay makes several appeals to the theoretical paradigm of structuralism that seem to amount to assertions to the effect that a structuralist (or, as Jean-Claude Milner would prefer, a "hyper-structuralist")[4] version of analysis would qualify as strictly scientific in a certain sense (a sense related to the history of modern science according to the French historian and philosopher of science Koyré, upon whom Lacan, and, as already noted, both Badiou and Meillassoux after him, avowedly relies).[5] On the other hand, although these appeals to structuralism betray a continuing preoccupation with the issue of whether or not psychoanalysis is some sort of science, many other instances in "Science and Truth" testify to the unfolding of something more than the pursuit of the prize of scientific status for analysis.[6] Incidentally, near the end of his life, Lacan comes to renounce the idea that there is anything scientific per se about the "babbling practice" (*practique de bavardage*) of the Freudian clinic;[7] however, already in 1964, Lacan, in the second session of the twelfth seminar, acknowledges "the difficulty of establishing a psychoanalytic science," albeit not necessarily "insurmountable," due to analytic theory and practice tending to defy capture by scientific-style formalizations.[8] As is common knowledge, one of Lacan's favorite formal sciences is topology, upon which he draws extensively (especially in his later seminars of the 1970s). As regards "Science and Truth," one could say that this *écrit* begins to delineate a twisted, multifaceted topological space simultaneously conjoining and disjoining psychoanalysis and the various sciences. This nuanced, subtle delineation—in it, neither domain is simply collapsed into the other, although points and areas of overlap are highlighted[9]—might well be the most promising and enduringly relevant aspect of Lacan's 1965 musings on scientificity.

Before tracing the more complex topology of the psychoanalysis-science link in "Science and Truth," I will touch upon this text's comparatively less complicated appeals to structuralism as means to broaden the scope of the term "science" (beyond familiar accepted images of the empirical sciences)[10] so as to include within its extension psychoanalysis. Early on in this essay, Lacan repeats a gesture familiar from his 1950s-era "return to Freud," the gesture according to which Freud was a spontaneous Saussurean without knowing it: Freud is likewise said to be a post-Saussurean structuralist *avant la lettre*. However, whereas Lacan's 1950s coupling of Freud with Saussure draws primarily from the early Freud of the first topography (particularly from such analytically foundational writings as *The Interpretation of Dreams, The Psychopathology of Everyday Life,* and *Jokes and Their Relation to the Unconscious*), this 1965 characterization of Freud as a protostructuralist makes reference to the later Freud of the second topography inaugurated with 1923's *The Ego and the Id:*

> The doctrinal revamping known as the second topography introduced the terms *Ich, Über-Ich,* and even *Es* without certifying them as apparatuses, introducing instead a reworking of analytic experience in accordance with a dialectic best defined as what structuralism has since allowed us to elaborate logically: namely, the subject—the subject caught up in a constituting division.[11]

An inflection subsists in this quotation already signaling a distance between Lacan and classical French structuralism (as epitomized by someone like Claude Lévi-Strauss) despite his apparent reliance upon it in this *écrit*. So as to discern this subtlety, one should start by observing that Lacan's subject, the "barred S" ($) split in its very (non-)being, is not reducible to the positivity of one, two, or all three of Freud's psychical agencies as per the second topography (i.e., id [*Es/ça*], ego [*Ich/moi*], and super-ego [*Über-Ich/surmoi*]). Rather, Lacanian subjectivity is tied to the quasi-insubstantial negativity of intrapsychical rifts, namely, the tension-ridden gaps between the different sectors and functions of the psyche as *parlêtre* (speaking being).[12] Although the negativity of this subject-as-$ would not exist without the positivity of these psychical agencies (as themselves conditioned and shaped by signifiers and images), it nonetheless remains irreducible to them insofar as it circulates among them as their conflicts and clashes between one another. Moreover, the structuralist "logic" Lacan has in mind in this context, a logic capable of capturing both temporality and dialectics, is not that of an orthodox, textbook version of a structuralism privileging static synchrony at the expense of kinetic diachrony. Instead, it would be closer both to the temporal logic Lacan first struggles to sketch in his 1946 *écrit* "Logical Time and the Assertion of Anticipated Certainty: A New Sophism"[13] as well as to the Frege-based mathematical rendition of the Lacanian distinction between "the subject of the utterance" (*sujet de l'énoncé*) and "the subject of enunciation" (*sujet de l'énonciation*), being two sides of $ as the subject of the signifier, offered by Jacques-Alain Miller in his essay "Suture" (published in the same issue of the *Cahiers pour l'Analyse* as "Science and Truth").[14]

Perhaps what Lacan values most about structuralism is its pronounced antihumanism. At first, he associates an antihumanist rendition of subjectivity with science: "All humanist references become superfluous in science, the subject cutting them short."[15] This assertion is promptly and forcefully reiterated: "There is no such thing as a science of man because science's man does not exist, only its subject does."[16] In his only other contribution to the *Cahiers pour l'Analyse,* appearing in its third issue and entitled "Responses to Students of Philosophy Concerning the Object of Psychoanalysis," Lacan again insists that "in point of fact, psychoanalysis refutes every idea heretofore presented of man."[17] In 1970, during a question-and-answer conversation with auditors in front of the Panthéon, he bluntly states, "the discourse of science leaves no place for man."[18] Of course, a significant red thread running through "Science and Truth" and related to these remarks consists in Lacan's twofold efforts to one, connect the birth of modern science via Galileo's mathematization of the experimental study of nature with the emergence of the modern subject à la Descartes's cogito;[19] and, two, demonstrate that these thus-connected events in the early seventeenth century are historical conditions of possibility for the advent of Freudian psychoanalysis, with its distinctive conception of subjectivity.[20] Although I will address these efforts in "Science and Truth" in passing below, they will not be my primary focus.

In line with Koyré, Lacan considers mathematical formalization to be essential to scientificity in its modern sense.[21] Related to this, he warns, in "Science and Truth," about "what has been trumped up about a supposed break on Freud's part with the scientism of his time."[22] Against this view, he contends:

> it was this very scientism—which one might designate by its allegiance to the ideals of Brücke, themselves passed down from Helmholtz and Du Bois-Reymond's pact to reduce physiology, and the mental functions considered to be included therein, to the mathematically determined

terms of thermodynamics (the latter having attained virtual completion during their lifetimes)—that led Freud, as his writings show, to pave the way that shall forever bear his name.[23]

Lacan immediately adds: "I am saying that this way never sheds the ideals of this scientism, as it is called, and that the mark it bears of the latter is not contingent but, rather, remains essential to it."[24] Lacan's stress on the mathematical side of the "scientism" endorsed by Freud throughout his lifetime of labors is indispensable for the former's purposes. Freud himself remains focused on the more biological side of his psycho-physicalist influences conveyed to him through his early training in neurology; he never entirely leaves by the wayside his formative relations with this field. However, Lacan's structuralist-inflected "return to Freud," drawing on cybernetics, formal logic, game theory, knot theory, and topology as well as Saussurean linguistics,[25] prefers to emphasize the deeper Galilean undercurrents connecting the nineteenth-century psycho-physicalism coloring Freudian psychoanalysis to the modern regulative ideal[26] (or what Lacan identifies as "*La science*"[27] over and above given existent sciences) according to which the degree of scientificity is directly proportional to the degree of mathematization of the area under consideration.[28] To cut a long story short, Lacan, in "Science and Truth," proclaims yet again his fidelity to a psychoanalysis that is scientific precisely in the sense of grounding itself on a mathematical-type formalism liquidating the humanist image of individual persons in favor of an antihumanist theory of subjectivity-beyond-the-ego,[29] a subjectivity decipherable through the matrices of combinations of differentially codetermined signifying units distributed simultaneously in synchronic and diachronic dimensions (this being one of the several things referred to in this mid-1960s context by Lacan's use of the phrase "the subject of science").[30] But, as I will urge later, perhaps the biological facets of Freud's scientism, which Lacan tosses aside as a superficial naturalist shell hiding a core mathematical kernel, ought to be reexamined in a different, new (post-)Lacanian light.

Referring to the same passages quoted above, Miller comments that "in this sense, psychoanalysis can be considered as the manifestation of the positive spirit of science in a domain which has been specially resistant to the conceptual grasp of science."[31] In other words, as Lacan and many of his interpreters (including Serge Leclaire, another key psychoanalytic contributor to the *Cahiers*)[32] regularly maintain, Freudian analysis properly understood is not, as some might erroneously believe it to be, an obscurantist mysticism celebrating the unconscious as a dark underbelly, an irrational depth of primordial profundities forever evading the grasp of scientific-style reason's secular reflections.[33] If anything, psychoanalysis shares in the Weltanschauung of scientific modernity and the Enlightenment insofar as it pursues a hyperrationalist project of attempting, speaking loosely, to discover logic in the ostensibly illogical, reason in apparent unreason, and method in manifest madness.[34] Furthermore, like mathematized modern science, it also eschews positing any sort of deep meaning at the basis of the Real material base of being.[35] To borrow a turn of phrase from, of all people, Richard Rorty, analysis tries to "eff the ineffable" in the belief that the ineffable can be effed much more than is usually assumed—and, when it fails to do so, it at least tries to eff with conceptual-theoretical precision exactly why and how the ineffable cannot be effed directly in a particular case.[36]

§2 Analyzing Science: Lacan's Extimate Object

Seemingly in resonance with his recourse to modern science as involving an antihumanist mathematical-type formalism, Lacan proceeds to mention examples of specific sciences in which portraits of humanity are effaced. He points to, among other formalized discourses, game theory: "A case in point is game theory, better called strategy, which takes advantage of the thoroughly calculable character of a subject strictly reduced to the formula for a matrix of signifying combinations."[37] If this formalism alone is what garners a scientific status for structuralism generally and structuralist psychoanalysis specifically, then, as Lacan admits here, subjectivity (i.e., the subject of science, including the subject of an analysis constitutively indebted to modern science) is indeed entirely dissolved into the networked structures of transindividual symbolic orders.[38] Such a structuralist paradigm, as Milner describes it, amounts to a nonmathematical-but-literal (i.e., formally symbolized) dissolution of the nonformalizable qualities of humans as objects of investigation, echoing the Galilean privileging of primary (i.e., quantitative) over secondary (i.e., qualitative) properties in the scientific observation of material bodies.[39] But, passing without delay to the example of linguistics, the discipline of origin for structuralism and the key "scientific" partner of analysis in Lacan's Saussure-inflected "return to Freud," Lacan indicates that the subjectivity he is concerned with theorizing is not simply the subject as fully subjected to the constellations and movements of formally delineable representational units: "The case of linguistics is subtler as it must take into account the difference between the enunciated and enunciation, that is, the impact of the subject who speaks as such (and not of the subject of science)."[40] This sentence is crucial in that Lacan herein refers to his distinction between the subjects of enunciation and utterance so as to clarify that the former in particular (which consists of much that eludes formally delineable structures, including multifaceted affective and libidinal dimensions) is different from "the subject of science," itself associated with the cogito.[41] (As Bruce Fink helpfully explains, the Cartesian skeleton of the subject of the unconscious is an "unsaturated" subjectivity posited at the hypothetical level of metapsychological theory, whereas the subject actually dealt with in clinical practice is a subjectivity "saturated" by concrete affective and libidinal contents, permeated by drives, desires, fantasies, *jouissance,* and so on.)[42] The subject of the utterance, insofar as it is constituted on the basis of chains of concatenated signifiers differentially codetermining each other within the contexts of enveloping webs of larger batteries of signifiers forming surrounding symbolic big Others, looks to be amenable to treatment by game-theory-variety reductive formalism. And yet, it too cannot be straightforwardly equated with the symbolically subjected subject, the passive puppet or plaything of (in Hegelese) the "objective spirit" of autonomous signifying systems. Why not? Simply put, the subjects of enunciation and utterance are bound together in an oscillating dialectic of entangled, bidirectional influences making it such that they cannot actually be handled separately from one another.

Soon after these references to game theory and linguistics, Lacan turns to topology, reaching for one of his favorite topological objects: the Möbius strip.[43] He employs this object to underscore and complicate the demarcation between subjectivity and scientificity: "structuralism . . . ushers into every 'human science' it conquers a very particular mode of the subject for which the only index I have found is topological: the generating sign of the Möbius strip that I call the 'inner eight.'"[44] He then proposes that "the subject is, as it were, internally excluded from its object [*en exclusion interne à son objet*]."[45] The image of the Möbius strip, both in "Science and Truth" and elsewhere, is brought into association with, among other topics, the distinction between "knowledge" (*savoir*) and "truth" (*vérité*), a distinction bound up, especially in this 1965 presentation, with Lacan's interrelated readings of Descartes's philosophy, this philosophy's rendition of subjectivity à la the cogito, and the genesis of the break with premodern "science" via Galileo's mobilization of mathematics as the language of nature (as the physical universe).[46]

At this juncture, I want to underline the following: Lacan's structuralist psychoanalysis of the mid-1960s (itself really already a poststructuralism of a specific type) traces a convoluted topology of subjectivity such that psychoanalysis, although having been made historically possible by the advent of mathematized modern science and its subject (i.e., the cogito as subject of science) with Galileo and Descartes, peels away from such scientificity. As Alain Lemosof puts it, "if the subject is the correlate of science, it is a correlate which is . . . absolutely antinomic to science."[47] A plethora of other commentators concur, emphasizing the same point in slightly varying fashions.[48] Using one of Lacan's own neologisms, one might say that the subject, as psychoanalysis conceives of it, is "extimate"[49] (i.e., an intimate exteriority as an internal exclusion, a foreign void at the heart of the familiar) with respect to the sciences of post–Galilean/Cartesian modernity. Lacan and his disciples frequently speak of science as involving the *Verwerfung* of foreclosure, a "success-ful" paranoid psychosis, primal repressions of the truths upon which its knowledge rests, fetishist-style disavowal (*Verleugnung*) of that which defies treatment by its methods, motivated blindness to the ideological mechanisms enveloping and supporting it, and a death-drive-like com-pulsion toward knowledge at all costs come what may.[50] This recourse to the vocabulary of psychopathology unambiguously serves to advance the thesis that the sciences presuppose yet simultaneously exclude from con-sideration specific facets or kinds of subjectivity illuminated by psycho-analysis; that is to say, the sciences have an unconscious of sorts in the form of their defensively occluded foundational bases. Expressed in Lacanese, these disciplines "suture" such subjectivity[51] (although Miller, in "Action of Structure," draws attention to the difference between Lacan's use of the term "suture" apropos science and his own employ-ment of it in his 1966 article with this term as its title).[52] In the last sen-tence of "Responses to Students of Philosophy Concerning the Object of Psychoanalysis," Lacan, referring to a structuralism (or, again and more precisely, to his own brand of structuralism-beyond-structuralism) for-mally drawing the contours of the limits of its own formalizations, closes by remarking, "psychoanalysis as a science will be structuralist, to the point of recognizing in science a refusal of the subject."[53] Years later, in the twenty-third seminar, Lacan returns to and summarizes much of the preceding by insisting that the divided subject ($) of analysis "puts in question science as such."[54]

One moment in "Science and Truth" in particular reveals how, in this pivotal essay, Lacan's attention begins to be turned toward the ques-tion "What would a science be that included psychoanalysis?" At this point, he indicates that science will have to change in order to accom-modate "the object of psychoanalysis" (here, *objet petit a* as inextricably intertwined with the subject-as-$ in the structural logic encapsulated by the "formula of fantasy," whose Lacanian "matheme" is $\$ \lozenge a$):[55]

> And let me remind you that while, certainly, to now pose the question of psychoanalysis' object is to reraise a question I broached upon first mounting this rostrum—that of psychoanalysis' position inside or outside of science—I have also indicated that the question probably cannot be answered without the object's status in science as such being thereby modified.[56]

Generally speaking, in Lacanian theory, the barred subject and object *a* coimplicate each other in the form of fantasies as fundamental formations of the unconscious.[57] This coimplication between the subject and object of fantasy invariably entails one or more schematizing incarnations of conjunction ($\wedge$), disjunction ($\vee$), and relative positions of being greater than ($>$) or less than ($<$), with the "lozenge" of the "*poinçon*" ($\Diamond$) designating all of these possible permutations fleshed out by various fantasies of union or fusion, rejection or abandonment, domination or mastery, submission or slavery, and so on.[58] Lacan, in "Science and Truth," clearly maintains, first, that $ is extimate as "internally excluded" from the sciences of modernity (structuralist sciences too), and, second, that *a*, the fantasy-correlate of $, can be digested by the sciences only if they themselves are transformed in the process.

Fink makes reference to the passage quoted above on a couple of occasions.[59] He claims that "science itself is not yet capable of encompassing psychoanalysis. Science must first come to grips with the specificity of the psychoanalytic object . . . Lacan's view is that *science is not yet equal to the task of accommodating psychoanalysis.*"[60] This claim, and those of Lacan it echoes, can be construed in several manners, especially depending upon how one understands "science" in this context. Recourse to the distinction between what the French (and Lacan, albeit with grave reservations)[61] call the "human sciences" (i.e., both the humanities and social sciences, and including structuralist versions of these as well as what Lacan designates as "conjectural sciences,"[62] an example of which would be game theory) and the physical sciences (i.e., physics, chemistry, etc.) is mandatory here (one also could cast this as the difference between the "soft" sciences of culture and the "hard" sciences of nature). As for the so-called human sciences, an obvious way in which the psychoanalytic conception of the unconscious creates profound difficulties for these disciplines is that it undermines a basic assumption supporting and justifying both their methods and results: the presupposition that the human subjects studied and interrogated as these disciplines' objects of investigation are willing and able to furnish investigators with accurate and truthful self-reports through reflexive conscious introspection. Some of the resistance to psychoanalysis met with in the humanities and social sciences likely stems from a dim awareness on the part of the resisters that any acknowledgment of Freud's fundamental theses regarding psychical subjectivity would require casting into doubt, if not chucking into the trash can, veritable mountains of gathered data, thereby undermining any number of valued research programs and cherished theories—programs and theories laden with the libidinal investments of their academic partisans, investments governed, like all investments according to the Lacanian account of desire, by the unconscious subjective templates of fundamental fantasies (\$ ◊ a).[63] Vast swathes of the human sciences would require radical reworking if psychoanalysis is truly taken seriously by these fields. As the title of one of Lacan's best-known *écrits* has it, the "dialectic of desire in the Freudian unconscious" entails a "subversion of the subject" specifically as imagined by those scientists who assume that subjectivity is exhaustively equivalent to the transparency of reflective self-consciousness, be it their own purportedly nonsubjective subjectivity (along the lines of the Cartesian cogito as the anonymous subject of science devoid of the idiosyncrasies of particular subjectivities)[64] or that of their objects of investigation.[65]

But what about the physical sciences, namely, the hard sciences of nature as opposed to the human sciences as the soft sciences of culture? What implications, in addition to those sketched in the preceding paragraph applying equally to practitioners of any and every sort of science, would a rapprochement between the natural sciences and Freudian-Lacanian metapsychology generate—a rapprochement in which the interlinked subject and object of analytic metapsychology are no longer extimacies sutured by the sciences within which these intimate exteriorities have previously subsisted in internally excluded states as repressed, disavowed, or foreclosed? Of course, in the context of a discussion of psychoanalysis vis-à-vis these sciences, the first association that comes to mind should be Freud's complex rapport with the life sciences, that is, his frequent flirtations and multilevel engagements with biology. This is not the place to launch a futile attempt at frantically surveying the full story and scope of the fraught relations between psychoanalysis from Freud onward and both biology and biologism.[66] Instead, given my agenda in this chapter in terms of providing a contemporary assessment of Lacan's "Science and Truth" in light of the present state of the physical sciences (especially the life sciences, including the neurosciences), the remainder of what follows will involve the compressed formulation of a vision regarding the future possibilities of a new alliance in which psychoanalysis and the life sciences are reciprocally transformed in being folded into each other such that neither is eliminated or reduced away in its specificity in the process. In the background of this vision is the wager that Lacan's mapping of the frontier between analysis and the sciences of nature, after over four decades packed with momentous scientific developments, has become partially obsolete and in need of careful reconsideration in the early twenty-first century.

§3 A Moment of Truth: Analysis and Science After Lacan

In "Science and Truth," Lacan, with reference to Aristotle's four causes, emphasizes that psychoanalysis is concerned specifically with material causality.[67] However, the materialities in question here are the acoustic and graphic substances constitutive of pure signifiers as meaningless sounds and images independent of the meaningful sign-couplings of signifier and signified: "The material cause is truly the form of the impact of the signifier that I define therein."[68] Similarly, in his other contribution to the *Cahiers pour l'Analyse*, Lacan, reiterating a protest he vocalizes again and again,[69] maintains that "the least you can accord me concerning my theory of language is, should it interest you, that it is materialist."[70] Soon after mentioning the notion of material causality, he concludes that this necessitates divorcing the conception of subjectivity à la a psychoanalysis tied primarily to formal apparatuses (as per structural linguistics and anthropology, conjectural sciences such as game theory, various branches of mathematics, etc.) from anything having to do with the life sciences: "Conveyed by a signifier in its relation to another signifier, the subject must be as rigorously distinguished from the biological individual as from any psychological evolution subsumable under the subject of understanding."[71] Lacan's conclusion warrants critical revisitation today.

In *The Ego Tunnel*, the 2009 popularization of his 2003 tome *Being No One*, cognitivist philosopher of mind Thomas Metzinger reminds readers that a neuroscientifically informed account of subjects forces an alteration of the images and ideas of these sciences and their objects as well as the images and ideas shaping not-strictly-empirical theories of subjectivity.[72] That is to say, rendering mind immanent to matter requires a changed envisioning of matter paralleling a changed envisioning of mind; as Lacan puts this in a passage from "Science and Truth" quoted earlier, "the object's status in science as such" is "thereby modified." Arguably, this point is discernible in Žižek's engagements with the sciences[73] as well as writ large across the span of Malabou's oeuvre. Moreover, François Ansermet and Pierre Magistretti, in their recent efforts to bring together Freudian-Lacanian psychoanalysis and the neurosciences, appeal to moments such as certain of those to be found in "Science and Truth" as justifying their brave defiance of Lacanianism's pervasive dogmatic hostility to the life sciences.[74] One could even go so far as to assert that Lacan's odd materialism centered on the "material cause" of "the impact of the signifier"—the word "impact" (*incidence* as an effect or repercussion)[75] clearly evokes the collision of two bodies in the form of the acoustic and/or graphic materiality of the signifier slamming into the physical body of the organism—necessitates an indispensable addition in order to be truly materialist: a scientifically well-founded explanation of how and why human beings as living organisms can be and are transformed into the speaking beings spoken of by Lacanian theory. Lacanianism needs a fleshed-out delineation of what endogenously holds open the "natural" body's potentials to be exogenously impacted and subjectified by the denaturalizing signifiers of sociosymbolic orders. A failure or refusal to pinpoint the contingent yet a priori material conditions of possibility for the biological emergence of more-than-biological subjects risks allowing for (or even encouraging) the flourishing of irrational idealisms and obscurantist spiritualisms—illusions that ought not to have a future within and between psychoanalysis and science.

Of course, in his 1965 presentation, Lacan does not have the sciences of the brain in mind when addressing the issue of the scientificity of psychoanalysis. However, Lacan's relationship to things biological over the entire span of his teachings is not nearly so unwaveringly straightforward and consistent as is maintained by the widely believed old story according to which he unreservedly purges Freudianism of all traces of biomateriality in favor of a thoroughly formalized and antinaturalist metapsychology having nothing whatsoever to do with biology and its offshoots.[76] Both before and after "Science and Truth," Lacan not only calls for radically altering, based on psychoanalytic considerations, the protoconceptual pictures and metaphors underpinning the notion of "nature" in the natural sciences[77]—he also explicitly discusses the brain,[78] undeniably anticipating subsequent scientific insights into neuroplasticity, mirror neurons, and epigenetics (like Freud before him, he awaits a vindication of psychoanalysis from the life sciences as well as the formal and conjectural sciences).[79] These still incompletely digested scientific insights signal the urgency and timeliness of revisiting anew the intersection between psychoanalysis and science. A nonreductive yet scientifically grounded materialist theory of psychoanalytic subjectivity (one capable also of integrating key features of both dialectical materialism and existentialism) is finally foreseeable on the horizon, thanks not to further developments in pure mathematics, symbolic logic, and similar disciplines, but to empirical, experimental investigations into neural systems and evolutionary-genetic dynamics.

Several of the psychoanalytically minded contributors to the *Cahiers* would be suspicious, if not entirely dismissive, of the shotgun marriage between Freudian-Lacanian psychoanalysis and the biological sciences being pointed to by this intervention. With regard to science in general, Jacques Nassif, in the ninth issue of the *Cahiers* devoted to the "Genealogy of the Sciences," reiterates a well-worn stock assertion in French psychoanalytic circles: Freud's lifelong leanings in the direction of the physical sciences amounts to a lamentable self-misunderstanding on his part of the epistemological break (to use a Bachelaridian-Althusserian phrase dear to the members of the Cercle d'Épistémologie of the École Normale Supérieure) he accomplishes at the turn of the century with the invention of psychoanalysis as a novel discipline unprecedented in several respects.[80] On the heels of repeating this standard downplaying of Freud's references to various things scientific, Nassif gestures at a problem with integrating psychoanalysis into the empirical, experimental sciences quite familiar to every school of psychoanalysis (not just Lacanian and/or French analytic orientations): the absolutely singular character of the analytic experience resists and thwarts the "cumulative model" central to scientific knowledge.[81] In other words, not only does the inherent, irreducible idiosyncrasy of each and every clinical analysis prevent the possibility of repeated experimental replications as a process crucial for and integral to post-Baconian scientific method—according to Nassif, an impossible adding-up of utterly unique analytic insights purportedly peculiar to incomparable subjects-of-analyses does not yield an accumulation of "data" to be enshrined in a catalog-style encyclopedia of "facts" known by psychoanalysis, established facts on the basis of which further data could be collected and integrated (a movement of accumulation visible in long stretches of the history of the sciences).

Nassif's remarks warrant several responses. To begin with, Lacan's institutional experiments in his École freudienne, inaugurated just prior to the publication of issue number nine of the *Cahiers,* with the (notorious) procedure of *"la passe"*—this procedure is a kind of rite of passage from being an analysand to assuming the position of an analyst[82]—aim at, among other goals, finding a way to build up a repository of transmissible knowledge (*savoir*) obtained from a countless multitude of unrepeatable encounters with the unconscious. What is more, Lacan seeks to do so in manners that, like Hegel's *Aufhebung,* somehow manage to preserve-in-negation the particularity of these encounters while nonetheless simultaneously forcing them (as in a Badiouian struggle of *forçage*) to "pass" into the universal medium of iterable symbolic-linguistic formulations initially conveyed through testimony and subsequently conveyable through teaching within a community of speaking beings (such as analytic communities).[83] In fact, in his "Proposition of 9 October 1967 on the Psychoanalyst of the School," in which he first outlines the procedure of *la passe,* Lacan, contra what Nassif says about analysis in relation to cumulative scientific knowledge, declares regarding the proposed procedure of passage that "this proposition implies a cumulation of experience, its compilation and elaboration, an ordering of its varieties, a notation of its degrees."[84] An excessive insistence on the science-defiant uniqueness of clinical analyses, in which the heart of all analyses is threatened with being portrayed as the mystical experience of an inexpressible *je ne sais quoi,* is in danger of neglecting to take into consideration (extimate) features of Freudian-Lacanian psychical subjectivity intimately involving the external mediation of the "objective spirit" of the big Other as symbolic order (i.e., transindividual social, cultural, linguistic, institutional, etc., mediators constitutive of the *parlêtre* with its unconscious). Although certain Freudian-Lacanian considerations require being somewhat sympathetic to Nassif's emphasis on the particularity of analyses, neither Freud nor Lacan would be wholly comfortable with leaving things at that. In this vein and once again echoing Hegel, one could maintain that the notion of concrete particular analyses apart from abstract universal structures is itself the height of abstraction; or, put differently, each analysis is "singular" in the strict Hegelian sense, namely, an individual "concrete universal" as a dialectical convergence/ synthesis of both particular and universal constituents. Lacanian analysis consequently would be a paradoxical "science of the singular."

Admittedly, Lacan, right before his death, expresses reservations and regrets about *la passe* soon after having announced the "dissolution" of the École freudienne.[85] In line with his late-in-life renunciation of any claims to the effect that psychoanalysis is or could be scientific (I will touch upon this 1970s-era change in perspective in more detail below), he says of speaking beings with their unconsciouses, "It cannot be said that even in piling up, they form a whole."[86] He goes on to state, "Now I have a pile—a pile of people who want me to take them. I am not going to make a totality out of them. No whole."[87] These proclamations preface the announcement of the abolition of *la passe* and the corresponding "Analyst of the School" rank as the highest institutional status conferred upon successful *passeurs* within the now defunct (as of January 5, 1980) École freudienne. However, instead of appealing to the impossibility of accumulating transmissible information upon which Nassif insists, Lacan deems his experiment in psychoanalytic training in his former Freudian school a failure precisely "for having failed to produce Analysts within it who would be of the requisite level"[88] (i.e., not for having failed to produce knowledge of analysis through the accumulation of testimonies of submitters to *la passe* registered by and preserved through the analytic institution itself).

Lacan's vacillations vis-à-vis the "cumulative model" of scientific knowledge referred to by Nassif can be put aside in the present discussion—and this because the issues of replication and accumulation are not problems for the specific rapprochement between psychoanalysis and science I am suggesting here. Why not? I am not in the least bit interested in trying to reduce-away without remainder the singularity of more-than-biomaterial subjects with their distinguishing, individuating peculiarities; no attempt is being encouraged or undertaken to lay the foundations for a "scientific" (or, rather, pseudoscientific) psychoanalysis in which analysands are indifferently subjected to treatment as the fungible patients of a replicable clinical framework, system, or method, a poor (and impoverishing) imitation of the experimental sciences. For anyone even minimally acquainted with psychoanalysis, this would be both ridiculous and unethical. Nassif is quite right that many (although not all) facets of analysands, with their unrepeatable analyses with their chosen analysts, are difficult or impossible to replicate through representations transmissible to uninvolved, nonengaged third parties. But what Nassif overlooks the need for (at least if one wants to avoid falling back into the nebulous nonsense of idealisms and spiritualisms), and what recent related developments in the neurosciences as well as evolutionary theory (with its growing appreciation of nongenetic epigenetic, behavioral, and symbolic factors in phylogeny and ontogeny)[89] promise to provide, is a secular scientific basis explaining the nonmetaphysical conditions of possibility for the immanent material genesis of exactly those sorts of beings of overriding concern in analysis. Simply put, what I am heralding here is the potential for forging, at the intersection of psychoanalysis and the physical (especially life) sciences, a scientifically backed account of the genesis and structure of subjects that come to evade the grasp of the sciences themselves (for example, Nassif's analysand-subjects). Such would be a post-Lacanian inflection to the sense of what the paradoxical phrase "science of the singular" might mean for analysis in the near future. It seems to me that, in the absence of such an account, advocates of an analysis irreducible to any naturalism (of which I am one) are left with the unappealing choice between ultimately relying on either ontological dualisms or idealist epistemological agnosticism.

I can clarify and sharpen further the preceding remarks by turning attention to Leclaire's contributions to the *Cahiers*. Whereas Nassif

offers objections to a type of absorption of psychoanalysis into science—
my project entails neither the picture of science he has in view nor any
sort of eliminative absorption as collapse of the analytic into the scientific whatsoever—Leclaire offers objections directly addressing the field
of biology. Hence, for me, his reflections are even more topical and
important to address. Very much in step with Lacanian sensibilities as
(mis)understood at the time, Leclaire insists upon "the primacy of the
signifying order."[90] Zeroing in on the place of the body in psychoanalytic
metapsychology, he defines the analytic body as *an ensemble of erogenous
zones*"[91] (Leclaire's later writings spill a lot of ink in the delineation of
a theory of these corporeal sites).[92] In this relatively early sketch of his
conception of erogenous zones, Leclaire defines them at four levels: the
clinical, the structural, the topological, and the historical.[93] In the *Three
Essays on the Theory of Sexuality,* the text in which the analytic concept of
erogenous zones is first introduced at length, Freud, as he does throughout his work, anchors these zones (and the libidinal economy of drives
in which they feature centrally) in the anatomy of the living being, in
"somatic sources."[94] By contrast, Leclaire's list of four dimensions said
to be relevant to an analytic handling of the sexual and affective body
noticeably leaves out the dimension(s) of the biological.

Leclaire soon moves to defend and justify leaving out all levels having to do with biology. With detectable disdain for *"the body of the biologist,"*
he alleges that

> it is not necessary to ask how the erogenous body is founded in the
> structure of the biological body. But it is necessary to understand, on
> the contrary, that the biological body is constructed starting from the
> Signifier, that is to say, from the erogenous body. It is the biological
> body that it is necessary to derive from the erogenous body and not the
> reverse.[95]

He immediately adds, "Psychoanalysis places the accent on the Body as
an ensemble of erogenous zones. Freudianism is the accent placed on
this point."[96] It is highly dubitable that Freud himself would agree that
this is "Freudianism."[97] What is worse, particularly with the benefit of
subsequent philosophical and psychoanalytic hindsight, these remarks
cannot but appear to be symptomatic of the most flagrant form of an
idealist conflation of ontology with epistemology illegitimately projecting without qualification the limits of one discipline's circumscribed
domain of knowledge onto the being of the material real (in this case,
a conflation of what psychoanalysis as an interlinked theory and practice can know and should posit about the body with the body *an sich*

in all its aspects). This distorted and one-sided depiction of Lacanian psychoanalysis lends support to the accusations of Jean Laplanche and Badiou that Lacanianism tends to devolve into an *"idéalinguisterie"*[98] (or, in Meillassouxian parlance fashionable today, a subvariant of "correlationism").[99] Furthermore, it fails to reflect Lacan's own comparatively much more sophisticated and nuanced considerations of the sciences, embodiment, and the Real, among many other matters.

One might be tempted to interpret Leclaire's apparent idealism of "the Signifier" more charitably. Perhaps he is asserting, with respect to biology, that the scientific image of human beings, as assembled by scientists (who themselves are embodied speaking beings with unconscious desires and fantasies) handling signifiers pertaining to the body, is the product of a process of construction that cannot help inevitably channeling and reflecting formations of the unconscious bound up with the libidinally charged bodies of the constructing scientists themselves (this would be in conformity with some of the above-glossed lines of thought in "Science and Truth"). Even if this is what Leclaire really means—evidence that Leclaire sincerely believes "the Signifier" literally to govern from the very beginning "the order of the body"[100] suggests otherwise—one must be on guard against a crude, sweeping exaggeration which would exploit such assertions so as to leap to the conclusion that all biological science is through-and-through nothing more than a massive derivative and distorted sublimation of the "true" body (i.e., the nonbiological body assembled out of the signifiers of the Other marking sites on the flesh as erogenous zones, the constructed non-/prescientific body out of which the body of science is later itself assembled as a second-order construction). Leclaire undeniably betrays a tendency to endorse such a hyperbolic simplification of the life sciences in their entirety.

Stuck within the constraining parameters of a false dilemma pitting essentialist biology against antiessentialist psychoanalysis in a winner-takes-all fight to the end—the falsity of this zero-sum game is even more glaringly apparent nowadays, with the sciences having long ago dispensed with the ideational image of a nature diametrically opposed to "nurture"—Leclaire seems wrongly to be convinced that the only alternative to science reducing-away psychoanalysis is an inverse analytic reduction of science (as the backlash of a defensive, reactionary counteroffensive). At one point, Leclaire appeals to Lacan's mirror stage in his account of the body.[101] Ironically, his science-versus-psychoanalysis death match stages, on the terrain of theory, a spectacle of Imaginary rivalry arising from a fundamental *méconnaissance*.

The unsatisfactory nature of Leclaire's pseudo-Lacanian idealinguism manifests itself in stark relief when a few basic questions are posed: From where does "the Signifier" (or, more broadly, the symbolic order) ultimately originate phylogenetically? On the ontogenetic level, what is it about the body that makes possible and inclines it toward being over-written by signifiers coming from Others? If none of this immanently emerges from the world of matter investigated by the physical sciences, then from where does it emanate: God, *Geist,* some sort of mysterious metaphysical heaven, an utterly enigmatic X . . . ? In the face of such questions, Leclaire has two unpalatable options: either, one, espouse a Kantian-style critical idealism dogmatically asserting that such queries cannot be asked and answered in the vain hope of knowing the unknow-able (arguably, the progress of the sciences apropos these riddles, not to mention the numerous glaring inadequacies of Kant's Newtonian-era epistemology in terms of its inability to do justice to the state of the sciences from the early twentieth century onward, makes such appeals to a priori unknowables ring hollow); or, two, shamelessly endorse an absolute idealism of the Symbolic, namely, a solipsism of the almighty Signifier as a gross misrepresentation of Lacanianism. Under the sway of a certain, and sadly still commonplace, protoconceptual fantasy-image of Nature with a capital N (and attributing this picture to biologists), Leclaire is rendered unable to envision the option of a scientifically grounded yet nonreductive materialist psychoanalytic metapsychology, one willing and able to respond to the preceding fundamental questions in a nonidealist, nonmystical manner.

An utterly antinaturalist, antiscientific materialism is no material-ism at all, being materialist in name only. Any materialism worthy of the title must perform, in order to be truly materialist yet simultaneously nonreductive, a sort of theoretical jujitsu trick, a vaguely Gödelian-style in-/de-completion of the physical sciences. Ansermet, reflecting on cur-rent scientific appreciations of the brain's plasticity from an analytic angle—this plasticity, of which, again, Lacan himself anticipates the dis-covery, enables the neurosciences to be linked with "logosciences" such as Freudian-Lacanian psychoanalysis[102]—speaks of "a beyond of all biol-ogism" situated "at the very interior of biology."[103] Lacanian topologi-cal figurations of internal exclusions might appropriately come to mind. What is more, Ansermet indeed invokes Lacan's employments of topol-ogy in reference to the issue of the relation between science and psycho-analysis considered in terms of the nonantagonistic distinction between the neurosciences and the logosciences respectively:

> In effect, recent developments in the neurosciences permit advanc-
> ing that it is not about opposing them . . . The non-correspondence

between the biological and the psychical that the concept of plasticity tries to grasp opens onto the question of language. The neurosciences therefore open up to the logosciences, on condition of respecting their incommensurability. One cannot relate them except across a joint that one should conceive of as paradoxically disjoint. A disjoint relation: it is a topological problem that Lacan perhaps already resolved in his last constructions.[104]

As his obsession with topology and knot theory steadily intensifies during the late 1960s and 1970s, Lacan certainly speculates in numerous fashions about such topological paradoxes (especially with regard to the notoriously nonexistent "*rapport sexuel*"). And, in "Science and Truth," the subject ($) as well as the object (*a*) of psychoanalysis are said to be connected through disconnection to the then established sciences of the mid-twentieth century. But what both Ansermet and I are suggesting, in Lacan's aftermath, is that the present era is more than mature enough, considering the state of the life sciences nowadays, for beginning to attempt what Freud and Lacan each awaited: a future in which the disciplines composing the field of biology have become ready to greet psychoanalysis in such a manner as to initiate a trajectory of mutual modification of these sciences and analysis (as simultaneously a theory and a practice).

Playing off an irreducible nonnatural subject, portrayed as a mystery wholly inexplicable in empirical scientific terms, against the fictional straw-man caricature of a neuronal machine governed exclusively by the blind mechanisms of evolution and genetics merely reinstates a version of those dualisms that rightly are so anathema to the tradition of authentic materialism. When it comes to the subjects of concern to psychoanalysis (i.e., human beings as speaking subjects), the real challenge is to pinpoint and link up two parallel, complementary nodes of explanatory incompleteness within scientific and psychoanalytic discourses. A properly formulated neuro-psychoanalysis does precisely this. It engages in the double move of, one, supplementing Freudian-Lacanian psychoanalysis with a naturalist/biological account of the material underpinnings of denaturalized/more-than-biological subjectivity and, two, supplementing the neurosciences with a sophisticated, systematic metapsychological theory of subjects whose geneses, although tied to brains, involve much more than bare organic anatomy (these emergent subjects also come to have significant repercussions for the biomaterial bases that are the necessary-but-not-sufficient aleatory conditions of possibility for their very existences). One can and should strive to develop a scientifically shaped (although not purely and strictly scientific) account of how humans defying and escaping explanatory encapsulation by the sciences become what they are. Correlatively, a materialist psychoanalysis must be, as Lacan would put it, not without (*pas sans*) its scientific reasons, at the same time maintaining itself as a specific discipline whose objects of inquiry cannot be unreservedly absorbed without remainder into subject-less material being(s).[105]

Panning back to the perspective of a broad overview, Lacan's attitudes toward the notion of scientificity undergo major changes during the course of his intellectual itinerary. To get a sense of this arc of alterations, one finds, in the 1950s, statements such as "our discourse should be a scientific discourse"[106] ("our discourse" being, of course, psychoanalysis). By the 1970s, as already observed, this ambition is abandoned and repudiated.[107] For instance, continuing to conceive of the essence of modern science under the influence of Koyré, Lacan remarks, at the end of a session of the twentieth seminar, that "the analytic thing will not be mathematical. That is why the discourse of analysis differs from scientific discourse."[108] "Science and Truth" is an odd text situated midway between these two extremes, both chronologically and conceptually. Lacan's contribution to the first issue of the *Cahiers pour l'Analyse* neither simply crowns psychoanalysis a science according to some already fixed standard of scientificity nor strictly separates one discursive domain from the other. But, rather than construe this midway neither/nor as merely a transitional moment of indecision, as a wavering waiting for eventual resolution, maybe one ought to read this 1966 article in a Hegelian manner (and this regardless of whatever Lacan's own thoughts regarding science, in terms of the intentions supposedly lying behind his shifting pronouncements apropos this issue, might be). To be quite precise, one should interpret what appears to be the temporary negative absence of a decisive insight into the psychoanalysis-science (non-)rapport as already a direct positive revelation of this interdisciplinary link pregnant with potentials. This revelation allows for envisioning an unprecedented scenario in which a materialist metapsychology attains a scientific grounding (specifically through neurobiology) and, in so doing, reciprocally acts upon this same ground, thereby delineating the immanent biomaterial genetic emergence of structures and phenomena subsequently irreducible to and (partially) independent of the explanatory jurisdiction of the physical sciences and these sciences' objects of research. For a psychoanalysis not without relationships with the sciences, such is the road ahead after Lacan and in his shadow. A moment of truth has arrived.

3

On Deep History and Psychoanalysis: Phylogenetic Time in Lacanian Theory

§1 Traversing the Phylogenetic Fantasy: Revisiting the Archaic in Psychoanalysis

Starting with Freud, the topic of phylogeny has remained a vexed, troubling matter for psychoanalysis. Freud's ambivalence with respect to this issue is rather evident. On the one hand, especially in his later works, he repeatedly appeals to a phylogenetic "archaic heritage" both as a subject of metapsychological speculation and as an explanatory device at the level of clinical practice.[1] Freud not infrequently goes so far as to echo the theory of recapitulation à la Ernst Haeckel's famous statement asserting that "ontogeny recapitulates phylogeny."[2] (Before proceeding further, it must be noted that "phylogeny" and "ontogeny" are employed throughout what follows primarily in their Freudian analytic senses, as opposed to their contemporary scientific meanings; as Daniel Lord Smail clarifies, "natural selection allows organisms infinite room for variation—but the variation is infinite within a set of phylogenetic constraints that evolved upstream ... There's a subtle but crucial distinction ... between a phylogenetic constraint and what Freud called 'archaic heritage.' The former determines what you can't be; the latter determines part of what you are.")[3]

On the other hand, Freud's reservations regarding phylogenetic hypotheses are testified to not only by textual evidence—the fact that he refrains from publishing his metapsychological paper focused on such hypotheses (entitled "Overview of the Transference Neuroses")[4] bears witness to his hesitancy (a copy of this lost paper was discovered by Ilse Grubrich-Simitis in 1983 amongst Sándor Ferenczi's belongings, with Ferenczi himself having avidly indulged in musings about phylogeny). In a brief letter to Ferenczi (dated July 28, 1915) accompanying this draft manuscript, Freud tells him, "You can throw it away or keep it."[5] If Ferenczi had not kept it, this text would have been lost forever.

In print, the negative side of Freud's ambivalence vis-à-vis phylogeny comes through on a couple of occasions. The case study of the Wolf Man, although containing an instance of recourse to the claim that a reservoir of ancient, collective human experiences provides stock material for "primal phantasies" springing into operation when the individual's ontogenetic life history fails to furnish the psyche with such material,[6] harbors a moment of wavering with implications for his phylogenetic theories. Therein, Freud expresses this skepticism in a footnote:

> I admit that this is the most delicate question in the whole domain of psycho-analysis. I did not require the contributions of Adler or Jung to induce me to consider the matter with a critical eye, and to bear in mind the possibility that what analysis puts forward as being forgotten experiences of childhood (and of an improbably early childhood) may on the contrary be based upon phantasies created on occasions occurring late in life. According to this view, wherever we seemed in analyses to see traces of the after-effects of an infantile impression of the kind in question, we should rather have to assume that we were faced by the manifestation of some constitutional factor or of some disposition that had been phylogenetically maintained. On the contrary, no doubt has troubled me more; no other uncertainty has been more decisive in holding me back from publishing my conclusions. I was the first— a point to which none of my opponents have referred—to recognize both the part played by phantasies in symptom-formation and also the "retrospective phantasying" of late impressions into childhood and their sexualization after the event . . . If, in spite of this, I have held to the more difficult and more improbable view, it has been as a result of arguments such as are forced upon the investigator by the case described in these pages or by any other infantile neurosis—arguments which I once again lay before my readers for their decision.[7]

Later, in *The Ego and the Id* (1923), he very quickly performs a sort of intellectual *fort-da* game with phylogeny, remarking:

> With the mention of phylogenesis, however, fresh problems arise, from which one is tempted to draw cautiously back. But there is no help for it, the attempt must be made—in spite of the fear that it will lay bare the inadequacy of our whole effort.[8]

Of course, in the longer of these two passages from 1918's "From the History of an Infantile Neurosis," the thesis positing the effective existence of a deeply buried, hardwired archaic phylogenetic heritage is not itself directly in question; indeed, it is spoken of as established ("we should rather have to assume that we were faced by the manifestation of some constitutional factor or of some disposition that had been phylogenetically maintained"). Instead, the supposition of the actual, factual historical reality of early infantile/childhood episodes as the concrete ontogenetic basis of fundamental fantasies is manifestly what is explicitly at stake.

However, considering that Freud elsewhere concedes a reciprocity between phylogeny and ontogeny such that the former is reverse-engineered out of the latter—this indicates that factors pertaining to the ontogenetic dimension can and do entail implications for the phylogenetic dimension[9]—Freud's worries circling here around retroactive deferred action (i.e., *Nachträglichkeit, après-coup*) ought to apply to the phylogenetic as much as to the ontogenetic. That is to say, not only is a healthy skepticism warranted when analytically confronting the traces of unconscious fantasies apparently originating in very early life events, namely, in the singular subject's prehistory—serious doubts should be entertained in reaction to narrative tableaus purporting accurately to depict the shared ordeals of humanity transpiring long, long ago, namely, in the transindividual group's prehistory. In short, Freud has no reason to abstain from raising the same reservations in connection with phylogeny that he raises in connection with ontogeny. (Also, it is worth observing that these reservations regarding retroaction in ontogeny surface only a few pages after a seemingly quite confident deployment of the notion of archaic heritage in the same text—maybe a displacement of uncertainty is at work on this occasion.)

Lacan cuts the knot of Freud's ambivalent rapport with things phylogenetic by more or less jettisoning them. Unlike Freud, he has no sympathy whatsoever for the idea of the ontogenetic recapitulating the phylogenetic.[10] He mocks Ferenczi's wild imaginings in these Freudian veins.[11] For a thinker committed to a conception of both individual and collective histories as essentially staccato movements, as propelled and marked by sharp breaks and ruptures thwarting consistency through repeatedly introducing irreparable discontinuities,[12] Lacan detects the suspect assumption of too much substantial, underlying temporal continuity dwelling at the heart of the ontogenetic-phylogenetic couplet—a couplet he sees as indissociable from a problematic, nonpsychoanalytic developmental psychology of well-ordered, sequential stages organically flourishing out of a preordained (perhaps "natural") program.[13] At one point, he compares the recapitulationist version of the ontogeny-phylogeny link to the protorationalist Socratic-Platonic doctrine of reminiscence, an epistemological doctrine resting on an ontological theory of a unified soul (*psuchê, âme*) harmoniously enmeshed with the organic polis, the enveloping cosmos, and the timeless heaven of pure forms[14] (needless to say, for Lacan, Freudian analysis, with its split subject [$], irreversibly shatters this ancient vision of ultimate, seamless unity).

The agenda of this chapter is, in essence, simple: to challenge the Lacanian prohibition of phylogenetic speculations in psychoanalytic metapsychology (this includes Lacan's recurrently pronounced ban on asking after the origins of language). As will be seen, doing so does not mean thoughtlessly endorsing the shakiest, most dubitable versions of such speculations as articulated by Freud; it is not as though the concept-term "phylogeny" is inherently and necessarily wedded to a Haeckel-style recapitulationism automatically entailing the continuity and consistency of a fundamental, macrocosmic totality, a grand One-All as "the great chain of being." What is more, given relatively recent advances in relevant fields (biology and its offshoots first and foremost), Lacan's now somewhat dated arguments (primarily of an epistemological variety) against investigations into archaic origins and sources are much less convincing than they once were. They arguably might not hold water anymore. Harvard historian Daniel Lord Smail's important and intriguing 2008 book *On Deep History and the Brain* will play a key role in this critical reassessment of phylogeny in relation to Lacanian theory.

§2 "In the Beginning Was the Word": Lacan's Sacred History

Lacan periodically identifies himself as a materialist, hinting that he is inclined in the direction of Marxist-inspired historical and dialectical materialisms in particular.[15] Moreover, as observed earlier (see the first chapter), he indicates that one of the remaining crucial tasks bequeathed to contemporary materialists is the surprisingly incomplete and difficult struggle exhaustively to secularize materialism, to purge it of camouflaged residues of religiosity hiding within its ostensibly godless confines. As argued at length in the first chapter above, carrying out the mission of forging a fully atheistic and materialist Lacanian theoretical apparatus requires, among other things, forcing psychoanalysis and the life sciences dialectically to interpenetrate each other. Thus far, my efforts here and elsewhere[16] to meet this requirement have been centered on constructing scientifically informed yet nonreductive/noneliminative accounts of various aspects of ontogenetic subject-formation. But insofar as these ontogenetic accounts take for granted the established framework of transindividual sociolinguistic scaffoldings preexisting the being of the living entity thrown into processes of subjectification, the question of whether these collective historico-representational structures (i.e., Lacanian big Others) themselves are amenable to and ought to be brought into the orbit of (quasi-)naturalist, biomaterialist strategies of explanation remains open. In other words, for an ontogenetic theory of subject-formation elaborated at the intersection of Freudian-Lacanian psychoanalysis and the life sciences not to presuppose tacitly, in the phylogenetic background, the enigmatic, impossible-to-see-behind "Holy Spirit"[17] of a mysteriously always-already given big Other as symbolic order—such a presupposition hardly becomes any position purporting to be anti-idealist, immanentist, and atheist—scientifically guided investigations into the early emergence of the properly socio-representational dimensions of humanity (i.e., inquiries into phylogeny) must be pursued and integrated into analytic theory. This chapter is a first, rough and preliminary gesture in this direction.

In the third seminar, Lacan bluntly admits that "I'm not interested in prehistory"[18] (the full significance of this admission will become glaringly apparent in the last section of this chapter). Later, in the ninth seminar, he makes clear that, in line with a very standard view among historians themselves, he privileges the invention of writing as demarcating the boundary between prehistory and history proper.[19] Even later, in "L'étourdit," Lacan speaks of "the misery of historians" as their being confined to investigating "documents of signification" (i.e., writings of which they can make sense, in relation to which they can establish a *connaissance* and/or *méconnaissance*).[20]

One of Lacan's invariant principles affirmed regularly across the lengthy span of his intellectual itinerary is that the constellations of his register of the Symbolic must be treated as always-already given, established realities preexisting any and every particular subject.[21] He describes the "symbolic dimension"[22] as "the whole symbolic, original order—an environment"[23]—as an "environment," this "dimension" entirely envelops those living beings delivered into subjectivity, not only surrounding them, but making their forms of life possible to begin with. Appealing to the authority of Heidegger (someone incarnating anything but a Marx-inspired historical/dialectical materialism indebted to the physical, experimental sciences of modernity), Lacan maintains that "language is there before man, which is evident. Not only is man born in language, exactly as he is born into the world, but he is born by language."[24] As mentioned above, Lacan, while tending to defend his interdict of queries probing the origins of language on epistemological grounds, sometimes blurs together epistemological and ontological strata of reflection without explicit explanation and justification.[25] In these just-quoted assertions, the ontological emphasis (under Heideggerian influence) is to the fore, with the human being qua *parlêtre* (speaking being) owing his or her very existence to the eternally prior Symbolic big Other into which he or she is thrown. Similarly, Lacan elsewhere claims that "the best anthropology can go no further than making of man the speaking being."[26] As François Balmès insightfully remarks in a study focusing on the Heidegger-Lacan relationship, "At the very moment where he solemnly proclaims not to have an ontology, Lacan forges the term *parlêtre*."[27] The fact that Lacan doesn't consistently restrict himself to a Kantian/Wittgensteinian–style epistemology in which the prison-house of language (to borrow a phrase from Fredric Jameson) sets limits rendering the non-/extralinguistic inaccessible to linguistically constituted and mediated knowledge is on display in declarations like "reality is *at the outset* marked by symbolic nihilation"[28] ("*la réalité est marquée* d'emblée *de la néantisation symbolique*")[29] and "the symbolic universe exists first, and the real universe comes to settle itself down in its interior."[30]

Similarly, in what one might suspect is a less-than-secular bend of his knee to the Bible, Lacan again and again redeploys as one of his axioms the appropriated announcement, "In the beginning was the Word."[31] He insists that "it's an enigmatic beginning."[32] No wonder, then, that he earlier, in a session of the fourth seminar entitled by Jacques-Alain Miller "The Signifier and the Holy Spirit," proclaims that "the Holy Spirit is the entrance of the signifier into the world."[33] But why must the genesis of "*le Verbe*" (i.e., the logos of sociosymbolic orders as signifiers and linguistic-institutional systems) be left shrouded in (sacred) mystery? How does Lacan justify this insistence on the emergence of language (or, at least, language-like structures) as a timeless enigma?

One line of argumentation insinuated by Lacan quietly trades on Freud's premise that one is able to move back and forth between ontogeny and phylogeny such that findings at one level can be applied to the other level (i.e., there is a reciprocity in which ontogenetic phenomena reveal aspects of phylogenetic sequences and vice versa). Throughout the course of his teachings, Lacan contends that, ontogenetically speaking, the "preverbal," as what comes before the acquisition of language by the young, nascent subject-to-be, is capable of being (mis)recognized exclusively through *après-coup* retrojections arising from and conditioned by the "verbal"; speaking beings seeking to apprehend what they were prior to sociolinguistic subjectification are doomed to project backwards the verbal onto the preverbal,[34] to be stuck straining in vain to reach an inherently inaccessible transcendence.[35] Along these lines, in a 1956 paper coauthored with Wladimir Granoff, Lacan straightforwardly states:

We must first recall that psychoanalysis, which permits us to see farther into the psyche of children than any other science, was discovered by Freud through the observation of adults—more precisely, by listening to them or, rather, to their speech. Indeed, psychoanalysis is a "talking cure."[36]

Lacan and Granoff continue:

To recall such generally accepted truths may at first seem an imposition; upon reflection, it is not. It is only a reminder of an essential method-ological point of reference. For, unless we are to deny the very essence of psychoanalysis, we must make use of language as our guide through the study of the so-called pre-verbal structures.[37]

This "methodological" constraint bearing upon ontogeny as the tem-porally elongated emergence of the *parlêtre* also gets applied by Lacan to matters pertaining to phylogeny. In particular, the problem of the ancient creation of languages is handled by him exactly as is the prever-bal in the life history of singular speaking subjects. One of the ironies in the current context is that this move partially assumes and accepts the mutually mirroring parallelism between the phylogenetic and the onto-genetic proposed by Freud, a proposal Lacan, as pointed out above, dis-misses as analytically wrong-headed. More generally, as the engagement with Smail's work below will show, the presumed equivalence between speechless infants and archaic human beings has become extremely con-tentious and debatable.

Exemplary instances of Lacan's unwavering stance vis-à-vis the question of the origin of language are to be found both relatively early and quite late in his corpus. Relatively early, at the very start of the sec-ond seminar, he says:

When something comes to light, something which we are forced to consider as new, when another structural order emerges, well then, it creates its own perspective within the past, and we say—*This can never not have been there, this has existed from the beginning.* Besides, isn't that a property which our own experience demonstrates?[38]

As seen, Lacan himself recurrently expresses the view, as regards lan-guage, that *"this can never not have been there, this has existed from the begin-ning."* Hence, a plausible interpretation of this passage is that, in tension with his stronger ontological claims about the primordial, ground-zero originarity of "the Word," he is on this occasion content to rest with a weaker epistemological claim to the effect that the initial advent of the "structural order" of the Symbolic big Other engenders a Kantian-type necessary/transcendental illusion, a mirage in which this order appears as always-already established and present. Immediately following the preceding quotation, Lacan turns to the topic of language's root-source:

> Think about the origins of language. We imagine that there must have been a time when people on this earth began to speak. So we admit of an emergence. But from the moment that the specific structure of this emergence is grasped, we find it absolutely impossible to speculate on what preceded it other than by symbols which were always applicable. What appears to be new thus always seems to extend itself indefinitely into perpetuity, prior to itself. We cannot, through thought, abolish a new order. This applies to anything whatsoever, including the origin of the world.[39]

Human history prior to the surfacing of language-as-speech is, for Lacan, Real as impossible. This archaic phylogenetic *an sich,* although admitted to exist, if only as a spectral preexistence outside the domain of acknowledged existence proper (i.e., the being of existence as constituted by the logos of an onto-*logy*), is an epistemologically out-of-bounds, off-limits time before time, a Real beyond the Imaginary-Symbolic realities of speaking beings.

Moreover, following closely in Kant's footsteps, Lacan alleges that illegitimate speculative attempts to overstep the linguistically demarcated border between the prehistorical-as-prelinguistic and the historical-as-linguistic generate fictions and phantasms.[40] As he has it, efforts symbolically to comprehend the pre-/nonsymbolic inevitably result in the production of mere confabulations (i.e., "organized deliriums"):

> Well understood, the question of the origin of language is one of those subjects which best lends itself to organized deliriums, collective or individual. This is not what we have to do with. Language is there. It is an emergent. Now that it has emerged, we will never again know when or how it commenced, nor how things were before it was.[41]

Although the first occurrence of "we" in this quotation ("This is not what we have to do with") almost certainly refers to "we analysts," the second occurrence of "we" ("we will never again know") has a much wider semantic scope, referring to all agents of knowing. That is to say, while Lacan starts with what initially sounds like a stipulation holding strictly for analytic clinical practitioners (i.e., a methodological principle, in the spirit of what is said in the earlier-quoted paragraphs from the "Fetishism" essay coauthored with Granoff), he quickly jumps to the broadest of theoretical levels stretching well beyond psychoanalysis alone. One reasonably might wonder what, if anything, licenses this abrupt leap across the span of many wide chasms. But, for the time being, attention should be paid to the absolutism of the final sentence of these lines. Therein, Lacan emphasizes the ineliminable permanence ("never") of this fantasy-inducing ignorance.

Well after the 1950s, in the seventeenth, eighteenth, and nineteenth seminars, Lacan once again underscores what he puts forward as a theoretically fundamental law against raising the question of origins with respect to the symbolic order. In the seventeenth seminar, he comments, "We all know that to structure knowledge correctly one needs to abandon the question of origins," specifically "the origins of language."[42] In the eighteenth seminar, Lacan attributes the historical progress made by linguistics to this discipline's abandonment, in the nineteenth century, of the problem of the primordial historical sources of languages; it thereby bids farewell to a "period of genetic mythification."[43] In the nineteenth seminar, Lacan adamantly endorses this prohibition.[44] Knowledge gets nowhere if it wastes its precious time getting entangled in the semblances of hallucinations, imaginings, and rantings.

Returning to the highlighted issue of Lacan's unqualified absolutism (à la the "never" in "we will never again know"), he subtly introduces qualifications on other occasions. For instance, subsequently in the second seminar, he speaks of a conceptual grasp of the birth of language in a conditional mode ("if") and replaces "never" with "for a long time" ("if we had an idea of how language is born—something which we must renounce any knowledge of for a long time").[45] In the seventeenth seminar, he hints that insights into the origins of language can be inferred retroactively from within and out of language itself.[46] And, in 1967, Lacan rearticulates himself thus:

> Do not imagine that man invented language. You're not sure of it, you have no proof, and you've not seen any human animal become before you *Homo sapiens* like that. When he is *Homo sapiens*, he already has language. When one, and especially a certain Helmholtz, wanted to interest oneself in it in linguistics, one refused to raise the question of origins. That was a wise decision. It does not mean that this is a prohibition it would be necessary to maintain forever, but it is wise not to tell fabricated tales, and one always tells fabricated tales at the level of origins.[47]

In the section dealing with Smail to follow shortly, Lacan's appeal to ignorance ("you have no proof") will be submitted to harsh interrogation. Additionally, whether strictures productive for certain domains (for example, linguistics and/or psychoanalysis) are applicable and conducive to other domains is highly questionable. Related to this and at an intrapsychoanalytic level, whether a (methodological/epistemological) limit appropriate to clinical analysis (in which ontogeny predominates) directly and as a matter of course holds for analytic metapsychology is also vulnerable to fierce dispute. However, the preceding quotation is especially curious for its last sentence: "It does not mean that this is a prohibition it would be necessary to maintain forever, but it is wise not to tell fabricated tales, and one always tells fabricated tales at the level of origins." It contains a tension, if not an outright contradiction. On the one hand, Lacan concedes that the interdict forbidding inquiry into the origins of linguistic-symbolic configurations, an interdict he unflinchingly upholds, need not be taken as eternally unbreakable. On the other hand, he goes on to postulate, in the very same sentence and in accordance with his own orthodoxy, that any and every eventual breaking of this taboo inevitably ("always") gives rise to confabulations, fantasies, fictions, illusions, etc. ("fabricated tales"). Is this to suggest that, some day in the indeterminate future, people ought to resume constructing stories of phylogenetic origins, even if the products of these activities amount to nothing more than that, namely, just-so stories? Does this indicate that Lacan believes some tales yet to be told have the chance to be less false and misleading than the tales told thus far in and about human history (in the same manner in which Christianity is, for him, "the one true religion"[48] as the least false of all religions)?[49] Are certain artificial, contrived narratives of phylogeny somehow (potentially) preferable or superior to others? These unanswered (and, perhaps, unanswerable) questions aside, I am interested in gambling on the hypothesis that the moment Lacan casts into a hazy, distant, not-guaranteed-to-arrive future (i.e., the "long time" [*Seminar II*] of the not "forever" [*"Place, origine et fin de mon enseignement"*]) has, indeed, finally arrived—and this maybe sooner than expected (at least for Lacan and most Lacanians).

§3 The Damning Witness of Material Signifiers: Toward a Lacanian Deep History

Daniel Lord Smail's 2008 *On Deep History and the Brain,* a book using the neurosciences to dismantle firmly entrenched, long-standing perceptions regarding prehistory as distinct from history proper, not only is incredibly relevant to the topic of phylogeny (as archaic heritage) in Freudian-Lacanian psychoanalysis—this compact text deserves careful attention from today's philosophers and theorists concerned with novel varieties of materialism and realism. Before examining *On Deep History and the Brain* in light of the preceding analyses of Lacan, Smail's position should be situated with respect to Meillassoux's realist speculative materialism in particular. Smail unearths a zone neglected by partisans of various versions of "speculative realism" (a movement spawned by Meillassoux's 2006 programmatic treatise *After Finitude: An Essay on the Necessity of Contingency*).

Without providing a synopsis of *After Finitude*—this clear, concise book has been summarized thoroughly in other contexts[50]—suffice it to say that Meillassoux's focus on "ancestrality"[51] in his assault on idealist "correlationism"[52] obviously is fixated upon the labor of thinking a time before thought (i.e., an "ancestral" real[ity] prior to the coming-into-existence of sentient and, eventually, sapient beings). One of Ray Brassier's supplements to Meillassoux's critique of correlationist idealism consists in foregrounding a future after both sentience and sapience (i.e., "life after humans" as well as all other forms of [self-]aware existence, up to and including the death-by-dissipation of the physical universe itself) in addition to a past before any and every consciousness.[53] What is more, as Badiou and Laplanche, among others, already indicate well before the recent birth of speculative realism as an orientation,[54] Meillassoux and Brassier undoubtedly likewise would identify the Lacan discussed in the preceding section as a structural linguistic correlationist for whom the pre-Symbolic (or, for Brassier, post-Symbolic as well) Real exists solely in and through a (co-)constituting correlation with the Symbolic.

And yet, what Lacan's "idealinguistic" correlationism obfuscates specifically with regard to the psychoanalytic problem of phylogeny, and what Smail renders palpably visible, is neither Meillassoux's ancestral time of the "arche-fossil"[55] nor Brassier's post-apocalyptic future of extinction. Smail too presents arguments against what could be labeled a certain sort of correlationism prevalent among historians and, as demonstrated at length earlier, shared by Lacan (especially when he addresses the question of the origin of language). However, what this correlationist creed denies is a real(ity) neither prior nor posterior to awareness/sentience, but, rather, a time of sentience, and probably even sapience, anterior to the currently remaining testimony of sociosymbolic written documents as, so to speak, linguistic fossils; Smail isolates not past or future times entirely external to human beings, as do Meillassoux and

Brassier, but instead he pinpoints, in Lacanese, a time that is "extimate" in relation to humanity, an "arche," as it were, in history more than history itself. This time is casually labeled "prehistory" by both professional historians and the habits of everyday discourse. Smail convincingly contends that this is a loaded word implying that, before the invention of writing and related technical, practical, and ideational forms, humanity presumably dwelt in an unchanging natural stasis as opposed to the changing cultural kinesis supposedly ushered into being exclusively thanks to a sociosymbolic revolution inexplicably irrupting almost ex nihilo.[56] At the beginning of his text, Smail contrasts "prehistory" with "deep history": "Historians, for all intents and purposes, still regard deep history as prehistory, the time before history."[57]

How, exactly, does Smail define deep history in his precise sense? Right up front, he offers this preliminary definition:

> A deep history of humankind is any history that straddles this buffer
> zone, bundling the Paleolithic and the Neolithic together with the Post-
> lithic—that is, with everything that has happened since the emergence
> of metal technology, writing, and cities some 5,500 years ago. The result
> is a seamless narrative that acknowledges the full chronology of the
> human past.[58]

In Smail's view, the "full chronology" is, according to his deep historical ambitions, the long as opposed to the short chronology. For him, Lacan definitely would count as a proponent of the short chronology, that is, as an opponent of deep history (Freud, by contrast, would count as an advocate of a deep history [i.e., phylogeny as archaic heritage] constructed with the combined help of clinical analyses and Darwinian speculations—instead of, as in Smail's position, with the help of neurobiology). This truncated timeline, unlike the much vaster one favored by deep history, treats everything older than four- to five-thousand years as prehistory, not history per se.

One of the catchiest refrains in Smail's book is his assertion that the shallow history of the short chronology is a symptom of a lingering Judeo-Christian hangover.[59] Despite the nineteenth-century "time revolution" brought about by geological discoveries, an event in which the biblical account of creation and all its fruit rapidly were uprooted empirically,[60] Smail shows how historical consciousness (that of both historians and laypersons) lagged behind this revolution (in the well-known Lacanian terms of Octave Mannoni, unconscious fidelity to Judeo-Christianity results in historical consciousness resorting to a fetishistic "disavowal" [Verleugnung] of the "castrating" blow of the geology-driven time revolution, leading to variations of the line "je sais bien, mais quand *même* . . .").[61] To greater or lesser extents, this consciousness continues to fail completely to digest the revolutionary implications flowing from revelations of "deep time" brought about via such domains as geology and astrophysics. (Meillassoux and Brassier similarly draw attention to failures by philosophers and quotidian individuals to confront the consequences of a time whose depth and breadth exceeds the finitude of humanity itself.) Smail blames religiously inculcated habits of thought, engrained over the course of many, many centuries, for the absence of and resistance to an honest, thorough reckoning with deep time:

> Of all the obstacles to a deep history, the most serious may well prove to be simple inertia. For several thousand years, historians writing in the Judeo-Christian tradition were accustomed to framing history according to the short chronology of sacred, or Mosaic, history, the chronology that frames the story recounted in Genesis. The time revolution brought an end to the short chronology as a matter of historical fact. Yet the historical narrative that emerged in U.S. history curricula and textbooks between the late nineteenth century and the 1940s did not actually abandon the six thousand years of sacred history. Instead, the sacred was deftly translated into a secular key: the Garden of Eden became the irrigated fields of Mesopotamia, and the creation of man was reconfigured as the rise of civilization. Prehistory came to be an essential part of the story of Western Civ, but the era was cantilevered outside the narrative buttresses that sustain the edifice of Western Civilization. Its purpose was to illustrate what we are no longer. In this way the short chronology persisted under the guise of a secular human history.[62]

Smail provides helpful reiterations of this powerful thesis further on in his book. Addressing short chronological treatments of such "catalyzing events" as the invention of writing, he observes:

> The catalyzing events described in these accounts are secular. Nevertheless, they function in the narrative in a fashion identical to the infusion of God's grace. I make no claim, would in fact resist the claim, that the authors of these accounts were crypto-creationists. The problem lies in the grip of the narrative itself, whose rhythms and patterns were left essentially unchanged as the sacred was translated into the secular.[63]

In the paragraph summing up the chapter in which the above quotation is situated, Smail writes:

> By the early twentieth century, most professional historians had abandoned sacred history. Yet the chronogeography of sacred history and

its attendant narrative of rupture has proved to be remarkably resilient. History still cleaves to its short chronology. The otherwise meaningless date of 4000 B.C. continues to echo in our histories. Authors still use the narrative device of rupture to create an artificial point of origin, reducing the Paleolithic to the status of a prologue to history, humanity's "apprenticeship." And history's point of origin is still Mesopotamian, or even more recent than that, given how the myth of the medieval origins of the modern world has embedded itself in the historical community.[64]

Smail's lucid writing requires little by way of accompanying clarifications. So, circumnavigating promptly back to Lacan on phylogeny, one can make the claim, relying upon Smail, that Lacan himself (however wittingly or unwittingly) inhabits the prison of sacred history. To be more exact, even if Lacan's avowed psychoanalytic atheism guarantees that the contents of his theorizations regarding the ontogenetic and the phylogenetic are secular, Smail's insights compel an acknowledgment that crucial formal features of these same theorizations are far from secular, ultimately amounting to disguised vestiges of a traditional, conservative theology.

Here, Lacan falls victim to a trap he himself dissects better than anyone else: atheists who noisily trumpet the ostensible death of God usually tend to ignore the fashions in which, as Lacan puts it, "God is unconscious";[65] from the standpoint of psychoanalysis, the less one consciously believes oneself to believe, the more likely is it that one's beliefs will persist precisely by remaining unconscious and unanalyzed.[66] An analysis of Lacan, as atheistic in the ways in which Lacan insists any genuine analysis worthy of the name must be,[67] demands flushing out and liquidating his own conscious and unconscious stubborn investments in the theological and religious. That is to say, if Lacan is sincere in his rallying cry for the pursuit of the arduous, far-from-finished endeavor of secularizing materialism, then faithfulness to this Lacan dictates submitting to merciless criticism those other Lacans who deviate from this uphill path.

Related to the notion of materialism, Smail sees sacred history as an outgrowth of an onto-theology. Specifically, he links it to an idealist ontological dualism epitomized by, of course, Descartes:

> The short chronology of the standard historical narrative of the twentieth century was built on a rigid Cartesian distinction between mind and body: the body may be old, but the mind, for all intents and purposes, is young. This is why the standard historical chronology used in cultures influenced by Judeo-Christianity, beginning as it did around 4000 B.C., could afford to ignore humanity's deep history.[68]

One easily could substitute *"parlêtre"* for "mind" here to produce an accurate rephrasing of certain of Lacan's antiphylogeny sentiments. As seen, Lacan concedes that humans as biological organisms (i.e., as bodies) have existed for longer than the comparatively shorter stretch of recorded history (i.e., short/sacred history as based solely upon sociolinguistic remains). But he plunges these bodies into the dark noumenal abyss of an impossible as inaccessible Real forever after obscured and obliterated by the genesis of "mind" as symbolically mediated subjectivity. As noted previously, I have elaborated in detail on other occasions how a properly materialist and secular Lacanianism can and must articulate a theoretical account of ontogenetic subject formation grounded, in part, on the life sciences (primarily the neurosciences and evolutionary theory).[69] But, in order to go to the end, to finish the job thoroughly, the same sort of articulation has to be spelled out for the phylogenetic formation of the collective "objective spirit" (in Hegelian parlance) of Lacan's Symbolic big Other(s). Again, fidelity to the truly atheist Lacan forces a betrayal of the Lacan who categorically forbids phylogenetic inquiries.

In addition to the "inertia" of unconscious beliefs in sacred history, beliefs borne witness to by the forms (rather than the contents) of historical narratives, Smail draws attention to explicit epistemological objections underpinning resistance to the acceptance of deep history. Although *On Deep History and the Brain* unsurprisingly involves no engagement with Lacan (there is, however, a passing mention of "poststructuralism" therein),[70] Lacan's critiques of phylogenetic reasoning on the grounds of epistemology are, as should come as no shock by now, precisely the same objections made by the historians described in Smail's book who cling to the not-so-secular short chronology. Just as Lacan insists that history must begin with "the Word" (i.e., the "Holy Spirit" of the big Other as symbolic order),[71] if only due to the epistemological finitude/limitations of historically conscious subjects as speaking beings always-already ensconced in sociolinguistic constellations, so too do resisters rejecting Smailian deep history insist that "documents," conceived of as sociolinguistic records and remnants, are the sole basis for the (re)construction of any and every plausible, defensible history.[72] As Smail elegantly encapsulates this line of resistance, "That speechless past: no other phrase could capture so well the skeptical attitude toward the possibility of studying time beyond the veil."[73] This sentence could be applied directly to Lacan himself. Through mobilization of the explanatory strategies and resources of the life sciences, Smail demonstrates that investigators can and should tear aside this veil and cross the threshold beyond the shallowness of the sacred.

The crux of Smail's rebuttals of the epistemological objections raised against deep history is his distinction between "documents" and "traces."[74] Succinctly stated, documents are the written records, composed in natural languages, which advocates of the short chronology insist upon as the only reliable and valid foundations upon which to erect historical narratives. By contrast, traces, as defined by Smail, can be documents, but further encompass a much broader range of materials, including remnants left from before the time of history as recorded by written, linguistic documents as per the short chronological definition of these sources. Smail's examples of traces are "artifacts, fossils, vegetable remains, phonemes, and various forms of modern DNA"[75] as well as "cave paintings," "graves and grave goods."[76] Obviously, only vegetable remains and DNA are evidently troubling instances for Lacan, Smail's other examples of traces fitting Lacan's criteria for signifying elements of structural-symbolic systems. Lacan's short history would not be quite as restrictive as those of historians who turn up their noses at anything other than written, linguistic documents.

What is more, other Lacans are able to be rendered amenable to things close to the deep historical traces appealed to by Smail. Several times, Lacan grants that DNA can be construed as a series of "letters" as material signifiers, as signifying traces subsisting in the Real.[77] In the eleventh seminar, Lacan, anticipating cutting-edge scientific research into the dynamics shaping both genetics and epigenetics (research that takes off after his death), rightly hypothesizes that the persistent, enduring sociosymbolic mediation of Lévi-Straussian "elementary structures of kinship" in humans' patterns of mating and family formation across innumerable generations means that human DNA itself testifies, as a sequence of traces, to various historical Others.[78] Smail concurs with this hypothesis,[79] a hypothesis which points to the now well-established life scientific deconstruction of the nature-nurture dichotomy; and, with the implosion of this opposition, the partitioning of natural prehistory and cultural history proper (a partition Lacan the phylogenetic skeptic maintains) collapses too. Plus, apart from the later Lacan's increasing emphasis on the materiality of signifiers (an emphasis facilitating a rapprochement between Lacanian signifiers and Smailian traces), his expansion of Saussurean structuralism beyond the disciplinary confines of linguistics alone—this expansion informs his teachings from start to finish—indicates that the status of counting as a signifier has more to do with form than content. In other words, a Lacanian signifier is not always and necessarily a component (i.e., a word, phrase, sentence, etc.) of a given language as *une langue* (i.e., a "tongue"); nonlinguistic contents (such as sensory-perceptual mnemic materials and/or Smailian traces) qualify as signifiers too if they entertain determinative differential relations with various other contents bound together in organized, cross-resonating arrangements.[80] The Lacanian protests against a phylogenetic deep history scrutinized in the previous section of this chapter are contestable even on the basis of Lacanian principles.

But, what, if anything, might Lacan add to Smail? To cut a long story short, the fifth and final chapter of *On Deep History and the Brain*, entitled "Civilization and Psychotropy," employs a dialectical blend of history and neuroscience[81] to chart a deep historical thread running its winding way through time under the influence of human brains' modes of achieving enjoyment-producing self-stimulation.[82] To briefly and merely suggest a potential trajectory of future investigation bringing together Smailian deep history (itself having already begun to bring together the "hard" and "soft" sciences) and Lacanian psychoanalytic metapsychology (in this particular instance, drive theory), Lacan's complex, sustained reflections on libidinal economies indicate that history is as much driven along by continual struggles to cope with failures to enjoy as it is by techniques and technologies of pleasure, gratification, etc. (as per Smail's narrative).[83] The historical present provides perhaps the best evidence, the key case in point, for this: contemporary consumer (late) capitalism propels itself forward in historically fateful directions partially on the basis of how it continually and frenetically (re)produces dissatisfaction and lack.[84] Moreover, Lacanian sensibilities push for keeping in mind, even at the evolutionary and neuroscientific levels, the constitutive disharmony and dysfunctionality of human being, right down to the bare-bones, raw-flesh fundaments of these beings' physiologies—namely, the barred corpo-Real[85] of the kludge-like[86] anatomies of creatures internally generated out of a lone immanent-material plane of contingencies devoid of solid, underlying necessities, meanings, or teleologies. Biology itself has reached a juncture at which it unveils what Lacan, in 1955, characterizes as "the dehiscence from natural harmony, required by Hegel to serve as the fruitful illness, life's happy fault, in which man, distinguishing himself from his essence, discovers his existence."[87] Hence, an existential materialism positioned at the intersection of science and psychoanalysis, a materialism in which science too lends true credence to the postulated precedence of existence over essence, is a real possibility nowadays.[88]

In Lacan's mind, the phylogenetic perspectives he repudiates are associated with evolutionism. The latter is in turn associated for him with a temporalized, spontaneous substance metaphysics stressing smoothness, gradualness, continuity, and teleological directedness[89] (hence the association between Haeckelian recapitulationism, which Lacan erroneously takes to be the one-and-only version of the phylogenetic, and evolution). The name "Stephen Jay Gould" (not to mention many other names) stands for the empirical, intrabiological demolition of this wholly false image of evolution in (post-)Darwinian evolutionary theory, a demolition that clears space for alternate dialectical reconceptualizations of phylogeny in which discontinuities immanently arise out of a background of biomaterial bases.[90] (Given his guiding intention to break down the barriers separating prehistory from history, Smail understandably emphasizes continuity against discontinuity—but both psychoanalytic and scientific considerations cry out for a dialectics in which discontinuities of various kinds remain part of the historical picture.) A series of remarks by Smail waves in this same general direction: "With phylogeny, there is no blueprint";[91] "Darwinian natural selection . . . has a fundamentally *anti*-essentialist epistemology. That is the whole point. Species, according to Darwin, are not fixed entities with natural essences imbued in them by the Creator";[92] and, apropos the "futile quest to identify 'human nature' . . . Here, as in so many areas, biology and cultural studies are fundamentally congruent."[93]

Contra Lacan's famous counterintuitive thesis in the renowned seventh seminar according to which the originally Christian notion of creation ex nihilo is more authentically atheistic than ostensibly atheist Darwinian evolutionary theory[94]—this has everything to do with his problematic assumption that believing in evolution logically requires being committed to a fundamentally seamless monistic ontology allowing for no radical breaks or ruptures—an atheism inspired by analysis need not be left languishing in the spirituality-sustaining mystical void of the anti-scientific "out of nowhere." Near the end of his teaching, in the twenty-fifth seminar, Lacan, after asking what the definition of "the nature of nature" might be, shifts away from his 1960 thesis apropos the ex nihilo; here, in 1977, instead of "creationist raving" being superior to "evolutionist raving," they are said to be equivalent, the former no longer being deemed better than the latter.[95] They are both hypothetical.[96] But, since the 1960s and 1970s, a great deal has happened in the life sciences. The balance of the scales between these two hypotheses rapidly has tipped ever more decisively in favor of Darwin's legacy. If Lacanianism is to achieve the task of transforming itself into a soundly secular theoretical framework integrated with the historical and dialectical materialisms first delineated by Marx and Engels,[97] it must make its peace with neurosciences and evolutionary theories dramatically different nowadays from what Lacan himself had before him.

Enough enigmas! Down with veils! Holy Spirits be gone! It is high time for more profanation, more desacralization! As Smail declares, "All

that remains for us to shake off is the grip of sacred history."[98] To conclude with an enthusiastic call-to-arms that is simultaneously a warning
of the danger of the return of old (un)holy ghosts (*"Dieu, à en reprendre
de la force, finirait-il par ex-sister, ça ne présage rien de meilleur qu'un retour de
son passé funeste"*):[99] the future of the past awaits.

Part 2

Alain Badiou: Between Form and Matter

4

What Matter(s) in Ontology: The Hebb-Event and Materialism Split from Within

§1 "Frenchman, One More Effort If You Wish to Be a Materialist!": A Plea for Ontic Impurity

One of the most provocative and timely recent efforts at revitalizing materialism in the European philosophical tradition is that carried out by Badiou in a number of texts serving as linchpins of his intricate, sprawling theoretical apparatus. He unabashedly declares, "I would submit that my system is the most rigorously materialist in ambition that we've seen since Lucretius."[1] However, Badiou's materialism is of a rather weird kind, to say the least. As is well known, starting in *Being and Event* (the 1988 tome that forms the foundation for much of his subsequent work up through the present), Badiou outsources ontology from philosophy to mathematics, equating the ontological with the mathematical and identifying post-Cantorian trans-finite set theory as the science of "being qua being" (*l'être en tant qu'être*).[2] One of the justifications for this move is that only pure mathematics is supremely indifferent to any and every actual or possible ontic referent; mathematical discourse alone is able to elaborate an absolutely precise rational scaffolding for thought, for thinking about anything and everything, without recourse to invoking a specific this, that, or the other.[3] With an ontology founded on set theory alone, Badiou's materialism is mathematical rather than historical or dialectical.[4]

Despite the many differences between Heidegger and Badiou, Badiou's justifications for equating ontology with mathematics arguably rest, at least in certain respects, on Heideggerian foundations—more precisely, on Heidegger's notion of "ontological difference" as the distinction between the ontic and the ontological. The second sentence of *Being and Event* asserts that "Heidegger is the last universally recognizable philosopher."[5] A few paragraphs later, Badiou affirms a point of solidarity with Heidegger: "Along with Heidegger, it will be maintained that philosophy as such can only be re-assigned on the basis of the ontological question."[6] Badiou's fidelity to Heideggerian thought isn't simply a matter of agreeing on the importance of ontology for philosophy. Although Badiou takes issue with Heidegger's "suturing" of philosophical ontology to the aesthetic-symbolic resources of the language(s) of poetry,[7] he nonetheless accepts that ontology must somehow manage to avoid getting entangled and mired in the particularities of ontic disciplines and domains (something pure mathematics seems to enable thought to accomplish). Badiou does not challenge Heidegger's manner of differentiating between the ontological and the ontic; he merely proposes that being as such is sayable in mathematical rather than poetic terms, to be analyzed through lenses of crystalline conceptual clarity rather than evoked through resonant associations glancing off the edges of the ineffable.

In Badiouian terms, Badiou counters the Heideggerian tethering of ontology to poetry with an alternate tethering of it to mathematics. However, what follows below involves a plea for ontic impurity that aims to challenge the very possibility of simultaneously being a materialist (as Badiou professes to be) and (as Badiou allegedly does) accepting a clear-cut distinction between the ontological and the ontic. Authentic materialism, especially a materialism with a relation to dialectical thinking, must resign itself to the messiness of a theoretical account of the instances and types of being conditioned by the empirical results of such ontic fields as the natural sciences. A materialist should be deeply suspicious of the cleanliness of any ontology of pure being in and of itself.

Before launching into a critical analysis of Badiouian materialism, a marvelous merit of Badiou's in-depth engagement with mathematics deserves to be mentioned here. The majority of "continental" philosophers are all too ready to abandon mathematics, itself intimately entangled in the history of Western philosophy from its origins in ancient Greece onwards, in favor of more cultural, historical, and literary pursuits. Instead of simply ceding mathematical thought to the Anglo-American analytic philosophical tradition, Badiou, like Lacan before him—Lacan's interest in symbolic logic, topology, and knot theory, among other formal disciplines, is a prominent feature of his teachings—urges those of more European theoretical sensibilities to contemplate the many powerful implications for thought flowing from discoveries in mathematics reached over the course of the past two centuries.[8] Badiou hopes that his engagement with mathematics, disregarding the standard turf claims and lines of demarcation established and generally accepted over the course of the past several decades, will make apparent "an obvious fact," namely, "the nullity of the opposition between analytic thought and continental thought."[9]

The endeavor I am calling for here through a critique of Badiou's strictly mathematical ontology draws inspiration from the same hope, although my focus is on forging a materialist ontology in relation to the natural, rather than the formal, sciences. As with mathematics, so too with the life sciences—just as continental philosophers automatically tend to assume that such things as set theory are the exclusive province of analytic philosophers,[10] so also do they carelessly assume, with intellectually impoverishing consequences for their fields, that biology and the neurosciences are best left to analytically trained philosophers of mind.[11] The insights and ideas of the neurosciences are too precious to be unreservedly delivered over into the hands of their self-appointed analytic (mis-)representatives (who often distort the evidence uncovered by empirical scientists in fitting this evidence into the preexistent theoretical concepts and categories of such discussions as Anglo-American mind-body debates). Moreover, it could be argued that the neurosciences themselves cannot adequately and fully articulate the truths of their discoveries in the vernaculars that have thus far been offered to them by analytic philosophers.

One should bear in mind that, for the Anglo-American tradition, the history of philosophy generally stops with P. F. Strawson's Kant and does not resume again until Frege and Russell (analytic philosophy originally arises, in part, as a violent reaction to late-nineteenth-century British Hegelianism). This historical gap contains, among other things, the nineteenth-century developments of German idealism and historical-dialectical materialism, developments capable of furnishing today's neurosciences with a language through which they can, as Hegel would phrase it, raise themselves to the dignity of their Notion. This Notion is no less than a new materialist ontology, an ontology with a viable, non-reductive account of subjectivity as more than a mere epiphenomenon eventually to be eliminated through gradually refined physical descriptions limited to delineating nothing more than the efficient causes of corporeal mechanics.[12]

§2 Having One's Cake and Eating It Too: Pure Mathematics and Rigorous Materialism

Given its mathematical nature, there are doubts about whether Badiou's ontology is indeed properly materialist.[13] How on earth can one claim to be any stripe of materialist, let alone the most extreme and consequent materialist in the 2,000 years since Lucretius, if one equates being as such with intangibly abstract numerical structures? (Speaking of Lucretius, Lenin Bandres, in the concluding paragraphs of his essay on Badiou's engagement with Lucretius and ancient atomism, hints that Badiou, unlike the atomists and their philosophical progeny, refuses to grant a central place to corporeal bodies in his philosophy.)[14] What becomes of the conception of matter when the inconsistent, infinite multitudes of the sets and subsets of trans-finite set theory are the exclusive revelatory windows opening out onto the very "stuff" of the Real of *l'être en tant qu'être*?

In response to these reservations apropos Badiou's claims to have fashioned a rigorously materialist mathematical ontology, Fabien Tarby defends Badiou by explaining that, insofar as Badiou is a self-declared Platonist—he describes his mathematical ontology as a "Platonism of the multiple"[15]—Badiou rejects the portrayal of mathematics as a fabrication of the human mind overlaid onto the objective world, as an artificial language constructed by and existing (in a pure, non-applied state) solely in the ideational realms of subjective individuals. That is to say, for Plato and Badiou, the thinking of mathematics "touches upon" being qua being itself as that which is irreducible to either pole of any subject-object or knower-known dichotomies.[16] Thus, Tarby concludes, Badiou's mathematical ontology is materialist insofar as mathematical entities and configurations are viewed, by Badiou-the-Platonist, as enjoying ontological weight, as participating in real being.[17]

The naive reader might already be suspicious: what type of materialist would pledge allegiance to Plato, an arch-idealist if ever there was one? Tarby's defense of Badiou's materialist credentials arguably fails to allay such suspicions. Believing in the ontological reality of mathematics does not make one a materialist. Put differently, metaphysical realism is not equivalent to materialism—quite the contrary. Metaphysical realists tend to be, not coincidentally or by accident, idealists. At least in glancing back through the history of philosophy, one discerns a strong correlation between materialism and the diametrical opposite of metaphysical realism, namely, nominalism. The new materialism hailed by Tarby is at risk of being indistinguishable from spiritualist idealism. Endorsing a perhaps excessive purification of *l'être en tant qu'être* (or even the very idea of a pure "qua" or "as such" of being) entails the danger of embracing something other than materialism.

Consistent with his mathematization of ontology, Badiou sets himself against any sort of naturalism or organicism.[18] For him, "life" should not be singled out as the proper name of being per se. In the opening of a chapter of *Briefings on Existence* entitled "Deleuze's Vitalist Ontology," he rightly observes that "in philosophy, how to name Being always involves a crucial decision. It sums up thought. Even the name 'Being,' if chosen as the name of Being, involves a decision that is in no way tautological."[19] At the very end of this same chapter, Badiou depicts naturalism-organicism-vitalism, on the one hand, and formalism-mathematicism, on the other hand, as mutually exclusive ontological options; a fundamental, unavoidable choice ostensibly must be made between naming being either "carnal life" or "pure multiplicity."[20] Addressing the vitalist ontology of Deleuze elsewhere, he likewise contends that an ontological decision-without-guarantee is required of philosophers between organic and mathematical materialisms.[21] Badiou has both positive and negative justifications supporting his preference for "multiplicity" over "life" as the name of being qua being, the negative justifications being his reasons for rejecting the naturalism-organicism-vitalism option. In what follows, these reasons will be called into question, thus also calling into question the alleged philosophical-theoretical inadequacy of a materialism of carnality.

The ontology delineated in *Being and Event* obviously involves a pronounced antinaturalism[22] (as Brassier rightly notes, "Badiou will have no truck with naturalism").[23] In fact, "Part III" of this 1988 volume directly discusses the topic of nature, defining it in the terms of Badiou's set-theoretic ontological framework. For Badiou, "nature" signifies, first and foremost, seamless consistency, the cohering-together of multiplicities in a smooth, regular fashion.[24] Nature, as characterized by Badiou through, for instance, a contrast between "natural situations" and "historical situations," is depicted as being utterly homogeneous and devoid of internal contradictions and discrepancies.[25] He bluntly asserts that "there are no holes in nature."[26] Due to this supposed placid plenitude of natural situations, a plenitude purported to be undisturbed by any type of historical volatility, such constellations of being are portrayed as too static to give rise to anything on the order of events:[27] "Nature is too global, too normal, to open up to the evental convocation of its being."[28]

In addition to nature as stable homogeneity, Badiou also addresses the notion of Nature as a cosmic One-All, as the substantial sum of the universe taken as a whole (and, for him, conceding that "matter" or "life" could be names of being is tantamount to sealing up *l'être en tant qu'être* back within the confines of an englobing wholeness).[29] Apropos this notion, he reminds readers of a thesis already established earlier in *Being and Event* through the equation of ontology with trans-finite set theory: in the absence of a single, enveloping infinite as the sole universal medium of everything that is—Cantor mathematically demonstrates through rational proofs that there are an infinite variety of infinities without upper or lower limits on numerical proliferation—there is no ultimate totality or unity.[30] Succinctly stated, "the one *is not*."[31] Consequently, Badiou affirms the nonexistence of Nature insofar as this loaded and laden key term from philosophy's history signifies an all-encompassing cosmos, the omnipresent embrace of an exhaustively full presence of dense substantiality.[32] Furthermore, according to Badiou's arguments, if one acknowledges that Galileo's scientific revolution, his break with premodern "science" (à la Aristotle), resides in his mathematization of nature (i.e., mathematics is the signifying medium in and through which material being *an sich* reveals itself),[33] then, to the extent that the subsequent historical progress of mathematical thought through and after Cantor reveals the lack/nullity of a singular infinite One, Nature as All is an inconsistent, rationally untenable idea. At the intersection of the Galilean and Cantorian revolutions, one is compelled, Badiou asserts, to concede that there is no Whole.[34]

Badiou's thesis positing the nonexistence of Nature as a One-All notwithstanding, other aspects of his antinaturalism warrant two main criticisms. First, at the level of his set-theoretic definition of nature as stable arrangements of coherent, homogenous multiplicities, arrangements without cracks or fissures, he assumes the transhistorical validity of a distinction between the natural and the nonnatural (specifically, the historical)[35] that itself is highly questionable and dubious. In fact, empirically speaking, it is utterly false. Under the influence of an antinaturalism that leads him to dismiss and neglect the natural sciences in favor of the formal sciences (i.e., mathematics), Badiou seems unaware of the profound problematization of the natural-versus-nonnatural dichotomy being brought about by genetics and the neurosciences.[36] At least apropos the "natural" materiality of human being, drawing a clean, black-and-white line between the nature of this matter and its other(s) is now well-nigh impossible. Badiou's distinction between natural and historical situations apparently fails to take into account this impossibility. A second criticism here, related to the first, is that, in terms of the nature dealt with by the life sciences, Badiou is simply wrong to insist that nature is fundamentally self-consistent and internally integrated. On the contrary, nature, as manifest in condensed form in the bodies and brains of human beings, is inconsistent and heterogeneous, permeated by holes, gaps, and lags.

As seen, Badiou refers to Galileo's tethering of physics to mathematics as the birth of the modern natural sciences, as an epistemological break or cut sharply separating scientific modernity from what precedes it. However, Badiou's attitude toward the natural (as opposed to formal) sciences evinces a fair amount of ambivalence. Overall, his mathematical materialist ontology results in a refusal to grant a properly ontological status to material contingencies, to the states of the universe studied by the natural sciences.[37] Tarby claims (rather strangely) that it is precisely Badiou's desire to formulate a materialist ontology that leads him to view physics (and, by implication, all of the natural sciences taken together) as insufficient, as not up to the task of ontology; he explains that Badiouian philosophy, as focused on the "anti-essential" rather than the essential, must turn away from physics and toward pure mathematics.[38] Undoubtedly, Tarby accepts as well founded Badiou's contentious claims regarding the notion of nature as entailing a substantial plenitude enjoying a full, seamless coherence/unity.

In the introduction to *Being and Event,* Badiou briefly addresses the distinction between pure and applied mathematics. He notes that mathematized physics is still an application of mathematical structures to a particular (albeit pervasive) "situation," namely, the realm of physical matter.[39] As such, physics, the most mathematized of the natural sciences, remains stuck at a level of ontic-referential particularity below the ontological dignity of pure mathematics as the science of being qua being. A decade later, in an interview with Peter Hallward, Badiou echoes these thoughts concerning physics and natural science:

> The more you decompose the concept of matter into its most elementary constituents, the more you move into a field of reality which can only be named or identified with increasingly complex mathematical operations. "Matter" would simply be, immediately after being, the most general possible name of the presented (of what is presented) . . . Matter, in the sense in which it is at stake in physics, is matter as enveloping any particular presentation—and I am a materialist in the sense that I think that any presentation is material. If we consider the word "matter," the content of the word "matter," matter comes immediately after being. It is the degree of generality immediately co-present to ontology. The physical situation will then be a very powerfully mathematised situation and, in a certain sense, more and more so, the closer it comes to apprehending the smallest, most primordial elements of reality.[40]

Badiou clearly distinguishes between being and matter—pure mathematics deals with the former, and the applied mathematics of physics deals with the latter—and yet insistently proclaims himself to be an ultra-rigorous materialist. First, there is the ontological purity of being qua being; and, second, there is the not-quite-ontological domain of matter. Pure being *an sich* is strictly mathematical.[41] For Badiou, the sign that post-Galilean, mathematized modern physics is extremely close to (although nonetheless still separate from) the absolute abstractions of ontology per se is that, as exemplified by quantum physics, it bypasses the mediation of human-scale sensory-perceptual experience to treat matter exclusively with the algorithms, formulas, and numbers of mathematics. Along these lines, in stipulating that scientificity requires a combination of "mathematic formalism" with a "theoretically controlled experimental apparatus,"[42] Badiou tries to define "science" in such a way as to concede the scientificity of physics while stripping much of biology and its offshoots of their scientific status.[43] This maneuver is reflective of his general hostility toward naturalism, organicism, or vitalism. On the basis of what Brassier aptly characterizes as Badiou's "all-too-ideological antipathy to biology,"[44] Badiou wishes to deny these disciplines centered on living nature not only ontological import, but also, through quite debatable assertions, a standing as sciences.

In a 1994 interview entitled "Being by Numbers" (a title obviously referring to the mathematical nature of his ontology), Badiou says a few things that are directly relevant to the current discussion. At one moment, he candidly admits to viewing his knowledge of the natural sciences as insufficient:

> My silence about science is entirely temporary and contingent. There's absolutely no principle involved. A whole series of aspects of the sciences, and particularly of contemporary physics, are of great philosophical interest. I had launched into arid studies of quantum mechanics years ago. But for the moment I still don't feel sufficiently experienced or intimately acquainted with what's in question there to talk about it. You can't do everything![45]

One could respond with "fair enough"—this admission of ignorance is refreshingly honest. But is Badiou's "silence" really "temporary and contingent"? Is it even a silence? As observed, Badiou, in 1988, feels completely confident in decisively situating physics and the natural sciences in a certain relation to the formal science of set theory as the mathematical discourse of *l'être en tant qu'être;* put in their purportedly proper place, these fields dealing with nature are deprived of any say in matters ontological. So, Badiou isn't close-lipped about natural science—nor is his stance vis-à-vis such science an unprincipled and passing circumstance, since his basic, long-held philosophical principles lead him to withholding ontological powers from sciences other than one particular branch of pure mathematics.

In the same interview, shortly after the above remarks, Badiou explains why he indeed is a materialist. Responding to Sedofsky's indication that some perceive him as "having yielded to a philosophical idealism" in his more recent post-Maoist years, he retorts, "To be an idealist you have to distinguish between thought and matter, transcendence and immanence, the high and the low, pure thought and empirical thought. None of these distinctions function in the system I propose."[46] The sentence immediately following this quotation is the one already quoted in which Badiou crowns his philosophy "the most rigorously materialist in ambition that we've seen since Lucretius." Badiou's insistence that the distinctions he lists here have no role or function in his philosophical system is somewhat misleading. Most importantly, what raises serious questions and difficulties in this context is the firm line of demarcation partitioning being and matter (instead of "thought and matter"), a line drawn in accordance with the full-fledged mathematization of ontology. Moreover, this line, contrary to what Badiou maintains above, indeed does end up segregating "impure" empirical disciplines, keeping them outside the enclosure of ontology properly speaking. And, to Badiou's disadvantage, this is where Tarby's previously critiqued and problematic defense of the materialist credentials of the mathematical ontology of Badiou-the-Platonist returns with a vengeance: the manner in which Badiou differentiates between *l'être* and *la matière* is tied up with a Platonic ontology that, if deemed to be materialist, renders the very opposition between materialism and idealism entirely null and void. How is this not metaphysical realism, an otherworldly doctrine inextricably intertwined with idealist spiritualism?

§3 Materialism's Three Bodies: After the War between Democratic Materialism and the Materialist Dialectic

Badiou's more up-to-date work again speaks to the topic of materialism. In particular, the preface to *Logics of Worlds,* the 2006 sequel to *Being and Event,* contains the now familiar formal declaration of a war already underway between "democratic materialism" and the "materialist dialectic." For both Engels and Lenin, one must always keep a watchful eye on the antagonistic rapport between the "two camps" of materialism and idealism.[47] But, for Badiou, being a materialist is no longer enough, given that a rift has opened up within materialism, a rift splitting this philosophical category/position from within. On the one hand, there is a materialism (i.e., democratic materialism) wholly compatible and thoroughly complicit with the socioeconomic order of late capitalism. On the other hand, there is another materialism (i.e., the materialist dialectic), a materialism advocated by Badiou as an assault on the hegemony of late-capitalist ideology and everything that goes along with it.[48] Democratic materialism proclaims that "there are only bodies and languages."[49] The materialist dialectic counters this proclamation with a crucial caveat, more precisely, the exception of a *"sinon que"*: "There are only bodies and languages, except that there are also truths."[50] This split internal to materialism pits the "Two" of bodies and languages against the "Three" of bodies and languages plus truths.[51] Furthermore, Badiou assures readers that these truths, rather than being transcendent Platonic ideas standing above and beyond the nitty-gritty concreteness of inner-worldly being, are defined and deployed by him in a thoroughly materialist and immanentist way.[52]

The preface to *Logics of Worlds* associates democratic materialism with a biopolitical paradigm in which the notion of bare organic life, of living, breathing flesh-and-blood existence, is elevated to a central position ethically, politically, and epistemologically. With this in mind, Badiou comments that "man, in the regime of the 'power of life,' is an animal convinced that the law of the body holds the secret of his hope."[53] The phrase to take issue with here is "the law of the body." Subsequently in *Logics of Worlds,* Badiou, as will be seen, elaborates a concept of the body different from that of everyday speech or democratic materialism, a concept of the body compatible with his theory of the subject and materialist dialectics. But, in this quoted comment concerning the "power of life," he is talking about the tangible, fleshly body of biology and its biopolitical interpretations. Of course, there is a world of difference between the scientism of biopolitical ideology and biological science proper (although Badiou exhibits a lamentable tendency to conflate the two).[54] Along these lines, one could say that not all biology is biopolitical in Badiou's sense, meaning that the lawful body fantasized by the individual under the influence of democratic materialism is just that, namely, a fantasy with no real basis in genetics, neurology, or any other biological science.

Malabou, in the course of unfolding the ontological implications of the neurosciences, argues with forceful persuasiveness against the impression that the life sciences, as brought to bear on humanity, reveal human being as matter fated to a destiny dictated by a predetermined scaffolding of evolutionary and genetic components and conditions; for her, this is merely an ideological illusion.[55] Badiou is in danger of succumbing to this misleading impression arising from a gross distortion of the facts. He risks uncritically ceding the entire ground of the life sciences to democratic materialism's biopolitical scientism. These sciences are much too valuable to be hastily abandoned to the enemy as a result of a miscalculation taken in by this same enemy's blurring of the boundaries between the scientific and the pseudoscientific. One must ignore the ideological falsifications of the empirical data divulged by the neurosciences and their allied fields, falsifications sometimes unfortunately promulgated by these disciplines' own practitioners (as should go without saying, not everything scientists say is scientific), when drawing on these disciplines in the forging of a new materialism. If anything, the natural sciences undeniably indicate that the body is far from being wholly and completely lawful, that there is a lawlessness inhering within the very materiality of human bodily existence. If the individual of democratic materialism hopes to uncover secrets telling him/her what he/she essentially is in the form of scientifically guaranteed biopolitical norms, then he/she is in for severe disappointment. The sciences of the body, properly understood, are presently pointing to what could be called an existential materialism, a materialist doctrine affirming a fundamental deficit or deficiency of biological determinants hardwired into the blueprints of humanity's corporeal architecture[56]—and this contra Badiou's insistence that the Sartrean-existentialist inflections coloring his own theory of the subject are uncompromisingly incompatible with any naturalist materialism whatsoever.[57]

Logics of Worlds, as mentioned earlier, introduces a specifically Badiouian conception of the "body" into his philosophy. One of Badiou's concerns in this sequel to Being and Event is to illustrate in detail how subjects-of-events concretely operate within particular situations and existent worlds. With regard to this concern, Badiou maintains that there are no disembodied evental subjects, despite the claim that the event-generated truths to which such subjects remain faithful are not reducible to the specific locales of situations and worlds. However, the terms "body" and "subject" are used in a philosophically atypical fashion in this context. Embodied subjectivity is not necessarily personhood-in-the-flesh (for instance, embodied subjectivity à la Merleau-Pontian phenomenology). For Badiou, a subject-with-a-body easily could be, and often is, a collective political movement, the practices of an enamored pair, or the works of an organized artistic orientation.[58] The "body" of Logics of Worlds is simply a material condition of possibility for the inner-worldly efficacy of an event-subject-truth axis as instantiated within concrete circumstances.[59] This concept-term has no real referential connection with the bodies at stake in, for instance, the life sciences. Although Badiouian subjects-of-events necessarily are embodied, this is far from meaning that they entertain a significant relation with the corporeal matter of living flesh. In fact, given his persistent equivocation between biology and biologism, Badiou is committed to resisting the linkage of subjectivity to the bodies referred to by both quotidian and scientific discourses.[60]

"Section 2" of "Book VII" ("What Is a Body?") of Logics of Worlds is entitled "Lacan." Badiou turns to Lacanian theory so as to elucidate and buttress his account of the body, doing so with reference to a psychoanalytic thinker's reflections on the incarnate bodily being of suffering individuals lying on clinicians' couches (despite the alleged irrelevance of these sorts of bodies to those spoken of in this 2006 book). To make a rather long tale quite brief, Badiou reduces Lacan's conception of embodiment to the idea that the body is nothing more than a passive vehicle, a receptive surface, for extracorporeal influences and inscriptions[61] (whether these influences and inscriptions are said to stem from an Other-regulated Imaginary-Symbolic reality [Lacan] or emanate from the radical newness of an evental rupture with state-secured situations and/or transcendentally regulated worlds [Badiou]). Apart from the fact that Badiou's interpretation of Lacan's notion (or, more accurately, notions) of embodiment engages in selective oversimplifications that border on outright misrepresentations—addressing point-by-point the problems with the Badiouian appropriation of the Lacanian body in *Logics of Worlds* would require a separate essay unto itself—this depiction of bodily being, taken on its own terms, deserves some critical remarks.

To begin with, the body becomes, via the mouth of the Lacan-dummy ventriloquized through by Badiou, structurally isomorphic with the mind of seventeenth- and eighteenth-century empiricist philosophy (especially mind as posited in the philosophies of Locke and Hume). That is to say, the Badiouian version of the Lacanian body functions only as a tabula rasa, as a blank slate or an empty room vis-à-vis impressions impinging upon it from elsewhere. This figure of the tabula rasa is untenable both philosophically/theoretically and scientifically/empirically. On the philosophical/theoretical level, just as empiricism is vulnerable to the Kantian angle of attack—in Kant's eyes, Hume's empiricist account of mind fails to ask and would be unable to answer the question of how its impressions are possible in the first place—so too could one demand to know (in line with materialism instead of the idealism of Kant) what makes possible (i.e., the transcendental conditions for) the openness of bodies to event-driven transformations by truths. Minus an explanation and delineation of the biomaterial conditions of possibility for the genesis of a more-than-biological subject of evental truth, Badiou is left with obscurantist religious language, mystifying mere words that, at best, create the mirage of a solution to the enigma of the immanent material genesis of the more-than-material by simply replacing the explicit articulation of the enigma itself with evocative terms that deceptively make it sound as though the hard conceptual problems already are solved. Apart from his allegedly atheistic recourse to and appropriation of Pauline Christianity,[62] Badiou's persistent use of the theologically saturated signifier "grace" for a process of evental subjectification eerily resembling the Catholic notion of transubstantiation is one of the more visible symptoms of the return of the religious repressed once the vast

majority of the sciences have been categorically prevented from informing what presents itself as a materialist ontology.[63] The protests that signifiers like "grace" have been sufficiently "laicized," detheologized and
rendered adequately secular, ring slightly hollow in the same manner
as instances of Freudian *Verneinung*:[64] "Methinks thou doth protest too
much."

The scientific/empirical problems with Badiou's concept of the
body are closely tied to its philosophical/theoretical shortcomings.
Badiou, with his antinaturalism and correlative neglect of the life
sciences, erroneously assumes that the physical body can be reduced to,
with the assistance of a watered-down Lacanian metapsychology, an inert
hunk of flesh, an inactive slab of solid, uniform skin. Coming from the
field of cognitive neuroscience, both Changeux and Metzinger, among
others, argue against the legitimacy of a Lockean-Humean empiricist
framework or paradigm for the neurosciences. Nervous systems, rather
than being the subdued conduits for extracerebral information and
stimuli, are self-organizing arrangements of material being. Changeux
considers the brain's self-organizational activities to be functions that
any viable materialist approach to human subjectivity must acknowledge
and incorporate.[65] He contends that "at the heart of informed materialism is the notion that the capacity for organization is an essential part of
the very definition of matter."[66] Unlike the mind of the empiricists,[67] "the
brain is the seat of intense spontaneous activity arising independently of
interaction with the environment."[68] Metzinger likewise emphasizes that
the brain amply exhibits internally generated spontaneity and immanently arising endogenous dynamics.[69] The crucial ramification for
Badiouian philosophy is that the image of the body as a passive, receptive surface turns out to be a fiction falsified by the facts. This image is as
much a politically motivated distortion of things as its equally extreme
inverted, polar opposite, that is, the fantasy, frequently dear to those subjected to biopolitical democratic materialism, of a corporeal existence
utterly and completely determined by the new scientific God of preestab-
lished genetic codes dictated by the commandments of evolution.

§4 The Hard Work of Remaining Faithful to Atheism: Reconfronting the Fundamental Choice Between Religion and Science

In a 2006 interview, Badiou explicitly addresses the field of cognitive
science for the first time at any length in print (apart from a passing
mention of it in *Logics of Worlds*).[70] His remarks are, unsurprisingly, curtly

dismissive of this discipline. He begins by denying the scientificity of biology as a whole due to its lack of "mathematical formalisms" as well as its reliance on "concepts" that allegedly are "wholly insufficient."[71] Moreover, biology is said to "fail completely to present the phenomena concerned in the register of eternal truths,"[72] a criticism almost immediately reiterated apropos cognitive science:[73] "Since every truth is in-human, we can hardly hope to understand its genesis by poking around in the neurons of our brains!"[74] Besides this criticism (perhaps the most important one articulated in this interview), Badiou summarily issues two other condemnations of the relatively young emerging domains of brain studies. First, he states:

> Cognitive science . . . is a program rather than a theory. Even more so than biology, it is just a mass of facts and techniques, devoid of concepts or adequate formalisms. The truth is that we remain totally ignorant as to the real functioning of the brain. From what I know of the current state of research in cognitive science, I feel justified in concluding that, despite an impressive technical arsenal, it is no more advanced in its understanding of the phenomena than was Gall's phrenology, at the time when Hegel said the latter thought it had proved that "spirit is a bone." Today we think we have proved that thought is a neuron . . . Cognitive science is hardly further advanced than the theory of cerebral localisations in Broca, even if the active zones appear today in bright colours, displayed directly onto screens.[75]

This is Badiou, an admirable and lively thinker well worth taking seriously on multiple levels, at his very worst (perhaps he is at his very best as an inspiring political polemicist, rather than as a builder of grandscale philosophical/metaontological systems—thus resembling not so much Plato, as Badiou presents himself, but, instead, the figure behind Plato, namely, Socrates the gadfly). He here indulges in underinformed dismissals of other orientations just as crude and anti-intellectual as Heidegger's woeful recurrent tendency mindlessly to use the jargon of ontological difference to write off as errant and reductive ontic nonthought anything apart from his own "fundamental ontology." And these cursory dismissals of the life sciences repeat denunciations uttered elsewhere as regards "biology—that wild empiricism disguised as science."[76] Edoardo Acotto, speaking of Badiou, maintains that "there is in our philosopher something like a repression of the ontic, of the empirical,"[77] a repression arguably leading to a philosophically indefensible neglect of scientific knowledge regarding the role of the brain in thinking that is "idiosyncratic," "anti-scientific," and "incomprehensible."[78]

Many things can and should be said in response to the Badiouian reaction against cognitive neuroscience. To begin with, Badiou's obsessive fetishization of mathematical formalization as the hallmark of worthwhile science is wanting for adequate, satisfactory justifications. If he admits the irreducibility of biology to physics (as indeed he does earlier in the same interview under discussion here),[79] then why does he imply that the life sciences ought to strive toward the same degree of mathematization as, say, quantum mechanics? Why would the life sciences fall short of being scientific if they have not achieved this thoroughgoing mathematical formalization? Nothing very convincing or persuasive is offered in response to these obvious skeptical queries.

As for the next claim in the passage quoted above, if, for Badiou, "cognitive science" also encompasses the neurosciences (which it appears to as evinced by his manner of employing this phrase, despite the fact that cognitivism, as a research program in the neurosciences, is distinct from the neurosciences taken in their entirety), then, by most imaginable reasonable standards, the alleged "truth . . . that we remain totally ignorant as to the real functioning of the brain" is, in actuality, false. The unflattering comparison of cognitive neuroscience to early-nineteenth-century phrenology that follows this false allegation is prefaced by a conditional qualification: "From what I know of the current state of research in cognitive science. . . ." Not only are there several reasons (outlined in the preceding pages above) for speculating that Badiou deliberately does not know all that much about such research due to his philosophical-ontological principles—one might also suspect that his frank admission (quoted previously) in a 1994 interview to the effect that he understandably has not been able to keep pace with the vast ensemble of advances in the sciences holds in this 2006 context too. However, in this more recent case, no admission of ignorance is forthcoming.

Finally, Badiou's comparison of cognitive neuroscience with the phrenology of Franz Joseph Gall (as derided by Hegel in the *Phenomenology of Spirit*) is based on the incorrect assumption that the neurosciences and cognitive science pursue the determination of nothing more than "localizations" as one-to-one correspondences between faculties of the mind and regions of the brain. Admittedly, neuroscientific studies, starting with the famous case of the nineteenth-century railway worker Phineas Gage, have progressed over the decades thanks in part to observing individuals with brain lesions. These patients allow for certain cognitive, emotional, and motivational phenomena of mental life to be associated with specific sectors of neural anatomy by virtue of manifesting psychological disturbances exhibiting correlations with particular types of brain damage. But Badiou's belief that this method is the sole one used by the neurosciences and constitutes the only sort of knowledge (i.e., anatomical localization) yielded by them is dead wrong. Physical mapping is not all there is to cognitive neuroscience, not by a long shot.[80] Recent work in cognitive science and the neurosciences reveals that mental functions, as related to the brain, are anything but neatly localized in discrete anatomical boxes within the organic matter of the central nervous system. By contrast, the practitioners of these sciences now insist on the highly distributed nature of mind, on nonlocalization not merely within the internally differentiated material milieu of the brain itself, but also across the incredibly complex, dialectically interacting networks/webs interconnecting nature and nurture, the genetic and the epigenetic, genotypes and phenotypes[81]—a delocalizing distribution across brain, body, and both natural as well as social-historical-cultural surrounding environments.[82]

The second of Badiou's three criticisms of cognitive science mentioned in his 2006 interview "Philosophy, Sciences, Mathematics" concerns the issue of materialism. Apropos this issue, Badiou argues that neuroscientific approaches to philosophical topics are either banally tautological (i.e., it is ostensibly obvious that monistic/immanent matter is all there is) or clearly self-refuting (i.e., one cannot locate thought in matter characterized as that which also supposedly exists prior to thought itself). He maintains:

> That human intelligence should be a "material" phenomenon is in my eyes a mere truism. What else could it be? I am, if this is the issue, completely monist. I do not think that any principle of being can "double" indifferent multiplicities. What's more, I always speak of the "human animal" when speaking about us, including even our most sophisticated cognitive activities.[83]

A few paragraphs later, he adds:

> To reduce thought to nature is in general a tautology, or a contradiction. If you understand by "nature" the material state of all that is, it is a tautology: thought is certainly a part of that state. If you understand by "nature" that which, precisely, pre-exists all thought, then it is a contradictory reduction.[84]

Badiou's conjoined contentions that he is "completely monist" and that he invariably refers to "the 'human animal' when speaking about us" are somewhat strange. For instance, the discussion of materialism in *Theory of the Subject* includes indications that adhering to strict, uncompromising ontological monism is perhaps impossible.[85] Additionally, given his firm distinction between all-too-human animality, on the one hand, and inhuman evental subjectivity, on the other hand,[86] it does not seem that Badiou consistently describes all "cognitive activities" as immanent to the natural being of humanity. In fact, quite the contrary—the utterly unnatural subject-of-the-event "subtracts" itself from the animality of its human being so as to operate independently of the influences imposed by material nature. In the 1998 interview with Hallward entitled "Politics and Philosophy," Badiou, during the course of laying out what initially sounds like the same line of defense as above regarding accusations bearing upon his antinaturalist neglect of the life sciences, even ends up again invoking a "grace" (as the inexplicable catalyst for processes of subjectification breaking with animality) that descends upon the human animal so as to denaturalize it in creating an evental subject wedded to a given truth, a subject with no real, delineable relation to the natural matter of animality.[87]

The criticism that cognitive science and the neurosciences do not and cannot address truths as transworld fragments of eternity—Badiou affirms, against what he perceives as the reductive materialism of the life sciences, the irreducibility of truths to brains and flesh—has something to it. Badiou is correct that philosophy should not be collapsed without remainder into studies of the brain. Certain things dealt with philosophically indeed can and ought to be treated in registers not tightly bound solely to the languages of the natural sciences. And *Logics of Worlds* identifies a specific Badiouian philosophical conception of truth as the crux of the antagonistic difference between democratic materialism and the materialist dialectic; only the latter admits the existence of truths above and beyond (biomaterial) bodies and languages. For the materialist dialectic, "it is about knowing if and how a body participates, across languages, in the exception of a truth."[88] Soon after this statement, Badiou, tying together truths with the evental subjects that recognize, deploy, and elaborate them (so that the phrase "subject of truth" becomes, in his discourse, a pleonasm), insists that only his materialist dialectic, as opposed to democratic materialism, acknowledges the category of transcommunal, translinguistic subjectivity proper.[89]

However, today, a philosophically guided coordination between psychoanalytic metapsychology and cognitive neuroscience answers to these Badiouian stipulations concerning subjects of truths—and, it does so without an ideologically dangerous recourse to religious rhetoric (i.e., grace, transubstantiation, Christ-Paul, etc.) opening the door to and encouraging idealist hijackings of materialism to the benefit of theologies. This new materialist alliance between psychoanalysis and science is able lucidly and precisely to explain how subtractive subjectification is a possibility embedded within the immanent material being of human beings. If one wishes to preserve intact tiers of philosophy and subjectivity endowed with some sort of autonomy vis-à-vis natural matter and the sciences thereof, then one appeals either to mysterious, magical forces or occurrences (i.e., meta-physical as trans-ontological variables) or to matter itself. What is required in order to avoid lapsing into an obscurantist reliance upon hypothesized enigmatic happenings is a scientifically informed account of how trajectories of denaturalization (including subtractive subjectification) that achieve, as it were, an escape velocity relative to the materiality of nature emerge out of this natural material itself.[90] What is more, a merger of psychoanalysis and science producing a precise outline of such trajectories of natural denaturalization would be neither a democratic materialism nor an instance of Badiou's materialist dialectic. As regards a theory of the (emergent) subject, the choice is not between, as Badiou contends in connection with ontology, mathematical formalism (as per his ontology) and naturalist vitalism (as per, for example, Deleuze's ontology), but between spiritualist obscurantism and scientific clarity—either a delineation, shaped by an engagement with the natural sciences, of the self-sundering capacities/potentials internal to natural materiality . . . or worse, as Lacan might say (the "worse" option being recourse to notions and terminology flirting with blatant, shameless religiosity). Scientific clarity alone is truly consistent with a rigorously atheistic materialism.

I can clarify further the assertions in the paragraph above in relation to Badiou's fashion of contrasting himself with Deleuze. In his review of the latter's 1988 book on Leibniz (*The Fold: Leibniz and the Baroque*), Badiou explains this contrast thus:

> That there be excess (indifferently shadow or light) in the occurrence of the event, that it be creative, I agree. But my distribution of this excess is opposed to Deleuze's, who finds it in the inexhaustible fullness of the world.[91]

He continues:

> For me, it is not from the world, even ideally, that the event gets its inexhaustible reserve, its silent (or indiscernible) excess, but *from its not being attached to it,* from its being separated, interrupted, or—as Mallarmé would say—"pure." And it is, on the contrary, what *afterward* is named by minds or accomplished in bodies that brings about the global or ideal situation in the world of the event (a suspended effect, that I call a truth). The excess of the event is never related to the situation as an organic "dark background," but as a multiple, so that the event *is not*

counted for one by it. The result is that its silent or subtracted part is an infinity *to come,* a postexistence that will bring back to the world the pure separated point of the supplement produced by the event, under the laborious and unachievable form of an infinite inclusion. Where Deleuze sees a "manner" of being, I say that the worldly postexistence of a truth signals the event as *separation,* and this is coherent with the mathematicity of the multiple (but effectively is not so if we suppose its organicity).[92]

A materialist theory of natural denaturalization constructed at the intersection of psychoanalysis and the neurosciences reveals this forced choice between "mathematicity" and "organicity" to be a false dilemma. Nowadays, one no longer must (or ought to) accept the terms of the decision Badiou aggressively thrusts forward here between Deleuze and himself, between a certain sort of naturalism and an antinaturalism insisting on subtractive purity. (Incidentally, the idealist as antimaterialist flavor of Badiou's antinaturalism is perhaps most glaringly betrayed in this passage by a specific detail: the casually articulated disjunction ["or"] between "minds" and "bodies" in the second sentence of the second block quotation above.) The substance of organic being (in particular, the matter composing human beings) empirically has come to show itself not to conform to Badiou's pre-/nondialectical vision of nature as a static homogeneity internally consistent with itself as a stifling idiotic enclosure of asubjective, even subject-squelching, immanence; this vision is unjustifiably blind to the aleatory, plastic, and conflict-ridden characteristics integral to an inconsistent, fragmentary, and not-whole nature. The natural/vital produces out of itself (or, at least, allows for the production out of itself of) that which, to speak in Badiouian parlance, breaks with it in a subtractive manner. In other words, contra Badiou, organicity does not rule out "separation" as the genesis of trans-organic event-subject-truth constellations. One indeed can and should account for the immanent material genesis of these more-than-material configurations.

§5 Declaring the Hebb-Event: The Starting Point for a Revivified Materialist Theory of the Subject

Several commentators and critics of varying degrees of sympathy toward Badiou have formulated observations further highlighting the somewhat problematic status of Badiou's (non-)rapport with biology in particular. Hallward notes that, especially when compared with Deleuze's philosophy, Badiouian ontology appears to be very limited, even excessively minimalist.[93] He indicates that Badiou's austere formalism impedes the urgent task of moving forward with the articulation of the links between a mathematical ontology and "material or historical existence"[94] (although, arguably, this is what *Logics of Worlds,* the officially published version of which did not appear until three years after Hallward's book on Badiou, sets out to accomplish—whether it succeeds is another matter). Specifically as regards materiality, Hallward critically comments, "Badiou will need to develop a logic of material or organic situations that demonstrates how their structurings are indeed consistent with the basic axioms of set theory" and that, in the absence of such a development, "Badiou cannot flesh out the material, endlessly ramified identity of thought and being."[95] Not only, as Tarby observes, is it the case that Badiou has yet to demonstrate any compatibility between his mathematized ontology and the natural-material field covered by biology:[96] Hallward speculates that biology might be constitutively irreducible to or incompatible with the realm of pure set theory identified by Badiou as the thinkable point of intersection between thought and being.[97] Remarks by Badiou about the relations between mathematics, physics, and biology (remarks quoted earlier here) appear to confirm this suspicion. If Hallward is indeed correct, then, once again, a fundamental decision, a choice or wager, presents itself between a mathematical or material ontology.

Furthermore, as I already suggested above, Badiou's anti-naturalism, especially as manifested through the contrasts between his and Deleuze's ontologies, runs a very high risk of allowing for a relapse into theosophy. Both Brassier and Daniel Smith, among others, draw attention to this danger. Brassier explains:

> However unappetizing the prospect of a naturalized epistemology may be to Badiou in its pragmatist idealist guise, once one has discounted transcendentalism, as Badiou has, it becomes difficult to reconcile insistence on the autonomy of the sciences as discrete registers of cognitive production with an unqualified disdain for the one scientific discourse that is in a position to mediate between natural and cognitive production, or *phusys* and *praxis.* For is it not precisely the appeal to an absolute (theological) cleavage between two fundamentally different kinds of history, natural history and cultural history, or hyletic history and noetic history, that Darwin revoked?[98]

Along similar lines, Smith states:

> The path followed by Badiou in *Being and Event* is almost the exact inverse of that followed by Deleuze in *Difference and Repetition,* and these

two paths, finally, can be seen to exemplify Deleuze's own distinction between an immanent and a transcendent ontology. For Deleuze, a purely immanent ontology is one in which there is nothing "outside" Being or "otherwise" than Being . . . Badiou . . . is forced . . . to reintroduce an element of transcendence, which appears in the form of the *event*. For Badiou, there can be no ontology of the event, since the event itself produces an "interruption" in being, a "tear" in its fabric: the event is "supplemental" to ontology, "supernumerary" . . . Though Badiou is determined to expel God and the One from his philosophy, he winds up reassigning to the event, as if through the back door, the very characteristics of transcendence that were formerly assigned to the divine . . . Badiou's "taste" for discretization and axiomatization in mathematics . . . entailed an inevitable appeal to transcendence: the eruption, within Being itself, of a supplemental event that is *not* Being-as-being.[99]

Perhaps what is being indicated in these quotations, taken together, is that, despite Badiou himself repeatedly trumpeting the "death of God" as supposedly brought about in the nineteenth century by Cantor's infinitization of infinity itself,[100] it will take more than mathematics to kill (the idea of) God once and for all. As Brassier points out, biology after Darwin undermines, at the most basic and foundational levels, certain sorts of dualisms with a distinctly religious heritage/tinge relied upon by Badiou (this is carried much further still by post-Darwinian genetics, cognitive science, and the neurosciences). And, as Smith argues, Badiou's manner of mathematizing *l'être en tant qu'être* compels him, in order theoretically to encompass a range of philosophically interesting and relevant phenomena and structures (especially those involving subjectivity), to repeat the foundational idealist gesture of distinguishing between being qua being and something different from and in excess of being as such.[101]

A productive combination and compromise between Brassier and Smith is worth mentioning at this point: in line with arguments I advanced previously here on behalf of a reinvigorated materialism (one that is neither democratic materialism nor the materialist dialectic and is based on a philosophically mediated interfacing of psychoanalysis with the life sciences), a reenvisioning of "natural" matter in light of both Freudian-Lacanian metapsychology and dialectical materialism is possible. Such a reenvisioning permits the formulation of a thoroughly atheist-materialist ontology able to explain, with the exactitude of precise, rigorous terms (i.e., in scientific, rather than religious, language), the immanent production, out of the materiality of nature, of (non-) beings that come to circulate and operate within this material milieu in ways not entirely determined by this same milieu. In short, a natural scientific account of the emergence or genesis of things that themselves cannot exhaustively be accounted for by these very natural sciences is requisite if one is to fend off a regressive resurgence of religiosity. In *Logics of Worlds,* Badiou, referring to his "(formal) metaphysics of the subject," awaits a "still un-thought physics" as the materialist basis-yet-to-come for this (admittedly) meta-physical theory of event-subject-truth constellations as other than strictly mathematical being qua being;[102] at a prior point in this same tome, he describes "man" as a "voided animal."[103] Blinded by the restriction of ontology to set theory, Badiou cannot see that the materialist science *à venir* which he eagerly anticipates, a science of human beings as porous animals shot through with the empty spaces of cracks and gaps, already has arrived, albeit in the form of sciences he derides as unscientific due to their not-completely-mathematized statuses. In Badiou's own parlance, this arrival, arguably dating to 1949, can be named "the Hebb-event." In fidelity to this event, it is time to put some flesh back on the bones of materialism.

If, as Malabou suggests, the recentering of the neurosciences on neural plasticity is the beginning of a scientific revolution with the power to breathe renewed vigor into the dialectical materialist tradition, then Donald O. Hebb's 1949 text *The Organization of Behavior* could be said to mark the start of this momentous upheaval.[104] What is now known as "Hebb's law," based on the findings of this text, is usually encapsulated with the succinct slogan, "Neurons that fire together, wire together."[105] His physiologically grounded theory of learning processes in human beings postulates what has become a factual given: experiential, pattern-based associative activations of multitudes of neurons in the brain actually alter the calibration of the strength of synaptic connections between these neurons, thus resulting in physical changes in the folded matter of the nervous system. That is to say, mental phenomena literally sculpt and resculpt the brain, which itself, given this Hebbian dynamic, must be thought of as plastic (and, as plastic in both of the two senses brought to the fore by Malabou, namely, as both flexible and resistant, as moving between the malleability of reformation and the fixity of formation).[106] The plastic brain is simultaneously constituting (i.e., it shapes the mental life arising from it) and, as Hebb shows, constituted (i.e., it is shaped by the mental life arising from it).[107] A plethora of consequences crucial to a scientifically informed materialist model of the subject flow from the Hebb-event, including the collapse of standard versions of the nature-nurture distinction; the invalidation of reductively mechanistic/eliminative materialisms; and the debunking of vulgar genetic determinism in relation to human beings. These consequences make possible a new materialism and correlative conception of subjectivity.

In its broadest philosophical outlines, what might this new post-Hebb materialism look like, especially when set against Badiou's ontology? A brief return to Sartrean existentialist philosophy is warranted at this juncture (Badiou openly acknowledges Jean-Paul Sartre as a major source of intellectual inspiration for him from his youth up through the present).[108] In drawing out the ontological implications of the radically transformed image of natural substance disclosed by Hebb-inspired models of neural plasticity and their numerous ramifications, one should struggle to combine existentialism—for instance, select aspects of Sartre's conception of subjective autonomy deserve to be preserved and redeployed today—not so much with structuralism (as per Badiou), but with materialism. In particular, the long-assumed incompatibility of the existentialist depiction of autonomous subjectivity with any sort of materialism allied to the natural sciences has become questionable, perhaps even indefensible. Sartre, in his 1946 manifesto *Existenitalism Is a Humanism,* condemns naturalism insofar as he views all materialisms grounded in scientific references to the living body as positing, at bottom, a human nature heteronomously (over)determining the being of the subject. If subjects are free, as per the insistence of Sartrean existentialism, then there is no strong nature, no causally ultimate biophysical/corporeal matter, dictating unbreakable laws to beings subjected to what thus would be a godlike substance. Of course, the key slogan of Sartre's existentialist theory of the subject is "existence precedes essence." And, for Sartre, this automatically entails an antinaturalist stance due to the supposedly essentialist hypotheses regarding human nature ostensibly put forward by materialisms linked to the natural sciences.[109]

Sartre's lasting influence on Badiou includes an inherited antinaturalism apropos the topic of subjectivity based on exactly the same assumptions and assertions regarding the natural sciences, assumptions and assertions dating from the middle of the twentieth century that Badiouian philosophy continues to rely upon nowadays in the early twenty-first century (hence, one might sensibly suspect that these notions have become somewhat outdated). In the concluding chapter of his 2005 book *The Century,* a chapter devoted to mapping the points of convergence between Sartre's radical humanism and Michel Foucault's equally radical antihumanism, Badiou praises both of these twentieth-century French philosophical orientations for offering resistance against the relegation of humanity to the status of a mere "species," a relegation appealing to "a bad Darwin."[110] Equivocally sliding from biology to biopolitical ideology without the slightest hesitation, he mobilizes Sartre and Foucault, with their shared "fierce hostility to substantialist categories" and "genuine hatred" of naturalism, in an opposition to the "man of animal humanism," a figure purported to be inextricably intertwined with a pathetic humanitarian vision in which everyone is reduced to nothing more than a potential or actual suffering victim.[111]

Contrary to Badiou's antinaturalism, the moment is ripe to integrate the contemporary natural sciences into a materialist ontology with a corresponding account of subjectivity (the life sciences especially have undergone profound transformations since the days when Sartre condemned them as reductive by virtue of being mired in essentialist substantialism). A scientifically informed materialism of (human) nature as internally conflicted and plastically porous matter is far from incompatible with some of the fundamental tenets of antiessentialist existentialism. To put it in Sartre's words, there are loci of convergence within nature (human beings being the exemplary instance in this case) where natural essence is ultimately indistinguishable from unnatural nonessence; the essence of human beings, from a contemporary life-scientific perspective, is shot through with existence (in the Sartrean sense) from the very beginning. Such would be one of the founding axioms of a materialist existentialism, a doctrine positing the materially immanent "snafu" subject as precisely that volatile juncture at which existence and essence collide. Badiou professes that he aims to construct "a Sartrean thought of mathematics, or of science in general."[112] The time has come to attempt this in relation to the natural as well as formal sciences.

§6 A Metaontological Wager on Another Truth-Event in Science: Of Sutures and Fidelities

In closing, a certain possible objection that might be raised by Badiou or certain Badiouians should be mentioned and then laid to rest. According to Badiou's conception of the discipline of philosophy (as elaborated in *Manifesto for Philosophy* and elsewhere), philosophy does not generate its own truths internally out of itself. Instead, it thinks under "conditions." More precisely, philosophical thought is responsible for responding to the truths arising from events occurring outside it in the domains of the four "generic procedures" of truth-production: art, love, politics, and science.[113] The vocation of philosophy is to comprehend the "compossibility" of the contemporaneous artistic, amorous, political, and scientific truths of its time, to hear and echo the reverberations and resonances between evental revelations flashing across the surface of the present.[114]

One of the conditions under which Badiou himself philosophizes is the Cantor-event and its aftermath in the generic procedure of mathematics as science. Responding to the impact of the Cantorian revolution, Badiou's philosophy makes the "metaontological" decision to shift ontology from a philosophical to a mathematical jurisdiction (i.e., to trans-finite set theory). Badiou clarifies that practicing mathematicians need not and likely do not conceive of themselves as ontologists spelling out what can and cannot be said of *l'être en tant qu'être*. The philosopher's choice to hand over responsibility for matters ontological to mathematics and mathematicians is an intraphilosophical choice at the level of "metaontology," a level at which the difference between being qua being and whatever is not such being ostensibly can be discerned or drawn. Hence, for Badiou, given both his conception of philosophy as well as the historicity of mathematics as a science in which decisive shifts occur in its unfurling over time (he readily acknowledges the historicity of mathematics),[115] ontology itself and its accompanying philosophical/ metaontological mediating framework are bound up with and conditioned by events in science.[116] Ontology is "*a* situation" or a particular "world" affected and structured by scientific truths.[117]

As regards the conditioning of philosophy by the four generic procedures (as well as the conditioning of ontology, via metaontology, by truth-events in science), Badiou sternly warns of an occupational hazard to which philosophers too often succumb. He even blames select cases of this succumbing for instances of apparent crisis, malaise, exhaustion, disrepute, or death afflicting philosophy throughout the twentieth century in particular.[118] Badiou labels this hazard "suture":

> If philosophy is, as I defend it to be, the configuration, within thought, of the fact that its four generic conditions (the poem, the matheme, the political and love) are compossible *in the eventful form prescribing the truths of the time,* a suspension of philosophy can result from the restriction or blockage of the free play required in order to define a regime of passage, or of intellectual circulation between the truth procedures conditioning philosophy. The most frequent cause of such blockage is that instead of constructing a space of compossibility through which the thinking of time is practiced, philosophy *delegates* its functions to one or other of its conditions, handing over the whole of thought to *one* generic procedure. Philosophy is then carried out in the element of its own suppression to the great benefit of that procedure.[119]

He adds: "I shall call this type of situation a *suture*. Philosophy is placed in suspension every time it presents itself as being sutured to one of its conditions."[120] To take a pertinent example here of such a suturing to one of the four extraphilosophical generic procedures of truth-production, Badiou accuses the Anglo-American analytic tradition of having collapsed philosophy, to its detriment, into a positivistic scientism.[121] One must bear in mind that Badiou certainly would consider contemporary English-language theorizing in conjunction with the neurosciences and cognitive science as an exemplary part of this same bemoaned suture.[122]

For Badiou, philosophy can and should function in a meta-ontological capacity vis-à-vis science, bringing out what could be described as the "unconscious" ontological ramifications sheltered within the sciences. In line with this, he proposes that "science doesn't include an evaluation of its double nature. Philosophy is able to organize the discussion between science and science or to think the double nature of science, mathematics or physics, or biology."[123] Badiou continues:

> There is no intrinsic relation between science and philosophy. Philosophy is not an interpretation of science. Philosophy is the method for organizing the discussion between science and science, science on the side of specific production and science as a part of the thinking of being *qua* being.[124]

The "double nature of science" (i.e., "science on the side of specific production and science as a part of the thinking of being *qua* being") refers to the thesis that particular sciences contain implications for ontology extending beyond the confines of the more circumscribed regional sphere of recognized objects and methods constituting the scientific discipline in question. One of the jobs of philosophy is to extract such consequences from these scientific disciplines. Interestingly, Badiou mentions biology in his discussion of this. However, considering the inter-related factors of his general antinaturalism, his restriction of ontology to a single branch of mathematics alone, and his chastising of analytic philosophy for having unphilosophically sutured itself to the (natural) sciences, it seems unlikely that Badiou would take seriously the idea that biology too (including the neurosciences and cognitive science) contains ontological dimensions worthy of the attention of a philosophical metaontology (he mentions it here simply as one of the sciences philosophy can put into conversation with other sciences). Would he not deride the above declared Hebb-event as irrelevant to ontology?

In all likelihood, Badiou and/or certain Badiouians would accuse me of suturing philosophy to science, of disastrously diminishing it to the shrunken size of a mere appendage of the life sciences. Three rejoinders are appropriate in response to this accusation. First, fidelity to the Hebb-event is no more of a suturing of philosophy to science than is Badiou's fidelity to the Cantor-event (if anything, Badiou tries to tie philosophical metaontology to one subdiscipline of one formal science with a suture-like rigidity and inflexibility). Second, Badiouian fears that bringing ontology into the orbit of the natural as opposed to formal sciences inevitably leads to this suture through reductionism are based on false, out-of-date impressions of how nature and matter are conceived of in biology and related fields (in this regard, Badiou-the-philosopher has not lived up to his philosophical duty thoroughly to think his contemporary scientific circumstances). Third, Badiou's reasons for insisting that, of the sciences, only pure mathematics is suitable for ontological purposes due to its supreme abstractness are reflective of Platonic-idealist tendencies to devalue real material existence in positing a purified being-in-and-of-itself. Separating out a clean ontology of being *an sich* from the dirty, messy onticness of concrete entities, regardless of how this separation is executed, always brings one into the proximity of antimaterialist elements.

With respect to both philosophy and ontology, Badiou frequently speaks of bets, choices, gambles, and wagers. The metaontological decision-without-guarantee taken here is that the implications to be extracted from the historically disclosed truth of Hebbian plasticity make possible the construction of a transcendental materialism,[125] a materialism uniquely capable of formulating a theory of the subject in the absence of any sort of divine, otherworldly forces whatsoever. (More precisely, through positing a dialectical commingling of the Sartrean opposites of essence and existence within the single register of material-substantial immanence alone, a materialism capable of charting the immanent material genesis of the more-than-material transcendent is able to be articulated.) Only the continuation of a further dogged pursuit of these implications will determine retroactively whether this decision is productive and, hence, worth defending.

Phantom of Consistency: Kant Troubles

§1 Transcendentalism and Its Discontents:
Badiou's Synthesis of Existentialism and Structuralism

The most important aspect of the work of Badiou, as situated at the intersection of the history of post-Kantian European philosophy and contemporary theory, is his sustained project to bridge the seemingly unbridgeable gap between two distinct orientations represented by two twentieth-century figures avowedly influential for him in his youth: Sartre and Althusser. In terms of the topic of subjectivity, a topic Badiou insistently keeps on today's intellectual agenda despite so much talk of "the death of the subject" surrounding deconstructionism and the various "post" movements (postmodernism, poststructuralism, and so on), the former (i.e., Sartre) represents a notion of the subject as a kinetic negativity of absolute autonomy free from ultimate determination by nature, nurture, or any combination thereof; by contrast, the latter (i.e., Althusser) represents a notion of the subject as the heteronomous, re-ified by-product of transsubjective sociohistorical mechanisms, namely, the subject as subjected to ideologies, interpellations, and so on. One of the central philosophical matters separating phenomenological existen-tialism from Marxist structuralism is, obviously, the enigma of freedom. As Badiou remarks, for him, "the decisive philosophical task . . . would be to complete the Sartrean theory of liberty with a careful investigation into the opacity of the signifier."[1]

In an interview with Bruno Bosteels, Badiou discusses his interest in finding a way to surmount the apparent antinomy between Sartrean-style existentialism and Althusserian-style structuralism. He states:

> I have always been concerned in a privileged way by the question of how something could still be called "subject" within the most rigorous condi-tions possible of the investigation of structures. This question had an echo for me of an even older question, which I had posed at the time when I was fully Sartrean, namely, the question of how to make Sartre compatible with the intelligibility of mathematics . . . I remember very

clearly having raised the question, having formed the project of one day constructing something like a Sartrean thought of mathematics, or of science in general, which Sartre had left aside for the most part. This particular circumstance explains why I nevertheless have always been interested in the question of structural formalism while sustaining a category of the subject.[2]

A certain question Badiou poses in the introduction to *Being and Event* should be understood in relation to the above statements—"pure mathematics being the science of being, how is a subject possible?"[3] Articulating himself in this fashion, Badiou makes clear that his efforts to figure out how to remain faithful to the insights of existentialism regarding autonomous subjectivity while nonetheless fully embracing the framework of structuralism—Peter Osborne is not without justification in seeing Badiou's philosophy, especially its recourse to mathematics, as fundamentally structuralist in inspiration[4]—are at the very heart of his protracted endeavors across the full range of his many writings. He thus puts himself forward as taking on the task of resolving one of the great unresolved tensions bequeathed to contemporary thought by twentieth-century continental philosophy; and, like Lacan, he strives to do so by formulating a model of subjectivity compatible with the strictures of structuralism's emphases on the mediating influences of asubjective configurations and matrices.[5] What is required, as Badiou readily admits, is nothing less than a quite novel and unprecedented account of the subject.[6]

Paul Ricoeur, in reference to Lévi-Strauss, describes classical 1950s French structuralism (a set of which Lévi-Strauss is perhaps the only full member) as involving a "transcendentalism without a subject."[7] Admittedly, neither Lévi-Strauss nor Althusser seems to leave space open in their theoretical systems for anything resembling the subject of Sartre's philosophy of freedom. Badiou's theory of the event, arising out of the openings provided by the points of inconsistency embedded within structuring situations and states, allows for avoiding precisely such stifling subject-foreclosing closure. But not only does Badiou seek to delineate what one could characterize as a structuralism with a subject—his most recent philosophical reflections, coming together in the hulking tome *Logics of Worlds*, labor to construct a reworked conception of the transcendental as decoupled from any sort of transcendental subject (à la Kant). Like Ricoeur's version of Lévi-Strauss, Badiou indeed pursues, in his latest texts, a transcendentalism without a subject. However, unlike this same Lévi-Strauss, Badiou simultaneously is at pains to preserve the category of the subject, albeit a subject divorced from its usual partners in certain post-Kantian philosophical circles (especially such notions or themes as experience, finitude, and embodiment).

A thorough critical scrutinizing of Badiou's theory of evental subjectivities would require a book-length study unto itself. In this chapter, my focus will be on the argumentative tactics and strategies deployed by Badiou in his attempts to divorce transcendentalism and subjectivity, attempts aiming to elaborate both a nonsubjective transcendental as well as a nontranscendental subject. The attempted desubjectification of transcendental structures will be of primary concern in what follows, thus warranting a careful examination of the doctrine of the object whose elaboration occupies the central bulk of *Logics of Worlds*.

This exorcising of the specter of the mediating presence of finite epistemological subjectivity has everything to do with Badiou's struggles against Kantian transcendental idealism and its (phenomenological) offshoots. As with Deleuze,[8] so too with Badiou—Kant is one of his key philosophical enemies. But, given Badiou's tempered hostility toward Deleuze's vitalist thought, the enemy of his enemy is not, in this case, his friend (the young Badiou even goes so far as to accuse the anti-Oedipal duo of Deleuze and Guattari of being closet Kantians).[9] There are three fundamental reasons why Kant functions as one of the main nemeses for Badiouian philosophy. First, Badiou blames him for having invented the motif of finitude, a motif present nowadays in various guises.[10] Badiou's tirades against this motif recur throughout his writings in the form of attacks upon not only epistemologies of finite subjective knowledge, but also upon promotions of mortality, of death-bound being, as philosophically foundational and ultimate.[11] Second, Badiou balks at Kant's invocation of the ostensible "limits of possible experience" insofar as this boundary-line partitioning noumena from phenomena entails the prohibition of constructing a rational ontology.[12] The Kantian critical-transcendental apparatus insists that only a deontologized epistemology is philosophically valid and defensible, which, in light of Badiou's post-Heideggerian ontological ambitions,[13] is a position that must be eradicated. Third, for Badiou as a committed materialist, the idealism of Kantian transcendental idealism is simply unacceptable. Badiou's transcendental is both asubjective and (materially) immanent to the world of which it is, at one and the same time, both a structuring scaffolding as well as an internal component. With implicit reference to the Kantian gesture of enclosing subjects within the prison-houses and shadow-theaters of their own cognition, Badiou sneeringly dubs Kant "our first *professor*,"[14] the initiator of a sterile academic orientation in philosophy whose very theoretical content reflects the alleged practical fact of its lack of substantial connections to any sort of, so to speak, real world.

In the course of beginning to sketch the contours of his peculiar conception of the transcendental, Badiou poses a series of questions to which this conception supposedly answers. He enumerates them thusly:

> How is it possible that the neutrality, the inconsistency, the indifferent dissemination of being *qua* being, comes to consist as being-there? Or again: how can the essential unbinding of multiple-being present itself as local relation, and, finally, as the stability of worlds? Why, and how, are there worlds, rather than chaos?[15]

The terminology used in this quotation from *Logics of Worlds* cannot be exhaustively elucidated in the present introductory discussion; considering the range of connotations and functions with which this terminology comes to be endowed by Badiou, a thorough exegesis of these remarks is not possible in this current context. Nonetheless, a few things can and should be said here. Badiou carries out a radical dephenomenalization of ontology in *Being and Event*.[16] Therein, being qua being (*l'être en tant qu'être*) is said to be the infinite infinities of inconsistent multiplicities-without-oneness "subtracted" from any and every field of consistency-dependent presentation.[17] Given that he also remains an opponent of idealism, he is thereby left with the mystery or problem of how phenomena (i.e., "being-there" [*être-là*], in Badiou's more recent philosophical vocabulary)[18] arise from nonphenomenal being: what accounts for the genesis of the relative coherence and organization of "worlds" (i.e., structured domains of relations between presentable entities) out of the incoherence and disorganization of pure being *an sich*?

One might anticipate that it is in response to precisely this query that Badiou redeploys the notion of the transcendental. However, such is not the case. Badiou's transcendental is coextensive with what he calls "worlds."[19] More specifically, each Badiouian world, as a regional sphere within which multiple-being is made to appear in the form of localized/situated existences according to the relational logic of this same sphere, is ordered by its own "transcendental regime."[20] Additionally, he contends that there are indefinite numbers of worlds both possible and actual.[21] Hence, the Badiouian transcendental is not a concept-term denoting delineable (pre)conditions for the emergence of phenomenal being-there (i.e., the appearances and presentations of transcendentally structured worlds) out of ontological being qua being (as distinct from any and every phenomenology). To the extent that Badiou's transcendental is internal to and entirely entangled with the circumscribed domain of *être-là*, it cannot simultaneously operate in a mediating transitional role between this domain and *l'être en tant qu'être*. Badiou seems to be left with the unanswered questions of how and why being(s) give rise to worlds (the latter involving the transcendental as each world's organizing state/regime). In isolation from Kant's idealism, the broadest sense of his notion of the transcendental has to do with conditions of possibility. In this sense, Badiou's transcendental begs the question of the conditions of possibility for its own surfacing out of the Real of being. Who or what catalyzes the coming into existence of the being-there of appearances? Badiouian transcendentalism, if there is such a thing, would thus require supplementation by a metatranscendentalism, an explanation of that which makes possible this very catalyzing.

In the subsequent sections below, not only will I explain the positions of Badiou apropos Kantian transcendental idealism—I will put forward three far-from-insignificant problems with the Badiouian reaction against Kant and his legacy. First, in his quarrels with Kantian thought, Badiou repeatedly uses the term "subject" in equivocal fashions, creating confusions that risk generating misleading illusions of there being genuine debates and disputes where there are not any. Second, Badiou's antinaturalism (especially his curt rejection of the life sciences as philosophically interesting and relevant) interferes with his being able to account for the genesis of appearances out of being in a materialist rather than idealist fashion. Third, Badiou's mature philosophical edifice, from 1988's *Being and Event* through 2006's *Logics of Worlds,* integrally involves the function of an idea Badiou baptizes "counting-for-one." This idea continues to play a part in Badiou's more recent work in ways that keep him within the orbit of Kant's critical philosophy despite his violent repudiations of Kantian transcendental idealism.

§2 What Counts: The Lingering Specter of Kant

Badiou takes issue with both halves of Kant's transcendental idealism, both his conception of transcendentalism as well as his deontologized idealist epistemology. I will address later Badiou's critical transformations of the notion of the transcendental. Before doing so, it will be useful to discuss the anti-idealist fork of Badiou's two-pronged attack on Kant. Again and again, Badiou opposes the crucial move at the heart of the Kantian critical "Copernican revolution," namely, the insistence that knowable reality conforms to the mediating templates of subjective cognition (rather than this cognition directly apprehending real being in and of itself).[22] This insistence upon epistemological finitude, an insistence entailing a denial of the possibility of access to anything

enjoying, as it were, a degree of ontological heft, is utterly unacceptable to Badiouian philosophy. He protests that "against Kant, we have to
maintain that we know being qua being and that we also know the way
by which the thing as such appears in a world"[23] (incidentally, whether
Badiou adequately explains the latter is worth calling into question). As
regards the former (i.e., a direct knowledge of *l'être en tant qu'être*), he
claims, against Kant's maintenance of the limits of possible experience,
that cognition indeed can transgress these purported limits so as to seize
being qua being in an unmediated fashion.[24] For Badiou, being-in-itself,
unlike *das Ding an sich*, is "entirely knowable"[25] (for this same reason,
he disagrees with readings of Lacan in which the register of the Real is
treated as akin or equivalent to Kant's realm of noumena).[26] In *Logics
of Worlds*, he speaks of thought's ability to operate "beyond the limits
of sensibility" so as to "synthetically think the noumenal and the phenomenal" (Hegel's post-Kantian aspirations are mentioned here too).[27]
Later in this text, the image of worlds (i.e., transcendentally organized
regions in which being manifests itself in specific forms of being-there)
as having an external underside, an underside akin to the noumenal
realm of things-in-themselves imagined by Kant as inaccessibly dwelling
behind or beneath the façade of accessible phenomena, is deemed to be
entirely inaccurate and false.[28] Panning back to a more general level, this
aspect of Badiou's anti-Kantianism can be encapsulated with the axiomatic proposition that being itself appears, that *l'être en tant qu'être* discloses
itself in and through *être-là*.[29]

Elsewhere, Badiou states his opposition to Kant's deontologizing
epistemology of the limits of possible experience thus: "There are indeed a noumenon and a phenomenon, but the noumenon is knowable."[30] This particular manner of expressing himself reveals a detail
that it is important to note apropos his position with respect to Kant's
distinction between phenomenal objects-as-appearances and noumenal things-in-themselves: Badiou does not seek to dissolve this distinction—instead, he merely denies that it constitutes an uncrossable border
strictly separating possible epistemologies from impossible ontologies
(in a relatively early text, 1985's *Can Politics Be Thought?*, he even defends
the Kantian thing-in-itself against Hegelian criticisms of this idea).[31] In
Kant's language, one could say that *Being and Event* deals with noumena
(i.e., being qua being *an sich*) while *Logics of Worlds* deals with phenomena (i.e., being-there as transcendentally ordered appearances).

However, even at this basic starting-point, Badiou's means of taking
distance and differentiating himself from Kant are not always so clear
and convincing. One of the core concepts entangled with the ontology elaborated in *Being and Event* is that of "counting-for-one" (*compter-*

pour-un).[32] This unifying operation, as an operation, is not itself a being in the strict ontological sense (i.e., something inhering within *l'être en tant qu'être*).[33] Instead, Badiou defines this "count" as distinct from being, although (supposedly) always-already having acted upon it so as to render being-in-itself presentable[34] (as Tarby explains, "the unity of something is operational and not substantial,"[35] and "unity is transitory, evanescent, operational").[36] Any "situation," as a locality within which unified entities can and do appear, is structured by a situation-specific operation of counting-for-one. Furthermore, from within any situation arising as an outcome of such a count, one can, after-the-fact of this operation, infer something (i.e., being qua being as pure multiplicities-without-one) retroactively presupposed as prior to this process of counting.[37] This leads Badiou to propose a distinction between "inconsistent multiplicity" and "consistent multiplicity"; the former is what presumably precedes the consistency-producing intervention of counting-for-one, and the latter is what is created as a result of this unifying operation.[38] A situation structured by a count contains many ones (i.e., consistent multiplicities), while being as such, posited as anterior to this situational structuring and organization, "in-consists" of multiplicities without one-ness or unity[39] (hence, "being *qua* being, strictly speaking, is neither one nor multiple"[40]—with "multiple" here meaning many unified ones).[41] Bruno Besana provides a retranslation of these terms and concepts back into Kantian parlance. After remarking that, for Badiou, "the pure multiple and the count for one designate two different regimes which fall under the sphere of ontology and that of phenomenology respectively,"[42] Besana proceeds to describe, with reference to Badiou's 1998 *Short Treatise on Transitory Ontology* (a text Badiou identifies as a pivotal hinge situated between *Being and Event* and *Logics of Worlds*),[43] a passage from the noumenal (i.e., being as uncounted and inconsistent multiplicities) to the phenomenal (i.e., appearing as counted and consistent multiplicities).[44]

On the basis of the positioning of *compter-pour-un* between inconsistent and consistent multiplicities (i.e., in the vocabulary of *Logics of Worlds,* between *l'être en tant qu'être* and *être-là*), Badiou further complicates matters—with these complications already popping up as early as the first two meditations of *Being and Event*. In "Meditation One—The One and the Multiple: *A Priori* Conditions of Any Possible Ontology" (one cannot help but be struck by the Kantian language of this subtitle), he maintains that

> ontology can be solely *the theory of inconsistent multiplicities as such.* "As such" means that what is presented in the ontological situation is the

multiple without any other predicate than its multiplicity. Ontology, insofar as it exists, must necessarily be the science of the multiple qua multiple.[45]

Several facets within this passage deserve attention. To begin with, Badiou qualifies ontology as a "situation." Elsewhere in *Being and Event* as well as in various subsequent texts, he unambiguously treats ontology as one situation or world among others.[46] But, as such, how can ontology also address inconsistent multiplicities, given that these multiplicities of pure being *an sich* allegedly escape the grasp of any and every one-ifying count and, hence, any and every situation? I will return to this question momentarily. In the last sentence of the quotation above, one might wonder whether the caveat attached to ontology (i.e., "insofar as it exists [*pour autant qu'elle existe*]")[47] harbors a premonition of the contrast between being and "existence" so crucial for *Logics of Worlds* (wherein "existence" pertains to the being-there of appearing within a transcendentally governed world),[48] since, in the language of this 2006 tome, ontology itself is a world. Finally, apropos the quotation above, Badiou's definition of ontology as "the science of the multiple qua multiple" generates, in conjunction with remarks regarding the role of the count-for-one occurring in the immediately following pages of *Being and Event,* further difficulties requiring resolution.

Badiou proceeds to identify *compter-pour-un* as "the system of conditions through which the multiple can be recognized as multiple."[49] Of course, insofar as counting-for-one establishes situations in which multiplicities are rendered consistent, this operation's unavoidable mediation, a mediation turning even ontology itself into a situation, bars direct access to the unsituated inconsistent multiplicities of *l'être en tant qu'être.*[50] Badiou's introductory framing of his 1988 magnum opus hints at this from the very start: proclaiming an equivalence between mathematics (as post-Cantorian trans-finite set theory) and ontology is not tantamount to claiming that the "stuff" of being qua being in and of itself is numerical in nature;[51] rather, this is merely to assert that, for several reasons, a particular mathematical "discourse" is what is "pronounceable" or "expressible" of being *an sich.*[52] In other words, the necessary, always-already there intervention of a count-for-one imposes certain constraints and limitations on thought's relation to the (inconsistent) multiplicities of being per se.[53] The first meditation of *Being and Event* draws to a close with Badiou proposing, among other things, that ontology requires the inconsistent being made consistent so as to be addressed within its discursive parameters.[54]

The second and fourth meditations of *Being and Event,* in relation to the count-dependent distinction between consistent and inconsistent multiplicities, contain propositions that bring Badiou back into proximity with Kant-the-enemy. In the second meditation, he declares:

> The inconsistent multiple is actually unthinkable as such. All thought supposes a situation of the thinkable, which is to say a structure, a count-as-one, in which the presented multiple is consistent and numerable. Consequently, the inconsistent multiple is solely—before the one-effect in which it is structured—an ungraspable horizon of being.[55]

A few lines later, Badiou succinctly stipulates that "what thought needs is the—non-being—mediation of the one."[56] Subsequently in the second meditation, the inconsistency of being qua being as multiplicities-without-one is deemed to be "unthinkable."[57] In the fourth meditation, such inconsistency is similarly qualified as incapable of being "presented."[58] Kant speaks of noumenal things-in-themselves as thinkable but not knowable.[59] With respect to this matter, Badiou oscillates between two incompatible stances. On the one hand, when railing against Kantian epistemological finitude with its limits of possible experience denying direct access to noumena, he claims that the noumenal realm of Real being *an sich* indeed can be grasped cognitively in ways forbidden by Kant's deontologizing epistemology. On the other hand, he sometimes seems to reinstate essential features of the Kantian divide between the phenomenal and the noumenal when speaking of unsayable being-in-itself as inconsistent multiplicities-without-one inaccessible to all discourse and thought (even that of pure mathematics).

What could be called Badiou's "Kant trouble" becomes more apparent and serious once additional attention is turned to the concept of *compter-pour-un*. In a collection of papers on Badiou (*Writings Around the Thought of Alain Badiou* [2007]), three of the contributors to this volume articulate a series of unsettling queries and problems for the Badiouian philosophical framework on the basis of the role played by this operation of counting therein. Sam Gillespie's posthumously published paper "Multiple Being Presented, Represented, Rendered True" makes several important points. First, given the inescapability of the count-for-one (an inescapability constraining even ontology itself to be one situation or world among others), it becomes doubtful whether, in the absence of a possible position or perspective outside of a count-shaped situation, any delineable difference between consistent and inconsistent multiplicities can be legitimately and defensibly affirmed.[60] In this vein, Gillespie notes that it makes little sense to talk about being as inconsistent in itself (i.e., in an absolute, nonrelative mode), since inconsistency is a valid category or concept only relative to consistency.[61] Following Gillespie's indications, perhaps it also should be observed that Badiou fails to distinguish between structured and unstructured inconsistency, namely, between, as structured, an inconsistency arising from and inhering within the structures of situations (with their presentations as countings) and states-of-situations (with their representations as countings of countings)[62] and, as unstructured, an inconsistency presumably characteristic of being qua being apart from its manifestations both ontic and ontological. Arguably—this would be an argument to advance on another occasion—Badiou's failure to draw such a distinction is linked to what could be critiqued as, in *Being and Event,* an equivocal use of the word "inconsistency."

Additionally, Gillespie asks why Badiou denies counting-for-one any sort of ontological status.[63] Why should the operation of this count be entirely deontologized? Besana and Edoardo Acotto, in the same collection of essays, raise similar questions. Besana inquires into from where *compter-pour-un* comes; and, he rightly remarks that, given Badiou's adamant anti-naturalism, the ground, origin, or source of this operation remains mysteriously unspecified.[64] Acotto, discussing the count-for-one, likewise comments:

> Badiou defines it . . . as an *operation*. But who is, concretely, *the operator*? This is one of the mysteries of the philosophy of Badiou, and of its exclusion of perceptual and cognitive mechanisms from ontological discourse.[65]

Critically inquiring into whether there are, in fact, good reasons for denying operations an ontological status (one might inquire about this also as regards Badiou's later withholding of such status from relations), Jean-Toussaint Desanti similarly argues:

> It seems clear to me that the project of a pure ontology (an intrinsic theory of being as being) would stumble here with its very first step, were one to ask oneself this "preliminary" question: what is it to operate? Who operates here and in what realm? In this case, clarification of the object-act correlation would at least have to be the (transcendental) propaedeutic required for any meaningful ontology, if we are to avoid postponing indefinitely a pure theory of "being as being," or even annulling its object.[66]

What is at stake in the answers (or lack thereof) to these critical questions formulated by Acotto, Besana, and Desanti is nothing less than the matter of whether Badiou succeeds at moving beyond the Kantian-style idealism with which he presents himself as having broken. Moreover, Badiou's difficulties arising from the enigmas surrounding *compter-pour-un* do not go away, fading with time and through successive revisions to his system; long after *Being and Event* (at least up through *Logics of Worlds*), he continues explicitly to invoke this problematic concept. For instance, in 1998, he defines the one-ifying operation of counting as Kant's transcendent unity of apperception minus a self-conscious subject.[67] To this, one should respond as follows (a response revealing the complications created by Badiou failing to clarify the different meanings of the word "subject" at stake in his scattered readings of Kant):

> Throughout almost the entirety of the *Critique of Pure Reason*, Kant abstains from speaking of "the subject" or "subjectivity" in his delineation of the conditions of possibility for experience and its correlative forms of legitimate knowledge. A Kantian could nonchalantly reply to Badiou along the lines of, "Fine, the term 'subject' won't be used as somehow equivalent to the configuration of transcendental conditions for reality. So what? The essential framework of the critical system still stands, remaining serenely unaffected by this merely terminological concession." And, Kant may be even more radical than Badiou here. More often than not, criticisms of Kant's "idealist subject" fall into the trap of what a committed Kantian transcendental idealist could easily and convincingly condemn as crude metaphorical "picture thinking": the "Transcendental Aesthetic" of the first *Critique* clearly stipulates that spatiality is confined to being solely one of the two "pure forms of intuition." Hence, accusations that Kant ultimately relies upon a simplistic idealist inside/outside dichotomy (i.e., experience is somehow "in" a subject rather than being "out there" beyond the closed circle of cognition) is, from a Kantian perspective, a cheap and easy criticism ultimately reliant upon a simplistic, unrefined category mistake. That is to say, such a critique betrays the fact that the critics have yet to make the leap from picture thinking sorts of depictions of subjectivity (the *Innenwelt* of the subject versus the *Umwelt* of being)—Kant might note that the subject cannot be envisioned in this way, namely, according to criteria implicitly or explicitly derived from the limited domain of intuition—to a transcendental level in which the very question of "inside or outside" (i.e., the spatial "where?") with respect to subjectivity is simply irrelevant. The Kantian subject is not spatially localizable, whether literally or, as with most criticisms of it, figuratively. Properly envisioning this form of subjectivity demands dispensing with the prosthetic crutch of visual metaphors.[68]

Oddly enough, in *Short Treatise on Transitory Ontology* (the same book in which counting-for-one is equated with a subjectless transcendental unity of apperception), Badiou appears to acknowledge certain key points made in the quotation immediately above. Therein (as well as elsewhere),[69] he alludes to an anonymous "One" at work in the Kantian critical apparatus, an impersonal, selfless unifying dynamic not so different from the operation of counting described in *Being and Event*.[70]

Counting-for-one, as a disembodied, always-already prior structuring condition or principle of basic formal unity for situations as fields of both possible and actual object-level presentations/appearances, sounds awfully akin to how Kant discusses what is at the core of the "Transcendental Deduction" (which itself arguably is the very heart of the *Critique of Pure Reason*). But, on a more sympathetic reading, maybe Badiou succeeds at taking distance from Kant not so much through the concept of this count (as an ethereal, spectral operation of unification) in relation to ontology, but, instead, through his insistence (admittedly inspired, in part, by certain of Hegel's reactions to Kant) that being itself can and does appear within the parameters of circumscribed phenomeno-logical frames. To the extent that Kant's idealism commits him to consign any connection or link between appearances (as objects) and being (as things) to the darkness of an unknown about which nothing can be said, Badiou's post-1988 reflections (especially in and around *Logics of Worlds*) on the being-appearance rapport perhaps establish more convincingly that Badiou is indeed, by contrast with Kant, a committed anti-idealist. However, before addressing these reflections through a thorough analysis of Badiou's doctrine of the transcendentally constituted object (as elaborated in *Logics of Worlds*), assessing the differences between the Kantian and Badiouian notions of the transcendental is in order.

§3 Anonymous Appearances: The Asubjective Transcendental

Quickly encapsulated, Kant's transcendental, as characterized by Badiou, involves four features, with it being (1) subjective (this scaffolding of possibility conditions for a reality of presentable objects is associated with the mind of a cognizing individual agent); (2) singular as universal (there is one, and only one, fundamental skeletal structure of these possibility conditions shared by all mental agents); (3) necessary (without this singular, transindividual matrix common to all individual minds there is no reality); and (4) transcendent (this transcendental, of necessity, is not internally included within the field it nonetheless makes possible). Badiou's transcendental is the mirror-image inversion of this, with it being: (1) asubjective (there is no central mental agent or cognizing individual invariably organizing worlds of appearances);[71] (2) multiple as nonuniversal (given both the coextension of transcendental regimes with worlds as well as the alleged plurality of worlds, there are as many transcendentals as there are innumerable worlds—thus further justifying the denial of a unique transcendental subject à la Kant);[72] (3) contingent (given the open-ended multiplicity of worlds with varying transcendental regimes, no one transcendental configuration is absolutely necessary);[73] and (4) immanent (those things functioning as conditions of possibility for a particular world simultaneously appear as elements within this same world).[74] It seems Badiou could not be further from Kant as regards the transcendental, positioning himself as Kant's polar opposite here.

Addressing the topic of the Badiouian transcendental, Alberto Toscano sees in it the signal of a not-to-be-overlooked shift between *Being and Event* and *Logics of Worlds*. More precisely, he views Badiou as moving away from the vexed concept of counting-for-one as deployed in the former book:

> Where Badiou's recent work goes further is in the postulate that every arrangement (read "world") is endowed with one element (a multiple) which functions as its structuring principle, localising all other existent (or appearing) multiples and determining their degrees of existence (or appearance), in other words, their degrees of identity or difference from one another. This element is defined as the *transcendental* of the "world"—it is, so to speak, what individuates the world, providing it with maximal and minimal degrees of appearance and intensity.[75]

Toscano continues:

> Rather than relegating the structuring agency to the nebulous domain of a perennial and unquestionable law (a danger arguably incurred by the focus on the "count" in *Being and Event*), Badiou's determination of the transcendental as a structured *element* (or multiple) *within* the situation itself heralds the possibility of a far more immanent, which is to say, of a substantially more *materialist,* consideration of order and placement than the one provided in *Being and Event.* What we are given is not the ubiquitous pertinence of "structure" *per se,* but rather an abstract schema to consider how, rather than being shrouded in ontological invisibility, the organisation of a particular ontological region is determined by an identifiable element or complex . . . a collection of

multiples is articulated through the (transcendental) agency *of another multiple.*[76]

Toscano's lucid and insightful remarks highlight the important implications of Badiou's insistence on the immanence of those multiplicities operating as transcendentally structuring principles to the worlds they shape and regulate. The multiple-entities of a world are not evenly weighted relative to one another. Within a world, certain of its internal constituents (i.e., those functioning as components of the given world's transcendental regime) are more privileged than others to the extent that these certain constituents (like a Lacanian *point de capiton* or Laclauian hegemonic articulator) are endowed with the power to organize and govern the plethora of inner-worldly appearances. Through emphasizing the dimension of immanence in Badiou's post-1988 account of the transcendental, Toscano stresses that structuring, at least in *Logics of Worlds,* evidently is not imposed from anywhere else other than the immanent interiority of the worlds thus structured.

Several other details of Toscano's observations merit being noted and submitted to criticism. Following Badiou, Toscano, in the passages quoted above, obviously treats "existence" and "appearance" as equivalent (in the "Dictionary of Concepts" at the very end of *Logics of Worlds,* Badiou's definitions of these two terms make manifest this equivalence).[77] As will be seen shortly, this is not without major problems, especially considering the issue of Badiou's fraught relations with Kantian transcendental idealism. Prior to addressing the difficulties arising from the notion of appearing for Badiou's transcendentalism, one should also pay attention to Toscano's justified concerns about the potential (quasi-)idealist implications of the deontologized operation of *compter-pour-un* in *Being and Event.* Toscano believes that these anxieties about Badiou's less-than-fully-materialist status circa 1988 subsequently are assuaged in two ways after 1988: first, the 2006 conceptualization of the transcendental is purportedly less, as it were, mysteriously faceless than the anonymous count-for-one (and yet, in *Being and Event,* Badiou, as seen, actually does maintain that each situation has its own specific structuring count); second, the immanence of each transcendental regime to its respective world supposedly (re-)secures Badiouian thought as a form of strict materialism (a standing Toscano indicates is jeopardized by the enigmas and obscurities surrounding *compter-pour-un*). The most obvious flaw initially to be remarked upon here is a scholarly one: Toscano's comments erroneously imply—this is quite surprising, given his general scholarly scrupulousness—that the idea of counting-for-one is abandoned after *Being and Event* (nonetheless, it would be correct to claim that this idea is much less explicitly prominent in the current version of Badiou's system). Not only is this concept-term deployed in 1998's *Short Treatise on Transitory Ontology* (in passages referenced earlier here), the "small book" serving as a transitional bridge between the two "big books" of 1988 and 2006—it resurfaces again in *Logics of Worlds* itself. In "Section 2" (entitled "Kant") of "Book III" ("Greater Logic, 2. The Object") of this recent book, Badiou says, "one could construct a definition of the object common to Kant and me: the object is that which is counted for one in appearance."[78] It would now be appropriate to examine the Badiouian concept-terms "appearance" and "object."

Toscano emphasizes the immanence of Badiou's transcendental, this being one of the four characteristics of it. However, one of this notion's other four characteristics, its alleged asubjective character, is not established in as clear and unproblematic a fashion as its immanent character (and this not simply because of the downplayed post-1988 persistence of the not-so-obviously anti-Kantian operation of counting). Badiou and Toscano use "existence" (i.e., the being-there of entities in a particular world ordered by a specific transcendental regime) and "appearance" interchangeably as synonyms. Hence, transcendentals here are said to structure (phenomenal) logics of inner-worldly appearing. A question resembling that posed above (in agreement with Acotto, Besana, and Desanti) apropos the operation of *compter-pour-un*—"Who or what is the operator doing the counting?"—ought to be raised with respect to Badiou's phenomenology: to whom or what do appearances appear?

Badiou maintains that there can be worlds without subjects (insofar as there are asubjective transcendentals)—with "subjects" referring, in this case, to perceiving or conceiving mental agents (what Badiou takes to be the referent of Kant's notion of transcendental subjectivity as the set of possibility conditions for experience).[79] A distinction absolutely central to *Logics of Worlds* is that between the being qua being of ontology (as extensive differences-in-kind) and the being-there of phenomenology (as intensive differences-in-degree);[80] or, as Badiou sometimes expresses it, this is a difference between "*onto*-logy" and "onto-*logy*,"[81] the latter signaling Badiou's equation of appearance with the relational structures of logics.[82] (As will be seen below in the exposition to follow of the Badiouian nonidealist doctrine of the transcendental constitution of objects, these logics interface with being itself, hence the "*logy*" remaining connected to the "onto.") For Badiou, insofar as there can be transcendental regimes without any subjective mediation, there can be worlds without subjects—and, consequently, there can be appearances without anything (i.e., a who or what) to which these appearances appear. But, Badiou's choice of the word "appearance" for localized asubjective organizations of multiple-being is still incredibly perplexing. Additionally, minus experience itself, can one convincingly claim to have constructed a phenomenology in the strict sense? And, more generally, does the very distinction between ontology and phenomenology stand up in the face of such doubts and questions?

Speaking of Badiou's anti-Kantian transcendental-without-a-transcendental-subject, Hallward warns readers that the word "appearing" is not employed in this context in a manner conforming to any of its typical quotidian or traditional philosophical meanings. Instead, appearances are simply the regionally constrained manifestations of being caught in the nets and webs of various relational matrices, within the "there" of a logically governed locality.[83] In an interview conducted soon after the publication of *Logics of Worlds,* Badiou indeed limits appearing to mere, bare being-there (not necessarily perceived or conceived by a perceiver/conceiver): "Appearance is being plus its place."[84] Hallward cites some key passages on this topic from the fourteenth and final chapter of *Short Treatise on Transitory Ontology* (a chapter entitled "Being and Appearing"). Therein, Badiou not only denies that appearances appear for anyone or anything (itself an extremely puzzling statement)— he insists that, in light of the nonexistence of Being as the totality of a One-All (ostensibly demonstrated via the post-Cantorian mathematical ontology of *Being and Event*), *l'être en tant qu'être* is always locally instantiated as *être-là*[85] (an insistence repeated in *Logics of Worlds*).[86] In this vein, he maintains that "appearing is an intrinsic determination of Being,"[87] and that "it belongs to Being to appear, and thus to be a singular existent."[88] Taking into consideration the lines of criticism suggested above, it seems that only one of two consequences, consequences distasteful to Badiou, can result at this juncture. The first consequence would be that the distinction between noumenal being and phenomenal being-there completely collapses—and this for two reasons: one, *être-là* is "an intrinsic determination" of *l'être en tant qu'être* as a detotalized non-All not-One; two, there are no phenomena present here strictly speaking due to the hypothesized absence of any locus of experience. The second consequence would be that, as is risked earlier in *Being and Event* thanks to propositions about *l'être en soi* being separate from ontology-as-discourse (i.e., a "logy") as what can be said in consistent terms regarding inconsistent being, the distinction between noumena and phenomena is reinstated in its classical Kantian guise—with being qua being, apart from its (potential) accessibility as always-already formed into the oneness of the unified consistency of the being-there of worldly objects, remaining unpresentable, unsayable, and unthinkable. Put differently, either there is no being-in-itself distinct from being-there or the being distinct from being-there is noumenal in the old Kantian sense of an inaccessibility exceeding set limits. Once again, Badiou's self-proclaimed distance from Kant is in question.

§4 The Ghost of Unity: Badiou's Unfinished Materialist Project

Perhaps the key place for achieving a definitive assessment of Badiou vis-à-vis Kant is the Badiouian theory of objectivity as carefully formulated at length in *Logics of Worlds*. Apart from blaming Kant for allegedly inventing the modern (and postmodern) motif of finitude, Badiou credits him with inventing the philosophical category of the object too.[89] As with his version of the transcendental, so too with his version of objectivity— Badiou's object, unlike Kant's, is without a corresponding subject (as an idealist power of constitution). All of the facets of the Badiouian critique of Kantian transcendental idealism appear together in condensed form in this new doctrine of the subjectless transcendental constitution of objects (a doctrine elaborated primarily in "Book III" ["Greater Logic, 2. The Object"] of *Logics of Worlds*).

Badiou proclaims that he conceives of the transcendentally constituted object as existing without a corresponding subject.[90] If there are transcendentals independent of transcendental subjects (the latter in the Kantian sense), then there are objects minus any subjectivity whatsoever. Badiou maintains that his object is not an idealist category for two reasons: one, its being *an sich* can be known in its pure multiplicity through a mathematical, set-theoretic ontology of *l'être en tant qu'être;* two, it is composed of constituents drawn from (material) being.[91] This second reason makes reference to what Badiou calls "real atoms" (to be defined and analyzed soon below). Unlike Kant's idealist doctrine of the experiential object-as-appearance as lacking any specifiable rapport with the presumed-but-inaccessible ontological density of *das Ding an sich,* phenomenal being-there is always tethered to noumenal being.[92] One of the fundamental postulates of materialism, according to Badiou, is the declaration that "every atom is real."[93] This axiomatic materialist thesis asserts that there can be no purely virtual, free-floating appearances unanchored in and completely disconnected from actual multiple-being(s), namely, no entirely deontologized phenomena;[94] worded differently, "Every object is the being-there of the being of an entity."[95] A Badiouian object is a transcendentally indexed multiple (i.e., a constellation of being localized as being-there by virtue of its being situated within the coordinates of a given world) consisting of real atoms[96] (again, these atoms will be discussed here shortly). To the extent that the object takes shape at the intersection of the ontological domain of *l'être en tant qu'être* and the (phenomeno-)logical domain of *être-là*, the object is "onto-logical" (i.e., both noumenal-ontological and phenomenal-logical).[97] It consists of a synthesis of pure multiple-being(s) and the relations prescribed by the transcendental regime of a world (with its other thus-constituted objects). Of course, the Kantian object is a combination of the transcendental and the empirical (with the latter presented through the receptivity of intuition), and both of these halves are situated within the nonontological realm of epistemological subjectivity. By contrast, the Badiouian object is a combination of the ontological and the (phenomeno-)logical.[98] Furthermore, Badiou suggests that this onto-logical synthesis is not an entirely smooth and harmonious affair. Insofar as the object involves being as irreducible to being-there, it "objects" (i.e., offers and poses resistance) to its "fixation" (*fixion*) as a "one" (i.e., an entity as counted unity) within "the transcendental fiction" (*la fiction transcendantale*) of a world of appearances.[99]

What about these strange "real atoms" which Badiou invokes in his discussions of the category of the object? Turning to the "Dictionary of Concepts" at the back of *Logics of Worlds* is again helpful. There are two separate entries relevant in this context: one for "atom (of appearance)" and the other for "real atom." The definition of "atom (of appearance)" makes reference to "the authority of the One in appearance" as "that which counts for one in the object"[100] (the resurfacing of the concept of *compter-pour-un* should be noted). The immediately subsequent entry for "real atom" states that "an atom is real when the authority of the One in appearance is dictated by that of the One in being: the atom of appearance is prescribed by an element (in the ontological sense) of the multiple that appears."[101] For someone familiar with the Badiou of *Being and Event*, this talk of "the One in being" ought to sound very odd. According to Badiou's post-Cantorian mathematized ontology, is not any instance of oneness a result of the nonontological operation of counting-for-one superimposing its structuring influence upon a being (*l'être en tant qu'être*) depicted by Badiou as, in and of itself, devoid of structure?[102] Is not being qua being said to be infinitely proliferating multitudes of multiplicities-without-one, neither (at the macroscopic level) the unity of an all-encompassing cosmic totality nor (at the microscopic level) the unities of indissoluble, indivisible atomic kernels?[103] In "Meditation Two" of *Being and Event*, Badiou even speaks of "the dissemination of all supposed atoms"[104] (i.e., the liquidation of any minimal, lower-level stopping-points to the infinite proliferation of multiplicities-without-one[s]).

This initially baffling shift concerning the One (plus the count-for-one) between *Being and Event* and *Logics of Worlds* becomes somewhat more comprehensible with Badiou's introduction of the notion of what is described (subsequently in the latter book) as "the retroaction of appearance on being."[105] He claims that the objectification of *l'être en tant qu'être* (i.e., the situating of bits of being as being-there within the frame of a world) "inscribes the transcendental in multiple-being itself."[106] This has to do with a question asking, "What are the ontological consequences of logical seizure?"[107] One aspect of what Badiou is concerned with at this point is the danger of lapsing into either a crude reductive monism (as in mechanistic or eliminative materialisms that treat appearances as residual, powerless epiphenomena of no ontological consequence) or an equally crude idealist dualism (in terms of an absolute dichotomous split between noumenal being and phenomenal being-there—something Kant's transcendental idealism arguably entails). Instead of an unbridgeable divide between being and appearing, he posits a dialectical interaction/oscillation between these two dimensions, a dialectic in which appearing, unlike the ineffective epiphenomena of vulgar materialisms, has real effects within ontological registers of (material) being. Badiou proposes that "the non-being of existence makes it such that it is otherwise than according to its being that being is. It is, precisely, the being of an object."[108] The object, as an onto-logical conjunction of *l'être en tant qu'être* and *être-là*, is the condensed crossroads at which this interaction between being and appearing takes place, an interaction in which appearing comes to leave its marks in being itself.

Having cast his object in the terms of this dialectical movement between the noumenal and the phenomenal, Badiou proudly proclaims to have found a solution sought after in vain by Kant, namely, "an ontico-transcendental synthesis."[109] In other words, whereas, with Kant, the object is reduced to being nothing more than a deontologized phenomenal appearance without specifiable links to the noumenal being of *das Ding an sich,* with Badiou, the object is a point of tension-ridden convergence for the ontological (i.e., being qua being irreducible to worlds) and the transcendental (i.e., being-there in a world).[110] It seems that, in Badiou's eyes, Kant is compelled to assume some sort of rapport between object-as-appearance and thing-in-itself, but ties his own hands through the critical insistence on the limits of possible experience and thereby traps himself in the enclosure of a sterile idealism unable to explain how phenomena entertain connections with noumena; these connections, purportedly delineated in the Badiouian system, are left languishing as aporias in the Kantian system.[111] Interestingly, Badiou's above-cited admissions that he and Kant agree apropos the notion of the object as "that which is counted for one in appearance" occur a couple of pages after these assertions.[112] And yet, despite an idealist shadow remaining cast over Badiouian thought thanks to the continued role of *compter-pour-un* (I will say more about this momentarily), in the 2006 interview "Matters of Appearance," Badiou insists that the commingling dialectical dynamic he allows for between being and appearing assures that the current version of his theoretical apparatus is thoroughly materialist.[113]

Later on in *Logics of Worlds,* Badiou adds two more embellishments to his doctrine of the onto-logical object worth highlighting. First, he argues that objects determine relations, and not, as per certain types of idealism, the other way around.[114] For Badiou, it is not the case that an ephemeral network of relational structures (i.e., concepts, logics, etc.) prefigures, in the form of a previously established template, the possible contours of appearances that can and do come to be "there" in the guise of objects (obviously, this sounds a lot like Kant's account of the part played by the faculty of the understanding with respect to the faculty of intuition in the [subjective] constitution of experience). Rather, the network takes shape around its nodes, not vice versa; to be more precise, already-constituted objects dictate the organizations and rules of relations, instead of being constituted by these same organizations and rules. Second, Badiou, further buttressing his de-Kantianization of the transcendental, maintains that the contingency of transcendentals is legible in objects themselves, given that all objects contain a surplus of being in excess relative to being-there.[115] There are components and traces of *l'être en tant qu'être* sheltering within the transcendentally constituted object embedded as a localized instance of *être-là*. Succinctly stated, the Badiouian object is never entirely situated in and structured by its respective world without reserve (or, in Lacanese, "not all" of the object is in its world).

In closing, I should explain why, up to this point at least, my analysis still contends that Badiou fails to separate himself convincingly and sufficiently from Kantian transcendental idealism. For instance, at one moment in *Logics of Worlds* during the elaboration of the doctrine of the object as summarized in the preceding pages, he goes so far as to permit viewing his vision of possible worlds as equivalent to Kant's conception of possible experience.[116] What might this mean juxtaposed side by side with Badiou's paradox-plagued struggle, in this same book, to forge a dephenomenalized phenomenology in which there are appearances (ostensibly) without a who or what to which they appear? Is this not to suggest, quite unlike Kant (and many others in the philosophical tradition, including Descartes, to whom Badiou is very sympathetic), that it somehow makes sense to speak of experiences without experiencers?

However, to phrase things once more in Lacanian parlance, perhaps the phenomenal beings-there of Badiouian transcendentally structured worlds are not without (*pas sans*) a who or what. Recall that, in defining "atoms" (as situated within both appearances and an ontological Real) as well as in describing the onto-logical object's function as a locus of intersection in which appearing (*être-là*) "retroacts" on being (*l'être en tant qu'être*), Badiou reinvokes the operation of *compter-pour-un* first deployed in *Being and Event*. Also recall that, in the latter text, it remains troublingly unexplained who or what performs this enigmatic, mysterious operation as well as from where it comes. Worse still, Badiou ties his own supposedly materialist hands with a virulent, ideology-driven antinaturalism that leads him, in *Logics of Worlds,* to dismiss perception and the brain as utterly irrelevant to his endeavors.[117] So readers continue to be presented with an unaccounted-for count. This count is a unity-producing synthesizing function or process as an ephemeral non-being arising from God-knows-where, albeit not from precisely those multiple-beings that might appear, from the viewpoint of a non-Badiouian perspective, to be the only real candidates for the status of elements able to serve as immanent material constituents of transcendental regimes in which worlds, objects, and appearances exist—namely, the bodies of certain sorts of living beings as analyzed at the levels of the life sciences, psychoanalysis, and phenomenology. Kant-the-idealist, with the specter of his disembodied transcendental unity of apperception, remains just around the corner.

Part 3

Quentin Meillassoux:
Between Faith and Knowledge

The World Before Worlds: The Ancestral and Badiou's Anti-Kantian Transcendentalism

§1 From Badiou to Meillassoux: The Antifinitude Front

Badiou describes *Logics of Worlds* as a phenomenological framework erected specifically on the basis of the ontological foundations laid in *Being and Event*. He refers to Hegel's oeuvre in clarifying the position and status of this recent substantial addition to his philosophical apparatus: "*Logics of Worlds* is to *Being and Event* what Hegel's *Phenomenology of Spirit* is to his *Science of Logic*."[1] As Badiou explains it, whereas *Being and Event* deals with "being" as "being qua being" (*l'être en tant qu'être*), *Logics of Worlds* addresses "existence" as "being-there" (*être-là*).[2] The phenomenal appearances of being-there (i.e., existence at the phenomenological level) are said to be constituted by virtue of the "transcendental regime" of a "world" (*monde*) configuring given multiplicities (i.e., being at the ontological level). Real beings appear in a world, a domain of organized, interrelated phenomena, thanks to the structuring intervention of a transcendental architecture responsible for distributing varying degrees of "visibility" across the multiplicities of which a particular situation consists.[3] The "logics of worlds" spoken of by the title of this 2006 book are none other than the ordering networks and webs allegedly making possible the localized appearings that compose the tableau of varying phenomenological regions of situated, differentially codetermining manifestations.[4]

As examined in the previous chapter, Badiou, in *Logics of Worlds*, struggles to develop a conception of the transcendental divorced from Kantian transcendental idealism, namely, a, so to speak, de-Kantified transcendental. Such a nonidealist transcendentalism—Badiou aspires toward a transcendentalism compatible with his vehemently avowed (but questionable) materialism (see the fourth and fifth chapters above)—involves the notion that there can be and are appearances in worlds without any corresponding Kantian-style transcendental subject being there as a necessary condition enabling these worldly manifestations to manifest themselves. Put differently, Badiou envisions the possibility of sub-jectless worlds of appearances that appear to/for no one whomsoever.[5]

As argued in the preceding chapter, Badiou himself doesn't pro-vide all of the arguments required to desubjectify transcendentalism (i.e., to forge a non-Kantian conception of the transcendental) in a per-suasively complete and exhaustive manner. In fact, he delegates some of this labor to his protégé Meillassoux. At a key juncture in his discussions of decoupling transcendentalism from transcendental idealism and its theory of the subject, Badiou explicitly appeals to lines of thought contained in Meillassoux's very interesting debut book *After Finitude,* avowedly relying upon the latter's materialist critique of the idealist dogma according to which objects are phenomenal appearances depen-dent, for their existence, on a conscious individual human animal or sentient mind to whom they appear.[6] Badiou and Meillassoux both iden-tify Kant's critical-transcendental framework as an exemplary instance of the idealist faith of what Meillassoux christens "correlationism," a belief system insisting upon the primacy of finite epistemological subjectivity as the ubiquitous mediating milieu for all actual and possible knowledge of objects (each and every object supposedly being constituted exclu-sively in and through this same milieu).[7] Post-Kantian variants of cor-relationism share in common an antirealist, deontologized epistemol-ogy denying that subjects can and do, as Lacan would put it, touch the Real (i.e., gain direct, unmediated access to the ontological domain of being in and of itself). For correlationists, the smudging fingerprints of knowing subjectivity and its constraining limitations always and necessar-ily cover over the entities taken up into the grasp of this subject. Badiou, especially as a self-proclaimed materialist deeply indebted to Marxist dia-lectical materialism, has a number of reasons for being uncompromis-ingly hostile toward this orientation, an orientation quite prominent in philosophy up through today (along these lines, one wonders whether Engels, Lenin, and Althusser, among others, are absolutely right to main-tain that professional academic philosophy exhibits an incorrigible ten-dency toward antimaterialist idealism).[8] But whether Badiou succeeds in entirely stepping out from under Kant's long shadow arguably depends on whether Meillassoux succeeds in thoroughly debunking Kantian and post-Kantian correlationism. So, appropriately, it is to Meillassoux's work that I now turn.

Before proceeding to a detailed engagement with Meillassoux's *After Finitude,* a few words of warning are in order. To be more precise, the reading of this text offered in what follows is partial and selective in two ways. One, it focuses almost exclusively on the critique of correla-tionism mounted by Meillassoux (i.e., the negative part of his endeavor), with his case made, in the aftermath of this critique, for an anti-idealist "speculative realism"[9] (i.e., the positive part of his endeavor) thereby being largely neglected (this will be taken up in the seventh chapter to follow). Two, it scrutinizes *After Finitude* with an eye to what light this book casts on Badiou's efforts to formulate a transcendentalism entirely separate and distinct from Kantian transcendental idealism. This discussion is crucial for a satisfactorily thorough assessment of Badiou's relationship to Kant. I will argue for two claims here: first, in the end, Meillassoux does not furnish Badiou with what the latter needs (and claims to get) from the former for the consolidation of his break with Kantian transcendental idealism; second, particular aspects and moments of *After Finitude* actually are at odds with the system deployed by Badiou in *Logics of Worlds*. Indeed, Meillassoux himself warns that there are major differences between his and Badiou's philosophies, despite his having been a student of Badiou.[10] Likewise, Graham Harman notes, "Meillassoux's vision of the world is not Badiou's, and certain aspects of the former even cut against the grain of the latter."[11] However, approving remarks uttered by Meillassoux with respect to Badiou's anti-Kantian transcendentalism indicate that, at least apropos this specific topic, he is not fully cognizant of the fundamental incompatibility between his realist anticorrelationist speculative materialism and Badiouian transcendentalism.[12]

§2 What Remains After Kant: The Arche-Fossil and the Worldless Earth

The first question to be asked and answered here is: what is "correlationism"? Like the Badiou of *Logics of Worlds,* Meillassoux considers one of the hallmarks of idealism (at least in and after Kant) to be the positing of the primacy of relations over the entities between which these relations hold—with this antimaterialist transcendentalism going so far as to suggest that such entities (as knowable) are produced by these deontologized relations, rather than vice versa. (Badiou is careful to stress the opposite, namely, to assert that, in actuality, really existent material objects create relations, and not the reverse.)[13] Meillassoux claims that, whereas pre-Kantian early modern philosophy generally centers on inquiries into the ultimate nature of substantial being, the Kantian "Copernican revolution," in banishing the ontological speculations of substance metaphysics (especially of the seventeenth-century continental rationalist sort) from the restricted realm of legitimate philosophical investigation, arranges everything around the "co-" relation (more specifically, the co-relation between the finite epistemological subject of limited experience and its co-occurring, deontologized objects-as-appearances).[14] This "co-" of correlationism, in all its multifarious forms, is treated by Kant and his idealist successors (including, according to Badiou and Meillassoux, the whole phenomenological tradition from Husserl onwards) as "always-already" established, as an unsurpassable background or horizon ostensibly framing and mediating the totality of what can be deemed to be reality, an enclosure allegedly without an accessible outside.[15]

Meillassoux later argues that, in the wake of Kantian transcendental idealism, idealist tendencies are carried much further. With the liquidation of *das Ding an sich* initiated by Kant's immediate German idealist successors, he contends that correlational structures are absolutized without reserve, supposedly without any noumenal or ontological residue remaining in place as external to subject-object relations.[16] (In tacit agreement with Badiou,[17] Meillassoux insinuates that the Kantian distinction between noumena and phenomena should not be eliminated entirely, that there are valuable philosophical virtues to the thing-in-itself unfortunately discarded in the post-Kantian criticisms of this notion.) In Meillassoux's view, European philosophy up through the present remains, for the most part, caught up in the consequences of Kantianism and its fallout. Correlationism, the still-reigning creed of "continental philosophy," automatically condemns in advance any and every realism as "naive."[18] Meillassoux maintains that, whereas philosophy proper departs from Parmenides's affirmed equivalence between thinking and being as axiomatic, "anti-philosophical" correlationism rejects this axiom, proposing instead that thinking and being are "entirely other" with respect to each other.[19]

For Badiou's purposes, the most important part of *After Finitude* is the "arche-fossil" argument, an argument serving as the crux of Meillassoux's critique of correlationism. This is the very argument referred to by Badiou when he enlists Meillassoux as purportedly arming him with a means for prying away the transcendental scaffoldings of worlds from any and every form of constitutive transcendental subjectivity. So, in the course of the ensuing examination of Meillassoux's arche-fossil, I will pay particular attention to whether or not these reflections actually do provide Badiou with support for his theory of transcendentals-without-subjects.

Meillassoux begins by observing that disciplines dealing with realities supposedly existing before or independently of the existence of human beings create serious problems for post-Kantian correlationist idealisms.[20] In particular, he has in mind such natural scientific disciplines as paleontology, geology, and astrophysics, sciences seemingly able to speak of the earth and the universe as they were and are apart from the mediating experience of microcosmic human minds.[21] He points out that most scientists, due to the obvious difficulties generated for correlationism by such natural sciences, are instinctively closer to the rationalist realism of Descartes than the critical idealism of Kant.[22] (In his 1908 *Materialism and Empirio-Criticism*, Lenin similarly appeals to the spontaneous "naive" realism of the scientists in his invectives against antimaterialist idealisms[23]—Ray Brassier, citing Damian Veal, notes this Leninist aspect of Meillassoux's text.)[24] The "ancestral utterances"[25] of the paleontologist, geologist, or astrophysicist (i.e., statements about the earth or the universe as they were prior to the coming-into-being of the human race) allegedly are dealt with by correlationism through the superficial tactic of tacking on the qualification "*for humans* (or even for *the human scientist*),"[26] a caveat involving the irrefutable, cheap-and-easy trick (reminiscent of the un-falsifiable idealist assertions of Bishop Berkeley) of a present-to-past retrojection of epistemological subjectivity (i.e., the presubjective past is known only and exclusively as it appears in, through, and for the subjective present as the present subject).[27]

The basic trajectory of Meillassoux's arche-fossil argument consists in a sort of reductio ad absurdum strategy intending to make the above-mentioned correlationist response to the challenge posed to correlationism by the ancestral utterances of the natural sciences appear so ridiculous that one is compelled both to reject this response and, correlatively, to affirm a realism compatible with scientific sensibilities. From his perspective, rejecting correlationist antirealism (as antimaterialist idealism) entails six consequences: (1) being is not equivalent or reducible to its manifestations for a subject to whom it is manifest; (2) being precedes its manifestations, existing before and apart from them; (3) said manifestations are intraworldly occurrences, rather than being the mere, sheer givenness of the world; (4) these occurrences of manifestations can be dated; (5) thinking can think the emergence of manifestations out of a nonmanifest being prior to and independent of its subsequent manifestations; and (6) "the fossil-matter is the givenness *in the present* of a being that is *anterior to givenness;* that is to say, that an arche-fossil manifests an entity's anteriority *vis-à-vis* manifestation."[28] At this point, it already is appropriate to inquire as to whether these consequences of adhering to the ontology of a realist materialism, as delineated thus by Meillassoux, are compatible and smoothly interface with Badiou's anti-idealism as articulated within the conceptual parameters of *Logics of Worlds*.

Problems arise for Badiou starting with the first of Meillassoux's six consequences listed immediately above. Whether, beginning with this first consequence, Meillassoux is using the words "*être*" and "*mani-*

festation" throughout *After Finitude* in the exact same manners as "being" and "appearing" are used in *Logics of Worlds* is itself a question demanding to be posed. The answer to this question is probably negative, insofar as, for Meillassoux, *l'être en soi* is addressed and apprehended by the natural sciences, whereas, for Badiou, such being is above and beyond the natural sciences, accessible, in its ostensible ontological purity, solely via the formal science of mathematics as post-Cantorian, trans-finite set theory. However, what must be remarked upon here is that Meillassoux speaks of "the past of events that do not manifest themselves for anyone." One might interpret this as in line with Badiou's problematic conception of inner-worldly appearances appearing to/for nobody and nothing (i.e., phenomena transpiring within the transcendental regime of a world without a who or what to register or witness these same phenomena). But, with the wording of his second consequence (a consequence entailed by the embracing of a reaffirmed realism), it becomes unambiguously clear that Meillassoux is not, as is Badiou, hypothesizing the existence of manifestations that manifest themselves to/for no one. In referring to "that which *is*" (i.e., being-in-itself) as "having preceded *in time* the *manifestation* of that which is," Meillassoux's ancestral world is not the same as Badiou's transcendentally structured world(s)-without-subjects. Why not? Badiou desires to preserve a distinction between *l'être en tant qu'être* (i.e., noumenal being *an sich* knowable through set theory) and *être-là* (i.e., appearing as phenomenal objects-in-worlds delineable through category theory) without positing a transcendental subject as coextensive with the latter field or stratum (i.e., the regions of appearances). But this leads Badiou to talk incomprehensibly about appearances without a who/what to which they appear—with this incomprehensible talk being what purportedly legitimates the idea of a transcendental decoupled from any transcendental subject. Meillassoux, by contrast, actually provides no support whatsoever for this decoupling, given his avoidance of characterizing the material beings-in-themselves referred to by the ancestral utterances of the natural sciences as paradoxical nonmanifest manifestations (i.e., appearances appearing to/for nobody and nothing). For the arche-fossil argument to buttress Badiou's hypothesis regarding worlds-without-subjects—this hypothesis expresses the essence of his attempt at conceiving a non-/anti-Kantian transcendental—the arche-fossil would have to belong to a world. But, although Meillassoux's arche-fossil belongs to an asubjective earth-on-its-own, it is not part of a world; in other (Badiouian) words, this ancestral being is part of a worldless earth, a world, as it were, before worlds. In the absence of this support he claims to find in Meillassoux's thought, Badiou is faced with the unappetizing prospects of the collapse of his distinction between being (as *l'être en tant qu'être* [being qua being]) and appearing (as *être-là* [being-there]) and a failure thoroughly to cleanse a retained transcendentalism of its associated idealism.

Additionally, Meillassoux's fifth consequence of anticorrelationist realism—it affirms the possibility of *"thinking the emergence of manifestation in being"*—arguably identifies a pressing, urgent task for philosophy that Badiou does not manage to execute himself. As I demonstrated in the prior chapter, Badiou's unaccounted-for count (i.e., *compter-pour-un*) continues to operate, albeit in a somewhat covert way, long after *Being and Event* (including in *Logics of Worlds*). And, insofar as the organizing function of this operation of counting literally establishes the distinction between being qua being and its situated being-there (the latter involving phenomenal worldly appearances), Badiou has no account whatsoever of "the emergence of manifestation in being"—and this because *compter-pour-un,* as an indispensable possibility condition for manifestation (i.e., appearing), remains shrouded in mystery, its origins obscured,[29] save for the antinaturalist stipulation that the material brain has nothing to do with it.[30] How is this not akin to transcendental idealism? A properly materialist transcendentalism must have a theory of how something like the structuring count-for-one immanently arises out of the materiality of *l'être en soi.*[31]

Carrying his arche-fossil argument further, Meillassoux insists that the ancestral utterances of the natural sciences present correlationists with an unavoidable decision to be made: did the earth (*la Terre,* not *un monde*) exist before human beings came into existence, or not?[32] With regard to Badiou, everything hinges on the meaning of the word "earth" here. One might suspect, not without justification, that Badiou reads "*la Terre*" as synonymous with "*un monde*" in his sense. But such a reading would be unjustified. Meillassoux's ancestral earth is a being anterior to manifestations, a (knowable) material Real *an sich* preceding any and every appearance (rather than a domain of anonymous asubjective-but-transcendentally-regulated appearances). Anyhow, briefly putting aside Badiou's *Logics of Worlds,* the reductio ad absurdum thrust of the arche-fossil argument becomes increasingly apparent at this point. As Meillassoux promptly proceeds to elaborate, "the ancestral statement . . . has a realist sense, and *only* a realist sense, or it has no sense at all."[33] That is to say, no compromise between the correlate and the arche-fossil is tenable.[34] Again like Lenin, Meillassoux denies the legitimacy and viability of any negotiated middle ground between antirealist idealism and realist materialism.[35] Coincidentally, in a book published the same year as *After Finitude* (2006's *Fear of Knowledge*), analytic epistemologist Paul Boghossian appeals to "facts about the world" preceding the existence of sentient and sapient human beings in his arguments against pragmatist and social constructivist antirealisms and relativisms.[36]

From Meillassoux's (Leninist) perspective, faced with the arche-fossil, all idealisms converge, with distinctions between such idealist philosophies as those of Berkeley and Kant becoming negligible. In combatively denying the realist implications of the natural sciences, these various idealisms dissolve themselves into a single correlationist creed/dogma presenting a united antirealist front.[37] In other words, if Berkeley's philosophy is a ridiculous solipsistic doctrine, then, at least as regards ancestral utterances, correlationism in its entirety is equally absurd. Moreover, Meillassoux heaps additional derision upon correlationist antirealism: in being forced into contesting the fact of the objective, independent existence of the earth prior to the existence of humanity (i.e., the coming-into-being of the subjective minds of human individuals), correlationists find themselves in the company of the silliest of Christian fundamentalist creationists (those who claim that scientifically uncovered evidence of the earth being significantly older than its age as indicated in the Bible is misleading, a test of faith engineered by God).[38]

§3 Qualities and Quantities: The Return to Galileo

Meillassoux goes on to point in the direction of a revived realism fully compatible with the natural sciences. Building on claims made at earlier points in *After Finitude* (claims to be critically analyzed shortly), he contends that mathematics in particular allows for a thinking of non-correlative (i.e., subjectless) states of being (such as ancestral facts). That is to say, mathematical discourse permits conceptually gaining access to a real(ity) without human beings, a realm of *l'être en soi* beyond, behind, or before the subjectively mediated experiential domain of manifestations—a realm Meillassoux calls a "great outdoors"[39] (*Grand Dehors*).[40] He refers to "the paradox of the arche-fossil," namely, the puzzle of, "how can a being manifest being's anteriority to manifestation?"[41] Meillassoux's brand of anticorrelationist realism, which he protests is not the same as naive realism, invokes the arche-fossil so as to exhibit the possibility of a strange subjective self-transcendence toward an asubjective Real.[42] This torsion-like dynamic of internal self-sundering, of "*getting out of ourselves*,"[43] is the central structure at the heart of Meillassoux's realist doctrine. Quite importantly, it intensifies the degree of difference between him and Badiou. The latter, in *Logics of Worlds,* wants to eliminate the mediating presence of traditional (transcendental) subjectivity altogether in trying to construct a theory of asubjective-but-transcendentally-regulated worlds (and, as observed, he appeals to Meillassoux's realism in the course of these endeavors). But, by contrast, Meillassoux leaves in place subjective mediation, arguing instead that, from within the confines of such subjectivity, one can, nonetheless, touch the Real (as Lacan would phrase it). Put differently, contact with subjectless being—this existence without subjects is not that of Badiou's appearances without a who or what to which they appear—occurs from within the circumscribed sphere of mediating subjectivity. Hence, as Meillassoux insists, he is not a naive realist—and this insofar as he does not talk about the reality of asubjective being as simply given in its brute, immediate stupidity via phenomenal experiences taken to be perfectly equivalent to what exists in and of itself. There are windows within (but, crucially, not apart from) the architecture of epistemological subjectivity, windows opening out onto the ontological objectivity of material existence *an sich*. For Meillassoux—his proximity to Badiou in this respect is obvious—these windows are mathematical.

At the beginning of the second chapter of *After Finitude,* Meillassoux briefly summarizes the ultimate upshot of the arche-fossil argument unfolded over the course of the preceding first chapter. Conveying the paradoxical flavor of the previously posited movement of subjective self-subtraction from the subjective ("thinking a world without thought"), he explains:

> To think ancestrality is to think a world without thought—a world without the givenness of the world. It is therefore incumbent upon us to break with the ontological requisite of the moderns, according to which *to be is to be a correlate.* Our task, by way of contrast, consists in trying to understand how thought is able to access the uncorrelated, which is to say, a world capable of subsisting without being given.[44]

In the exact same vein, the concluding sentence of the book declares, "If Hume's problem woke Kant from his dogmatic slumber, we can only hope that the problem of ancestrality succeeds in waking us from our correlationist slumber, by enjoining us to reconcile thought and absolute."[45] Meillassoux's vision of the absolute in relation to which his realist speculative materialism allegedly enjoys insight is beyond the scope of the present analysis (again, I will address this in the subsequent chapter). But, considering the concern with Badiou's philosophy driving this chapter's turn to *After Finitude,* paying additional attention to Meillassoux's discussions of mathematics and the sciences is crucial in this context.

The first chapter of *After Finitude* opens with a plea for resurrecting the early modern philosophical distinction between "primary and secondary qualities."[46] Starting with Kant, the correlationist paradigm rejects this distinction, given that primary properties refer to epistemologically accessible aspects of objects that are reflective of the ontological actuality of attributes and characteristics really possessed by these same objects in and of themselves (i.e., as they exist apart from the knowing mind of the experiencing subject). That is to say, primary properties (as invoked at the beginning of philosophical modernity by Galileo and Descartes) epitomize Meillassoux's conception of points at which, from within the coordinates of subjective cognition, direct contact is made with the Real of noumenal being *an sich*. Meillassoux sketches the basic contours of the pre-Kantian ideas of primary and secondary properties. Following a Galilean line, he defines secondary properties as affective and/or sensory-perceptual phenomena existing solely in the mode of a relationship (i.e., a "co-") between the sentient/sapient living being and entities as this being experiences them (in being affected by them). Meillassoux maintains that such phenomenal features are neither entirely "in me" nor wholly in the things themselves. Instead, these features arise at the intersection of subject and object as (epi)phenomena generated by a correlation between the subjective and the objective.[47]

If secondary properties are defined such that they depend on a subjective "me" to whom they manifest themselves through a (co-)relation between subject and object, the thing-in-itself (as distinct from the manifest object) must be thought of as utterly separate from this "me"— "the 'thing in itself' . . . is basically the 'thing without me.' "[48] Or, as Meillassoux articulates this later (in his third chapter), "the world in-itself would subsist despite the abolition of every relation-to-the-world"[49] (once more, this non-manifest "*monde*" is not the same as Badiou's appearing-yet-asubjective *mondes*). Meillassoux then defines primary properties, in fidelity to Galileo, as what can be formulated about objects in mathematical language (i.e., in quantitative rather than qualitative terms). Such quantifiable properties are alleged to belong to things-in-themselves (as things "without me").[50]

The fifth and final chapter of *After Finitude* underscores the Galilean-Copernican heritage of Meillassoux's realism, namely, its appeal to the mathematized natural sciences as guaranteeing epistemological access to a noncorrelational ontological *an sich*. Therein, Meillassoux refers to what he calls "*dia-chronicity*" as the world's in-itself existence before and/or after human existence[51] (i.e., an asubjective mode of being). He insists that Galileo's mathematization of nature is precisely what permits conceiving of a temporal cut or lag between natural materiality on its own and the reality of human experience[52] (contra the correlationist prohibition of this conception). The experimental sciences as a whole are said to open up the possibility of rationally thinking the genesis of manifestation (i.e., that which arises with sentient/sapient life) out of nonmanifest being, out of the world in and of itself before humanity's experience and its accompanying appearances arrive on the scene of existence.[53] Meillassoux, against Badiou's own assertions (made in the context of dismissively discussing the neural materialism of contemporary cognitive science),[54] believes in the power of thinking reflexively to think the emergence of itself out of that which is nonthinking (i.e., out of raw, insensate material nature). Although he does not explicitly mention such scientific disciplines as the neurosciences and cognitive science, Meillassoux appears to advance, during certain moments in *After Finitude* at least, lines of thought legitimating and substantiating the relevance of these disciplines to an understanding of the immanent material genesis of subjectivity itself—a relevance Badiou, with his antinaturalist hostility to the life sciences, staunchly refuses to recognize (but, as I will show in the subsequent last chapter and postface, Meillassoux ends up falling back into the company of this Badiou).

Meillassoux contends that the Galilean mathematization of nature and its philosophical deployment by Descartes entail hypothesizing the subjective capacity for *"the decentering of thought relative to the world within the process of knowledge."*[55] In other words, subjects (of science) can comprehend objects as "diachronic," namely, in their asubjective being as entities that can and do exist before or after the existence of these same comprehending subjects.[56] In a vaguely Badiouian fashion, Meillassoux, returning to early modernity, proposes that mathematizing natural being is tantamount to disentangling it from a correlationist-style dependency upon the mediating mind of an epistemological agent. Nature is supposedly desubjectified through being thought mathematically (i.e., at the level of primary as distinct from secondary properties).[57] Meillassoux bluntly asserts, "what is mathematizable cannot be reduced to a correlate of thought."[58] Already, one might ask in response to this assertion: is that which is not (thoroughly) mathematizable (automatically and entirely) reducible to a correlate of thought?

A little later in the final chapter of *After Finitude,* a fundamental Badiouian thesis is invoked in connection with the topic of mathematics. In several earlier contexts within his book, Meillassoux makes reference to Badiou's use of Cantor and trans-finite set theory to compel the ontological conclusion that there is no One or All of being, that being qua being is a "de-totalized" proliferating multitude of infinities without upper or lower limits.[59] In the final chapter of his book, Meillassoux, with recourse to Heideggerian ontological difference, differentiates between the ontic and ontological dimensions of mathematics as it relates to realism (as does Badiou before him in his 1990 treatise *Number and Numbers*).[60] The ontic dimension of mathematics involves the diachronicity of particular entities; more precisely, the applied mathematics of the natural sciences, describing the primary properties of these sciences' objects of investigation, deals with specific beings as thinkable in their supposed separateness from the mediating minds of scientific investigators. The ontological dimension of mathematics (i.e., that at stake in Badiou's mathematization of ontology as per *Being and Event*) does not address this or that given reality at the ontic level; rather, "the Cantorian non-All," as reflective of being itself, encompasses any and every possible reality, in addition to each actual reality.[61]

At least in relation to the Badiou of *Being and Event*, another discrepancy between Meillassoux and his teacher becomes apparent at this juncture. Badiou's 1988 magnum opus refrains from granting that applied mathematics furnishes access to the Real of *l'être en soi*,[62] whereas Meillassoux's retrieval of the early modern category of primary properties grants precisely this. Stranger still, one should remember that Badiou, understandably concerned that his equation of ontology with mathematics risks making him sound like some eccentrically anachronistic Pythagorian thinker believing literal numbers to be the very "stuff" of being (Meillassoux too is anxious to avoid this impression),[63] even utters several qualified denials that pure mathematics transparently discloses *l'être en tant qu'être*: counting-for-one invariably intervenes so as to render all multiplicities consistent;[64] inconsistent multiplicities as such hence are inherently inaccessible;[65] ontology itself is one situation or world among countless others[66] . . . and so on. Simply put, Meillassoux is more of a realist than Badiou to the extent that the former, unlike the latter, proposes that cognizing subjects engaged in mathematical thinking, applied as well as pure, can seize directly the structured stuff of the being of material nature as it is apart from all forms of subjectivity[67] (forms that arguably include Badiou's counting-for-one). Harman remarks that "I . . . miss a philosophy of nature in Badiou."[68] Both myself as well as Brassier have scrutinized and critiqued at length Badiou's hostility to the natural sciences and what he (mis)understands to be inherent to naturalism.[69] Implicitly at stake in the discrepancies between Badiou and Meillassoux as regards the distinction between pure and applied mathematics is the (materialist) question of whether or not one is going to differentiate strictly between being and matter.

But, picking back up the main thread of the critical examination underway here, what about the Badiou of *Logics of Worlds*? In this 2006 tome, he seeks to outline a phenomenology with a pronounced emphasis on the "logy" half—more precisely, a logic of appearing grounded on the quantitative rather than, as one understandably tends to expect from a phenomenology, the qualitative. In a short paper, he justifies this thus:

> To pit the "qualitative" against the reign of number has always been the rhetorical strategy of anti-scientific obscurantism. To be sure, there is a *truth* of pure qualities (in visual art, for example). But this is a generic creation, and not a logical given of worlds. The pure logic of appearance is marked in its form by the underlying mathematicity of the being of what appears.[70]

Although the mathematics resorted to in *Logics of Worlds* is different from that employed in *Being and Event* (category theory as opposed to set theory), the same basic impulse toward mathematical-style formalization as brought to bear on ontology in 1988 is imposed upon phenomenology in 2006. In a sense, Badiou desires to reduce the phenomena of phenomenology to its "-logy" half alone.[71] As is evident in the above quotation, he views any philosophical focus on qualia as necessarily obscurantist due to his fetishization of pure mathematical formalism as the only genuine form of scientificity.[72] Furthermore, within the same quotation, one can discern traces of the underpinnings for these remarks provided by the doctrine of the "onto-logical" object as delineated in *Logics of Worlds;* since the being of the appearing object is ostensibly bound up with the mathematical (specifically, the set theoretic), such appearances must reflect these structures.[73] Therefore, Badiou concludes, appearances themselves (i.e., the phenomena of phenomenology) can be reduced to their skeletal essences in the form of nonqualitative mathematical formalisms (akin to Lacanian "mathemes").

§4 "It Does Not Add Up": The Limitations of Mathematical Fixations

For both Badiou's dephenomenalized phenomenology as well as Meillassoux's realist redeployment of the distinction between primary and secondary properties, there are some major problems. As regards Badiou, no explicit justifications are offered on behalf of a very Kantian assumption hovering in the background of his thoroughly "logified" approach to phenomena, namely, the presumption that if one can descriptively formalize phenomena (i.e., appearances in worlds), then, in fact, these phenomena indeed are reducible to such formalizations (as conditions of possibility for said phenomena). Put differently, Badiou seemingly takes it for granted that his ability to recast qualitative phenomena in quantitative terms (in particular, the mathematical language of category/topos theory) somehow proves that these phenomena are shaped and determined by such formal structures (and any irreducible phenomenal remainders resistant to this approach are hastily dismissed by Badiou as qualitative epiphenomena obsessed over by "anti-scientific obscurantism"). But just because one can parse the objects of phenomenology in this fashion does not mean one should. Stronger arguments must be made openly in favor of the idea, evidently taken for granted by Badiou, that the possibility of a mathematical-style discourse about appearances demonstrates that formal/mathematical configurations actually dictate, as transcendental structures, the contours of phenomenal worlds.

As regards Meillassoux, his revival of the distinction between primary and secondary properties brings with it a series of unresolved issues from the early modern period of the history of philosophy. Most importantly, one should take note of the fact that, by contrast with Badiou's antinaturalist stance, Meillassoux's realism embraces the natural sciences, seeking to confirm the capacity of these disciplines to enable the subjective self-transcendence toward an asubjective Real of being *an sich* (for Badiou, only the deductive formal science of mathematical set theory, and not the experimental, inductive sciences of nature, has a chance to accomplish this). However, speculative, mathematized string theory aside—even this highly abstract, meta-level branch of contemporary theoretical physics is not without its relations to the empirical results observationally disclosed by experiment-driven physics—the primary properties addressed by the natural sciences reveal themselves in and through phenomenal experience. That is to say, both primary and secondary properties become manifest via the sensory-perceptual fields of observing individual subjects endowed with specific cognitive capacities. The difference, for the moderns, is that, amongst the diverse array of experientially disclosed aspects, features, and traits of objects, those amenable to quantitative (as opposed to qualitative) description are taken to be indicative of the nature of these objects as they exist in and of themselves apart from subjective mediation. Meillassoux's realism, as reliant upon the modern notion of primary properties, does not provide Badiou with what the latter needs and wants, that is, a notion of worldly transcendental structures wholly and completely without subjects, without any relations whatsoever to constitution and/or observation by subjectivity. Insofar as primary properties come to manifest themselves exclusively within the confines of cognition, they are not the utterly asubjective, nonappearing appearances posited by Badiou.

Casting a present-day glance backward, a glance informed by the advances of the natural sciences over the course of the past several centuries, one becomes aware of what could be designated as the historicity of the quantification of qualities. Put differently, the line of demarcation separating primary from secondary properties is itself historically variable, dependent upon technologically facilitated methods and practices of scientific investigation. Going back to Galileo's 1623 *The Assayer,* for instance, it is immediately obvious that those characteristics of observed objects then deemed by Galileo to be secondary properties, insofar as they seemed to him to be inherently qualitative in such ways as to be essentially resistant to quantification, could presently be spoken of as primary properties. Quantitative languages unforeseen by Galileo are now available for facets of phenomena which, to him (given the various limits imposed by his historical time), could not but appear to be intrinsically qualitative.

A strange obliviousness to the historicity of mathematics (at least the changing scope and boundaries of the applications of applied mathematics at the heart of the revolutionary Galilean mathematization of physical nature) is evinced by Meillassoux's appeal to the Galileo-influenced early modern distinction between primary and secondary properties. But, with respect to Badiou, Meillassoux is acutely aware that mathematics has a history. This discipline, despite presenting symbols and formulas appearing to trace the contours of eternal and unchanging conceptual constellations, has changed over time and, in all likelihood, will continue to change, at unpredictable rates and rhythms, through new hypotheses and discoveries. Indeed, Badiou too admits this.[74] However, Meillassoux meticulously elaborates the stakes and implications of this historicity for Badiouian (meta-)ontology in a rigorously lucid and consequent manner. With neither the time nor the space in these concluding moments of this chapter to summarize adequately the relationship between ontology and metaontology in Badiou's system, suffice it to say that he equates ontology with mathematics—the pure science of set theory is said to be the discourse of/on being qua being, even though most practicing mathematicians do not think of themselves as ontologists—and that this decision to equate ontology with mathematics is taken at the philosophical level of metaontology.[75] Meillassoux even maintains that, "For Badiou, the term 'meta-ontology' is another name of 'philosophy.'"[76] Speaking to the Badiouian equation of ontology with mathematics, he observes that one of the ramifications of this metaontological gesture is the historicization of ontology (and this to the extent that mathematics is a discourse with a history, including a historical-temporal trajectory in Badiou's precise sense of a "generic procedure" of "truth-production" [in this case, science, rather than art, love, or politics] in which events proper are the crucial motors propelling such production by faithful postevental subjects-of-truths).[77]

As spelled out by Meillassoux, the ultimate upshot of this, for Badiou, is that the very dividing line between the ontological and the evental (a line prominently drawn by the "and" in the title *Being and Event*—although Bosteels, appealing to Badiou's pre-1988 philosophical magnum opus, 1982's *Theory of the Subject,* contests reading this "and" thusly)[78] lacks any sort of ahistorical guarantee securing this distinction for all time. Badiou bets that no mathematics will ever be able to think events as he defines them in a consistent fashion. And yet, as with the future *tout court,* with the future of mathematics, a future that is an ineliminable, intrinsic part of its historicity, nothing forbids in advance the possibility of the arrival of a mathematics-to-come capable of accounting for the evental. What might happen if and when another Cantor or Gödel comes along? With current mathematics, if, as Badiou claims, this mathematics is what is sayable (at present) of *l'être en tant qu'être*—and, insofar as an event is not pronounceable within the structuring strictures of being-as-mathematical, the evental is said to be more-than-ontological (i.e., transontological)—this does not rule out intrascientific mathematical events-*à-venir,* unforeseeable insights and breakthroughs in the science that is mathematics. Such insights and breakthroughs could revolutionize mathematics so that, if mathematics is ontology, the ontological becomes able to absorb into its systematic matrices what formerly (in Badiou's eyes) could not be digested by the discourse of being qua being. Thus, Meillassoux legitimately characterizes Badiou's decision sharply to separate the ontological from the evental as a groundless gamble, a risky wager against the unknowns waiting in times ahead for the formal sciences[79] (Brassier too makes a similar point).[80]

Of course, in response to the preceding critical reflections, Meillassoux could construct several counterarguments in defense of the early modern version of the distinction between the qualitative and the quantitative upon which much of his speculative realist materialism rests. But, the problem of the historicity of the contrast between primary and secondary properties is not even raised by him in the first place, let alone addressed at any length—with this being quite odd in light of his above-discussed sensitivity to the issue of mathematical historicity vis-à-vis Badiou's ontology. Similarly, Meillassoux does not even bother noting and responding to old objections leveled against the Galilean-Cartesian primary-secondary distinction (such as those raised by Berkeley).[81]

This leaves a series of unanswered questions lingering: What about the historical role of technology, the history of instruments inextricably intertwined with the history of the inductive observational sciences, in the determination of the extent of the descriptive powers of quantification? Moreover, is quantitative description alone sufficient enough to guarantee access to *l'être en soi*, or are additional criteria needed in conjunction with mathematization—such as the experimental protocols of the scientific method tracing back to a source contemporaneous with Galileo, namely, Bacon's 1620 *New Organon* (not to mention Descartes's 1637 *Discourse on Method*)? Related to this, must a reliance, in practice, on empirical experimentation entail, in theory, a corresponding empiricism or pragmatism (to which neither Badiou nor Meillassoux are sympathetic)? Additionally, why should a reinvigorated realism not go even further than Meillassoux's version of it in claiming that primary properties indicate the ability of sensory-perceptual experience, at least in certain instances, to come into contact with a real(ity) standing apart from subjectivity (a possibility he casually alludes to, at the end of a question-and-answer session following one of his lectures, when he muses, "We cannot go outside our skin to know what is out there. Maybe the irony would be that this world is in itself exactly as it is for us—wow!")?[82] Asked another way, why (like Badiou and Meillassoux) should one categorically treat all nonquantified phenomena (i.e., secondary qualities) as nonontological, correlational epiphenomena, as ephemeral qualia and nothing more? Do or do not the results of scientific experiments situated in fields in which methods, objects, and data are not completely and exhaustively mathematized à la such branches of post-Galilean physics as quantum mechanics and string theory (at least not fully mathematized for the given historical time being, considering the historical variability of the line of demarcation maintaining a distinction between primary and secondary properties) deserve to be acknowledged as having a materialist or realist ontological status of some type? What is one to think if and when a secondary property becomes a primary property through the historical invention of a new means of quantification? Would this not suggest that at least some dimensions of non-/not-yet-quantified qualitative/secondary properties offer a nonmathematized access to the Real of being-in-itself?

The philosophies of both Badiou and Meillassoux, if they are to be taken seriously as genuine alternatives to correlationist idealism, must answer such queries. A materialism whose realism is restricted exclusively to the domain of mathematics (whether pure or applied) readily cedes in advance too much ground to such enemies as idealist phenomenologies, biopolitical scientisms, and any number of spiritualist obscurantisms.[83] If Badiou and Meillassoux, however intentionally or inadvertently, commit the fatal strategic error of surrendering all not-entirely-quantified territories to these antimaterialist, antirealist, and antirationalist foes, others must leave them behind and take up the fight for rational realist materialism on their own.

7

Hume's Revenge:
À Dieu, Meillassoux?

§1 The Trojan Horse of Divinology: Meillassoux's New Religion

Materialism certainly is enjoying a renaissance today. One of the defining features of contemporary theoretical work situated in the shadows of the traditions constituting continental philosophy undeniably is a concern with once again overcoming idealism, however varyingly construed. Perhaps the sole lowest common denominator among these multiple manifestations of materialism, apart from the shared use of the label "materialism," is an agreement with Engels and Lenin that the main fault line of struggle (or, as Mao would put it, the "principal contradiction")[1] within the field of philosophy and its history is the irreconcilable split between idealist and materialist orientations.[2] Borrowing additional concept terms from the lexicon of Mao's political thought, perhaps the time has come for the bouquet of the thousand blooming flowers of different recent currents of materialism to be sifted through with a nose to discerning which differences between these currents are non-antagonistic and which are actually antagonistic.[3]

Badiou, in his early Maoist period, rightly depicts materialism as "a philosophy of assault."[4] Of course, one of the main targets repeatedly attacked by this combative philosophical trajectory is nebulous spiritualism in its many varied forms and (dis)guises. Religiosity, insofar as part of its essence consists in positing that a being other than physical materiality lies at the base or pinnacle of reality, obviously is a primary natural enemy of anti-idealist materialism. But nowadays, something weird is happening: the materialist camp within domains intersecting with European and European-inspired theory has come to harbor individuals wishing to reassert, supposedly from inside the strict confines of materialism proper, the enduring validity and indispensability of theological frameworks. Marx and Engels must be rolling around in their graves. Despite the virulent theoretical and practical campaigns against religion carried out under the guidance of Marxist historical and dialectical materialisms, Marx's ostensible heirs in continental philosophy generally seem to be tolerantly treating the theologically inclined mingling among them as nonantagonistic rather than antagonistic others (sometimes even as sympathetic fellow travelers sincerely committed to the materialist cause). As asserted earlier (see the fourth and fifth chapters above), Badiou himself, in his later work starting in the mid-1980s, arguably has come to defend a specious sort of "materialism" suffused with metaphysical realism, hostility to the empirical sciences of nature, and barely concealed fragments of Christianity appropriated with little to no significant modification.

Badiou's student, Meillassoux, certainly would appear, at first glance, to be a thoroughly atheistic materialist. He even voices worries apropos his teacher's "troubling" religious leanings.[5] Meillassoux's *After Finitude* puts itself forward as an overcoming of the most potent and sophisticated strains of modern idealism (i.e., Kantian transcendental idealism and its offshoots, especially phenomenology beginning with Husserl). This overcoming ostensibly enables the affirmation of a realist speculative materialism in accord with, to paraphrase Althusser, the spontaneous philosophy of the experimental physical sciences.[6] Additionally, in his first book, Meillassoux also bemoans today's "exacerbated return of the religious."[7] More precisely, he maintains that the purported "end of metaphysics" ushered in at the close of the eighteenth century with Kant's critical philosophy has permitted, thanks to prohibiting self-assured atheism as a subspecies of a banished ontological absolutism, the flourishing of "fideism" defined as the faith of a hazy, diluted religiosity believing in an enigmatic Other transcendent in relation to that which can be grasped by secular reason. Fideism flourishes under the protection of a postabsolutist relativism, a tepid agnosticism obsessed with respecting purported epistemological (and ethical) limits associated with human subjective finitude.[8]

And yet, in an article entitled "Deuil à venir, dieu à venir" ("Mourning to Come, God to Come") published in the journal *Critique* at the same time as the release by Éditions du Seuil of *After Finitude,* Meillassoux strangely speculates that a God resembling the divinities of monotheistic religions, although he admits that such a deity has been and continues to be nonexistent, could come to exist at any moment in the future (as I will discuss in the postface, even more recent textual evidence reveals this quasi-religious twist to be central to Meillassoux's philosophy). Meillassoux's "thesis of divine inexistence" states that "God does not yet exist."[9] A component of the background to this is a particular distinction between "metaphysics" and "speculation":[10] metaphysics is defined as a philosophical position combining an epistemology of access to the asubjective absolute with an ontology in which some being thereby accessed is necessary in the sense of necessarily existent (early modern continental rationalism, with its substance metaphysics, exemplifies this position); non-metaphysical speculation—for Meillassoux, every metaphysics is speculative, but not all speculation is metaphysical—is defined as a philosophical position accepting the epistemological part of (pre-Kantian) rationalist metaphysics while rejecting its ontological part (i.e., for Meillassouxian speculation, with its denial of the principle of sufficient reason, absolute being in and of itself involves no necessity, resting on the baseless base of the ultimate fact of a brute contingency).[11] Traditional theologies are metaphysical,[12] whereas Meillassoux wants to advance what could be described as a speculative as nonmetaphysical theology (which he calls a "divinology").[13] Playing with the phrase "divine inexistence," he has it signify not only "the inexistence of the religious God" (i.e., the deity of metaphysical monotheistic theologies), but also, at the same time, the ostensibly irrefutable "possibility of a God still yet to come"[14] (Meillassoux's justifications for why this possibility is irrefutable will be addressed soon). What is more, this *Dieu à venir* ("God-to-come") might be willing and able to perform such miraculous gestures as resurrecting the dead and righting the wrongs piled up over the course of a brutal, unjust human history.[15] How could the author of *After Finitude,* with its polemics against the new fideism of "post-secular" thought sheltering under the cover of post-Kantian epistemological skepticism regarding claims about the objective nature of being *an sich*—ironically, the motif of the *à venir* is, as is common knowledge, dear to partisans of the post-secular turn in continental philosophy—simultaneously indulge himself in musings about a virtual, spectral *peut-être* interminably holding out the promise, however uncertain or unlikely, of the ex nihilo genesis of a divinity fulfilling the expectations of the most fanatical of the faithful?

Essential ingredients of this odd nonmetaphysical theology actually can be found within the pages of *After Finitude* itself. This flirting with religion is not dismissible as an extraneous article-length afterthought tacked onto an entirely separate and more substantial book-length manifesto for what otherwise would be a solidly materialist and atheist philosophical edifice. Without getting bogged down in exegetically unpacking this book in its entirety (solid summaries of it already have been written),[16] the focus in what follows partly will be on the role of Hume in Meillassoux's arguments for both his speculative materialism and its parallel peculiar divinology. The core maneuver lying at the very heart of Meillassoux's project is an ontologization of Hume's epistemology[17] (Meillassoux does with respect to Hume what Žižek's Hegel does with respect to the epistemology of Kant).[18] Through complicating the reading of Hume upon which Meillassoux relies, the former's empiricist philosophy can and should be turned against Meillassouxian speculative materialism, with its accompanying theology (however non-metaphysical), and wielded as a weapon on behalf of a real(ist) and atheist materialism worthy of the title. This non-Meillassouxian materialism is truly attuned to praxis, both in terms of the practices of the empirical sciences (I will allege below, in connection with the figure of Hume, that Meillassoux's appeals to science do not constitute a deep and defensible materialist philosophical engagement with properly scientific handlings of physical reality) as well as the ideological and institutional stakes of the practices of politics (speculative materialism/realism seems, at least thus far, unconcerned with these sorts of practical dimensions).[19] In fidelity to the materialist tradition inaugurated with Marx's 1845 "Theses on Feuerbach," this intervention insists upon keeping simultaneously in view the different praxes of the really existing natural sciences and those of the surrounding political circumstances of the times.

Apart from its denunciation of fideism, *After Finitude,* apparently irreligious but concealing kernels of religiosity which explode into plain view in "Deuil à venir, dieu à venir," employs a tactic repeatedly used by Lenin in *Materialism and Empirio-Criticism:* a reduction of all idealisms (including Kantian transcendental idealism) and fence-straddling agnostic stances between idealism and materialism, no matter how elaborate and intricate, to the absurdity of a Berkeley-style solipsism.[20] (Lenin's philosophically crude simplifications of Hume and Kant vis-à-vis Berkeley at least are arguably justified on the basis of "a concrete analysis of a concrete situation" in relation to his practical and theoretical conjunctures situated around the turn of the century.)[21] This absurd antimaterialist, antirealist dead end (i.e., Berkeleyian philosophy) is compared by Meillassoux to some of the more extreme and ridiculous characteristics of certain versions of Christianity.[22] Incidentally, to make an observation whose import quickly will become increasingly apparent, neither Lenin nor Meillassoux possesses open-and-shut, ironclad debunking refutations of a strictly logical-rational sort of Berkeley and his solipsistic ilk (as Hume would predict, radical idealism is dismissed by Lenin and Meillassoux as obviously preposterous, rather than rationally disproven for good through the proofs of philosophical logic). Along related lines, several authors have noted the striking similarities between Lenin's 1908 book and Meillassoux's debut text.[23] Žižek even claims that "*After Finitude* effectively can be read as '*Materialism and Empirio-Criticism* rewritten for the twenty-first century.'"[24]

As an aside appropriate at this juncture, Žižek's comments on Leninist theoretical (as distinct from practical-political) materialism frequently evince a marked ambivalence, the negative side of which is expressed in the objection that Lenin's naive materialist philosophy fails to include and account for the place and role of the mental observer of the nonmental objective facts and realities revealed by scientific siftings of cognitive representations of states of affairs in the world.[25] According to the Žižekian indictment, with which I agree, one cannot be an authentic materialist if one presupposes the being of a mind distinct from matter without delineating the material production of this very distinction itself. So, it might be the case that Žižek's comparison of Meillassoux with Lenin amounts to a backhanded compliment. In fact, as does the materialism of *Materialism and Empirio-Criticism* critiqued by Žižek, the speculative materialism of *After Finitude* simply assumes the existence of minds both sentient and sapient, consciousnesses through which mind-independent realities are registered (at least at the Galilean-Cartesian level of "primary qualities" as mathematizable-quantifiable features of objects and occurrences),[26] without offering anything by way of an explanation, essential to any really materialist materialism, of what Anglo-American analytic philosophers of mind, following David Chalmers, correctly identify as the thorny "hard problem":[27] an account of the relationship between mind and matter not just in terms of the former's epistemological access to the absolute being of the latter in itself, but in terms of whether or not mind can be explained as emergent from and/or immanent to matter (and, if so, what such an explanation requires epistemologically, ontologically, and scientifically). Brassier, the translator of *After Finitude* and a thinker profoundly sympathetic to Meillassoux, concedes that "Meillassoux's own brand of speculative materialism" remains haunted by the ghost of "the Cartesian dualism of thought and extension"[28] (however, Brassier's nihilism-prompted turn to the eliminative neuromaterialism of Paul and Patricia Churchland creates its own swarm of difficulties).[29] Similarly, it remains to be seen whether speculative materialism effectively can engage with nonreductive theories of subjects and, as per Žižek and related to such theories, the Hegelian-Marxian-Lacanian phenomena of "real abstractions."

As I will comment upon subsequently, Meillassoux, in an essay entitled "Potentiality and Virtuality," attempts to account for the vexing mind-body problem (and the equally challenging related mystery of the surfacing of sentient life) on the basis of his speculative position (Meillassoux's rehearsing of this attempted account elsewhere also will be addressed in the postface). But, as I will argue in response, this solution, as Martin Hägglund contends, is entirely out of step with the life sciences themselves.[30] One might be tempted to go so far as to charge that Meillassoux's explanation (or, rather, nonexplanation) of the "hard problem" amounts to an antiscientific sophistical sleight-of-hand that places

Meillassoux in undeniable proximity to the same Christian creationists he mocks in *After Finitude*. Considering this in conjunction with Žižekian denunciations of the "hidden idealism" of Leninist theoretical material-ism,[31] *After Finitude* suffers from the same major defect as *Materialism and Empirio-Criticism* without retaining one of the principal redeeming values of Lenin's text, namely, its merciless combative assault on any and every form of idealist religiosity or spiritualism. The door Lenin bravely tries so hard to slam shut, for practical as well as theoretical reasons, is thrown wide open by *After Finitude*. And, like Jehovah's Witnesses at the thresh-old of one's doorstep, who, with happily smiling aggression, will take a conversational mile if offered the inch of a cracked answered door, those faithful to theologies (especially advocates of so-called "theological materialism") likely will take heart from several characteristics of Meil-lassouxian speculation, including its rendering of their beliefs seemingly unfalsifiable and apparently not entirely irrational.

§2 Speculative Busts: Hume Troubles

Within the pages of *After Finitude,* the key kernel forming the germinal seed of Meillassoux's new "rational" speculative religion (i.e., his divinol-ogy) is his concept of *"hyper-Chaos."*[32] Through responding to Hume's empiricist version of the problem of induction via a non-Humean ontological move[33]—Meillassoux transforms the epistemological prob-lem of induction into the ontological solution of a radical contingency unbound by the principle of sufficient reason—reason's inability to prove that observed cause-and-effect patterns are expressive of under-lying "necessary connections" inhering within material reality apart from the mind of the observer shifts from being a privation of knowledge to becoming a direct positive insight into the real absence of any necessity in absolute objective being *an sich*.[34] Unlike the ontologies of the pre-Kantian rationalists, the ontology envisioned in *After Finitude* forbids pos-iting any necessities at all to what and how being is in and of itself (for Meillassoux, the one and only aspect of Kant's critical turn which should be affirmed as impossible to regress back behind is its rejection of the various versions of metaphysical necessity hypothesized by, in particular, early modern continental rationalism à la Descartes, Spinoza, and Leib-niz).[35] This leads him to assert the existence of a specific ultimate real as underlying material reality: a time of discontinuous points of instanta-neity which, at any point, could, in a gratuitous, lawless, and reasonless manner ungoverned by anything (save for the purely logical principle of non-contradiction),[36] scramble and reorder ex nihilo the cause-and-effect patterns of the physical universe in any way whatsoever and entirely without constraints imposed by past states of affairs both actual and possible/potential. This temporal absolute of ground-zero contingency, as a necessarily contingent, nonfactically factical groundless ground, is Meillassouxian hyper-Chaos.[37]

As regards Hume, whose treatment of the topic of causality with respect to the problem of induction is of paramount importance for Meillassoux's arguments leading to the ontological vision of a hyper-chaotic being, one should begin by considering the link conjoining his recasting of the idea of cause-and-effect relations with the distinction between the rational and the reasonable implicitly operative in the twelfth and final section (entitled "Of the Academical or Sceptical Philosophy") of Hume's 1748 *An Enquiry Concerning Human Understanding*. This distinction between the rational and the reasonable also is discernible already in Pascal's wager. Contra Descartes and those like him—this would apply to Spinoza and Leibniz too—Pascal maintains that the arguments, concepts, ideas, and proofs of philosophical reason (and of the human intellect more generally) cannot truly touch the infinitely transcendent superreality that is God. Obviously, this includes a ban on attempts to prove the existence of God. On the basis of faith rather than reason, one must take the leap of wagering on God's existence without prior rational guarantees vouching for the validity of one's decision to bet or gamble one way rather than another. However, through the presentation of the wager, Pascal tries to persuade one that wagering on the existence of God is reasonable given the permutations of possible consequences in terms of the outcomes of the different ways of wagering, although this wager on faith admittedly is not rational insofar as neither empirical/inductive nor logical/deductive reasoning is able decisively to determine the choice[38] (the matter of risk, associated with wagers, will resurface here in several significant incarnations).

Likewise, in the last section of *An Enquiry Concerning Human Understanding*, Hume, apropos the perennial philosophical difficulties posed by skepticism, pleads for a reasonable attenuated skepticism (such as he sees following from his analysis of causality) and against a rational hyperbolic/extreme skepticism (such as the denial of any possibility of knowing the world as it really is). In Hume's eyes, it is impossible rationally to refute, for instance, outright solipsism (a radical idealism) once and for all on the logical terrain of pure philosophical reason. In fact, if anything, the solipsist, as a figure of hyperbolic/extreme skepticism (i.e., "Pyrrhonism"), can put forward irrefutable arguments of a purely logical-rational sort in favor of his or her position against realist adversaries who cannot logically-rationally prove the superiority of their contrary stance. According to Hume, the sole refutation, a refutation of enormous force-fulness despite being deprived of the intellectual-philosophical strength of strict logic and reason, resides in practice, in the irresistible default inertia of practical doings beyond the artificial cocoon of the armchair of contrived speculative game-playing.[39] It is worth remarking here in passing that, in *After Finitude,* Meillassoux has counterarguments against nonabsolutist correlationisms but not against an "absolutization of the correlate,"[40] solipsism being subsumable under the heading of the abso-lute idealism of the latter. He merely tries to force nonabsolutist cor-relationists (such as Kantian transcendental idealists and various stripes of phenomenologists) to choose between realism (such as that of anti-correlational speculative materialism) and absolute idealism (which, as Meillassoux's reference to Berkeley reveals, is presumed without argu-ment to be prima facie untenable in its ridiculous absurdity). Similarly, in "Potentiality and Virtuality," a sheer preference, perhaps guided by the aesthetics of a certain philosophical taste, for a "strong" (i.e., onto-logical) response to Hume's problem of induction (as per *After Finitude*) over a "weak" (i.e., critical-epistemological) response seems to license Meillassoux's opting for the former resolution;[41] no logical-rational justi-fications are offered for choosing thusly in this context (presumably, one would have to return to the arguments in *After Finitude* against transcen-dental idealism to find the support for this favoring of the "strong" over the "weak" resolution).

For Hume, his empiricist reflections on epistemology, especially those concerning causality in light of the problem of induction, lead to a confrontation with the either/or choice between (1) a rational but unreasonable hyperbolic/extreme skepticism (including solipsism as absolutized subjective idealism, with its irrefutable refutations of "naive realism"); or (2) an irrational (as not decisively demonstrable by pure philosophical logic-reason alone) but reasonable realist faith (i.e., a "belief" in Hume's precise sense)[42] that, as Hume himself insists,[43] the mind is (naturally and instinctively) attuned to the world—albeit attuned in modes such that an attenuated skepticism equivalent to a nondogmatic openness to the perpetual possibility of needing to revise one's ideationally mediated knowledge of extra-ideational reality (in the form of conceptual structures of cause-and-effect patterns) ought to be embraced as eminently reasonable and realistic. From this vantage point, Meillassoux's alternate rational solution to Hume's problem (via his "speculative turn") would be, to both Hume and most (if not all) practicing scientists, utterly unreasonable. Why is this so? And what are the consequences for Meillassouxian materialism?

Hume devotes the tenth section of *An Enquiry Concerning Human Understanding* to the issue of (supposed) miracles. Therein, departing from the standard definition of a miracle as "a violation of the laws of nature,"[44] he offers arguments against the plausibility and existence of "miraculous" happenings. As regards the majority of ostensible instances, in which a miracle is attested to not by direct first-person experience but, instead, by the testimony of secondhand oral or written reports, Hume persuasively observes, on the basis of a number of reasons, that the weight of past first-person experience should outweigh secondhand testimony when the latter contradicts the former (in this case, when a purported miracle is reported that violates one's customary understanding of what can and cannot happen in the natural world with which one is empirically acquainted). As regards such instances, Hume's analysis raises the question of which is more likely: that a violation of what one takes to be the laws of nature, attested to by the weighty bulk of a mass of innumerable prior direct experiences, actually transpired as maintained by the source bearing witness, or that this source is distorting or lying about the evidence? For Hume, the second possibility is undoubtedly the more likely.[45] Meillassoux's deployment of the distinction between "chance" and "contingency" against such Humean considerations will be disputed shortly. For the moment, the upshot I am driving home in this context is that Meillassoux's idiosyncratic rationalism is utterly unreasonable.

But what about an instance in which one experiences oneself as witnessing firsthand the occurrence of a miracle as an event that violates the laws of nature? Drawing on his recasting of causality as decoupled from the assumption that observed and cognized cause-and-effect patterns immediately manifest the "necessary connections" of inviolable laws inherent to material being *an sich,* Hume is able to gesture at a stunningly simple but powerful argument against the very existence of miracles as violations of the (presumed) laws of nature: there is no such thing as a miracle because, if one experiences what is taken to be a violation of a law of nature, this means not that a real law of nature (as a necessary connection inhering within the natural world in and of itself apart from the minds of observers) actually has been violated, but that one was wrong about what one previously took to be an established law of nature.[46] Like a registered anomaly in relation to the practices of the sciences, a "miracle" ought to be construed as nothing more than a catalyst prompting the revision of features of the established picture of the world at the epistemological level of knowledge.

In "Potentiality and Virtuality," Meillassoux even employs the word "miracle" (albeit qualified in a fashion I will address here later) to characterize the instantaneous intervention of an omnipotent hyperchaotic temporal power of contingent change-without-reason.[47] And what Hume says about miracles would apply equally to Meillassoux's transubstantiation of the epistemological problem of induction into the ontological solution of absolute contingency. How so? Hyper-Chaos either appears as miraculous in the sense critically scrutinized by Hume, in which case it succumbs to Hume's objections, or it cannot appear at all. Why the latter? And, what does this mean?

A couple of additional questions warrant consideration at this juncture: How would one recognize an instance of the intervention of hyperchaotic temporal contingency? On the basis of what criteria would one distinguish between an anomalous observation as indicative of an epistemological error versus as indicative of being's ontological chaos/contingency? With these queries in mind, the example of the revolution in physics during the early part of the twentieth century—other examples of (to resort to Thomas Kuhn's [in]famous notion-phrase) "paradigm shifts" in the history of the sciences easily could be employed to make the same point just as effectively—calls for pause for thought. On the basis of Meillassoux's philosophy, what would prevent someone from claiming that this revolution was not a result of past physics having been wrong about the mind-independent material universe, but, instead, a consequence of a contingent change in the real patterns of the physical universe such that the universe itself underwent a hyperchaotic process of lawless transformation sometime early in the twentieth century in which it went from being Newtonian to becoming post-Newtonian? On this illustrative hypothetical account, which it is not evident Meillassouxian speculative materialism as a philosophical system is able to disqualify a priori in a way flowing consistently from its core tenets, the post-Galilean mathematically parsed world up through the beginnings of the twentieth century actually would have been Newtonian in and of itself, really becoming post-Newtonian *an sich* at some arbitrary instant of time at the start of the twentieth century. Incidentally, this example also highlights a serious problem with excessively and unreservedly privileging, with insufficient sensitivity to the history of science generally and the history of scientific and mathematical technologies/techniques of applied quantification specifically, Galilean-Cartesian primary properties, as quantifiable properties of perceived/observed objects, as directly revelatory of objects' objectivity as knowable things-in-themselves (see the sixth chapter above). If, as Meillassoux wants to maintain through his resuscitation of the distinction between primary and secondary properties, mathematics immediately manifests real material beings as they are in and of themselves,[48] then one is obliged to explain, which

Meillassoux does not, why Galileo and Newton, among others, were not already and automatically in firm possession centuries ago of the unvarnished truth about objective physical reality (reasonably assuming, from a post-Newtonian perspective, that they were not). The hyperchaotic early-twentieth-century becoming-post-Newtonian of the material universe in itself should strike one as an absurdity at least as absurd as the conceptual contortions Meillassoux claims correlationists and Christian creationists would resort to when faced with his argumentative mobilization of the "arche-fossil" in *After Finitude*.[49]

For reasonable scientific practitioners, Ockham's razor always would slice away from Meillassoux's hyper-Chaos and in a direction favoring the presumption that observed anomalies deviating from prior anticipations or expectations regarding cause-and-effect patterns appear as anomalous due to a deficit of past knowledge and not a surplus of anarchic being. In fact, just as miracles cannot appear as such in the domains of science—any miracle, traditionally defined as a violation of the laws of nature, merely signifies, as Hume indicates, that one was wrong before about what one previously took to be the laws of nature supposedly violated by the speciously miraculous—so too for hyper-Chaos. In terms of scientific practice, Meillassoux's speculative materialism, centered on the omnipotent sovereign capriciousness of an absolute time of ultimate contingency, either makes no difference whatsoever (i.e., self-respecting scientists ignore it for a number of very good theoretical and practical reasons) or licenses past scientific mistakes and present bad science being sophistically conjured away by cheap-and-easy appeals to hyper-Chaos. As regards the second prong of this discomforting fork, one should try imagining a particle physicist whose experimental results fail to be replicated by other particle physicists protesting that, in the intervening time between his experiments and their subsequent reenactment by others, an instantaneous contingent shift in the causal mechanisms of nature in itself intervened. Why should this physicist correct himself when he conveniently can blame his epistemological errors on the speculated ontological reality of hyper-Chaos? Insofar as Meillassoux's claims allow for (to the extent that they do not rule out) such highly dubious interpretive maneuvers, these maneuvers threaten speculative materialism with a reductio ad absurdum rebuttal. Moreover, they are an awkward embarrassment to a philosophy that proudly presents itself, especially by contrast with idealist correlationism (as both antimaterialist and antirealist) from Kant to Husserl and company, as rigorously in line with the actual, factual physical sciences.[50]

As regards the first prong of the above-wielded fork (i.e., speculative materialism makes no difference to the actual practice of science),

Meillassoux confesses that this is how he sees the relation between his theories and others' practices: "Our claim is that it is possible to sincerely maintain that objects could *actually and for no reason whatsoever* behave in the most erratic fashion, without having to modify our usual everyday relation to things."[51] One safely can suppose here that he would acknowledge scientists' presumptions apropos the stability of familiar patterns of causal sequences to be part of the outlook of quotidian nonscientific and nonphilosophical individuals too. This supposition later is confirmed when he, like Berkeley,[52] maintains that his ontology forces no changes whatsoever on the various sciences.[53] As I asserted previously (and as I will rearticulate below), all of this should signal again to any materialist influenced by the materialism of the Marxist tradition as developed specifically by Engels, Lenin, and Mao—recalling "Thesis XI" alone suffices—that Meillassoux relies on a strict separation between levels (i.e., the metaphysical-pure-logical-ontological versus the physical-applied-empirical-ontic) closer to the structures essential to idealism and anathema to authentic materialism. Related to this, Nathan Brown's defense of Meillassoux contra Hallward's criticisms of *After Finitude* ends up confirming that a Meillassouxian, when faced with the empirical evidence of scientific practice (not to mention everyday experience), quickly has to retreat to the irrefutable safety of a seemingly pure theoretical dimension unaffected by what are dismissed hastily as matters beneath the dignity of philosophy proper.[54] I side squarely with Hallward.

It must be observed that Hume's problem of induction arises in connection with the limited nature of finite human experience. Hence, Meillassoux's antiphenomenological rationalism of logic alone is not really based on pure reason only. It departs from an experience-based problem as its push-off point. Therefore, experience, the preponderance of which speaks in one loud voice against the truth of hyper-Chaos, is not without its relevance in evaluating Meillassoux's ideas. To be more precise, Meillassoux cherry-picks from the empirical realms of the experiential (seizing upon Hume's problem of induction) and the experimental (extracting the arche-fossil from certain physical sciences and also dabbling in speculations superimposed upon biology). Debates presently emerging around *After Finitude* seem to indicate that Meillassouxians, if they can be said to exist, believe it legitimate, after the fact of this cherry-picking, to seal off speculative materialism as an incontestable rationalism of the metaphysical-pure-logical-ontological (as pure *peut-être* as possibility) when confronted with reasonable reservations grounded in the physical-applied-empirical-ontic (as impure *être* as actuality or probability). But this belief is mistaken and this move intellectually dishonest: Meillassoux's arbitrary borrowings from and engagements with things empirical block such a path of all-too-convenient retreat. Advocates of a Meillassouxian rationalism want to pluck select bits from the experimental physical sciences without these same sciences' reasonable empirical and experiential criteria and considerations clinging to the bits thereby grabbed.

A line of pro-Meillassoux defense withdrawing to the purity of the *peut-être,* a line according to which his reflections are absolutely separate and distinct from the impurity of *être* (which here would include the domains of the empirical, experimental sciences of nature), might be a tempting counterargumentative option for Meillassouxians at this juncture. However, not only does this require deviating from Meillassouxian philosophy by jettisoning Meillassoux's own ventures into connecting his ideas to the sciences (about which I will say more shortly)—it saves Meillassoux's doctrine of hyper-Chaos from the preceding criticisms only by reducing his position to the vacuous tautological assertion that "what is logically possible is possible." Then, the empty void of this tautology is free to be capriciously filled in with arbitrary content through an activity of speculative projecting that is far from rigorous philosophizing proper and closer to the whimsical brainstorming of fanciful sci-fi scenarios, however improbable (one can always protest, "But it is still [logically] possible"). This defense of Meillassoux would end up making even clearer the fact that "speculative realism," as an orientation, risks easily degenerating into nothing more than a farcical, anachronistic recapitulation of the worst aspects of pre-Kantian metaphysics (with a mere shift of emphasis from necessity to contingency tacked on for a more contemporary feel). Additionally, as Aaron Hodges astutely observes, Meillassoux himself, in his utilization of the device of the arche-fossil, tacitly relies on the methods and results of the natural sciences; specifically, in tension with the implications of hyper-Chaos, he takes for granted the uninterrupted constancy of certain patterns and dynamics in nature (in particular, the reliability of carbon dating thanks to calculable half-lives and steady rates of radioactive decay as well as the unvarying speed of light traveling from distant celestial bodies).[55] In what at least counts as a sort of performative contradiction, Meillassoux, although he wishes to cast doubts on the continuity and stability of supposed natural laws, embarks on efforts to cast these doubts through recourse to an argumentative tool (i.e., the arche-fossil) which has built into itself the taken-for-granted indubitability of some of these very laws. He clings with one hand to what he struggles to cast away with the other.

Of course, Meillassoux would attempt to respond to the scientists for whom Ockham's razor invariably cuts against hyper-Chaos when they face anomalous data (i.e., data deviating from previous cause-and-effect patterns concerning similar objects and occurrences) with his arguments against the presuppositions underpinning the scientists' assumption regarding the constancy of causal configurations in material reality. These arguments hinge on a distinction between "chance" (*hasard*) and "contingency" (*contingence*) and involve recourse to Cantor's revolutionary alteration of the mathematical conception of the infinite as per his trans-finite set theory (as well as recourse to Badiou's metaontological reading of post-Cantorian pure mathematics). To be brief, Meillassoux's rationalist ontologization of Hume's empiricist epistemology of causality saddles him with the necessity of surmounting the problem of "frequentialism":[56] if material being *an sich* is contingent as containing within itself no law-like necessary connections, then why is reality and the experience of it not a violently anarchic and frenetic flux? Asked differently, how come there are apparently stable causal orders and structures if absolute being actually is hyperchaotic? Neither Brassier nor Harman, another "speculative realist" sympathetic to Meillassoux, are satisfied with Meillassoux's answers (or lack thereof) to this question, particularly as worded in the second fashion.[57] Meillassoux flatly denies that "the constancy of the phenomenal world" amounts to a "refutation of the contingency of physical laws."[58] But what buttresses this denial and its complementary affirmation that stable constancy, just because it is an epistemological precondition for the formation of empirical scientific knowledge, is not necessarily also an ontological condition of reality thereby known?[59]

§3 Infinitely Problematic: Cantor, Badiou, and Frequentialism

Although Meillassoux states that he is far from being simply a disciple of his teacher Badiou,[60] the Badiouian appropriation of Cantorian mathematics, as per *Being and Event,* is integral to Meillassoux's deployment of the chance-contingency distinction in response to the difficulty of frequentialism created by the introduction of hyper-Chaos as the consequence of ontologizing the Humean problem of induction. Without the time to do justice to Badiou in the constrained context of a critical evaluation of Meillassoux, suffice it to say a few things about the Badiouian philosophical framework circa 1988 so crucial to this feature of the project delineated in *After Finitude.* In "Part III" of *Being and Event* ("Being: Nature and Infinity. Heidegger/Galileo"), Badiou slides from pure to applied mathematics, displaying disregard for this distinction. He asserts that Cantor's infinitization of infinity itself—in the nineteenth century, the infinite goes from having been conceived of as the single grand totality of a unique One-All to being shattered into an infinite variety of incommensurable, nontotalizable infinities proliferating without end—not only kills (the theosophical idea of) God and renders invalid the entire enterprise of rational theology, but also, at the level of the applied mathematics indispensable to post-Galilean modern science, dissolves and destroys Nature-with-a-capital-N as the massive-but-unified totality of an all-encompassing cosmos, a singularly infinite material universe as a gargantuan sole whole.[61]

Meillassoux adopts this direct transposition of trans-finite set theory onto the mathematized physical reality of the Galileo-inaugurated natural sciences of modernity. Badiou and Meillassoux both reason that if the advent of modern science in the early seventeenth century marks a transition "from the closed world to the infinite universe" (as per the title phrase of the book by French historian and philosopher of science Koyré upon whom Badiou and Meillassoux each lean), then Cantor's subsequent radical reworking of the rational-mathematical concept of infinity also must apply retroactively to the infinite universe of the experimental sciences opened up by the Galilean gesture of mathematizing the empirical study of nature. Foreshadowing an objection to be formulated at greater length shortly, this teacher-student duo violates its own level-distinction between the ontological and the ontic, leaping without sufficient explanatory justification from pure mathematics as purportedly indicative of being qua being (*l'être en tant qu'être*) to applied mathematics as reflective of material entities. When Meillassoux, in *After Finitude*, explicitly appeals to Badiou in conjunction with his utilization of the difference between chance and contingency, he clearly assumes that Badiou's Cantor-inspired metaontological detotalization of ontological being qua being applies equally and immediately to the ontic spheres of the physical universe(s) too.[62]

So, how does Meillassoux distinguish between chance and contingency? And what does this distinction have to do with frequentialism? Meillassoux maintains that the probabilistic "aleatory reasoning"[63] employed by those who would recoil with horror at the idea of hyper-Chaos, being convinced that this idea leads inevitably and without delay to a hyperactively fluctuating anarchic abyss or vortex of a maximally volatile material real lacking any causal constancy whatsoever (i.e., a frequently changing unstable world manifestly at odds with the stable world encountered by experiment and experience), erroneously assumes the universe of possibilities for permutations of causal structures to be a totalized One-All. Such disbelievers in hyper-Chaos are said to cling to calculations of the likely frequency of change based on a mathematically outdated and disproven pre-Cantorian conception of infinity. They think in terms of chance, hypothesizing (whether implicitly or explicitly) the existence of an immensely large but nonetheless totalizable number of possible outcomes. Contingency, by contrast, is thought by Meillassoux in conformity with the post-Cantorian conception of infinity (or, more precisely, infinities) of trans-finite set theory. This unbounded infinite of multiplicities-without-limits rationally bars that upon which the probabilistic aleatory reasoning of chance allegedly depends, namely, the presumed existence of a totality of possible outcomes.[64]

But even if one concedes the validity of Meillassoux's (and Badiou's) questionable abrupt move from pure to applied mathematics and the ontic domains covered by the latter, an obvious question begs to be posed here: Why should the detotalization of the totality posited in connection with chance, a detotalization supposedly requiring the replacement of chance with contingency, make the flux of inconstancy less rather than more likely? How does this solve the problem of frequentialism raised against the speculative materialist thesis of hyper-Chaos? As Meillassoux notes, probabilistic reckonings tied to the notion of chance often rest upon metaphorical picture-thinking, imagining a die with however many sides repeatedly being cast. With this image of the die in hand, those who resist accepting the doctrine of being's absolute contingency ask: if the same face keeps turning up roll after roll (i.e., given the apparent constancy and stability of cause-and-effect patterns in the physical universe), is it not reasonable to conclude that the die is loaded (i.e., that something other and more than a random string of lawless and discrete isolated temporal instants, whether sufficient reason[s] and/or really existing laws of nature as necessary connections, is continually operative in material reality)? Meillassoux appears to believe that subverting the picture-thinking metaphor of the die is sufficient to solve the problem posed to the concept of hyper-Chaos by frequentialism. However, simply because one cannot probabilistically calculate chances in this mode does not mean that the glaringly and undeniably visible stable constancy of the world has been explained in anything close to a satisfactory manner. If contingency involves an incalculably and immeasurably vaster number of infinite possibilities than chance, is it not even more probable (although by exactly how much more cannot be determined with numerical exactitude due to the mathematics involved) that an ontology of hyperchaotic contingency would entail frequently fluctuating worlds as a Heraclitean flux of ceaseless, restless becoming? Just because trans-finite contingency is less readily calculable than pre-Cantorian chance does not mean that it is less chancy. If anything, it seems more reasonable to wager that it would be even chancier (as a chanciness beyond chance [*hasard*] in Meillassoux's sense), hence further inflating the entire problem of frequentialism facing speculative materialist hyper-Chaos. Even if there are an infinite number of possible universes in which what human knowledge here, in this actual universe, takes to be stable laws of physics are the same, why would it not be the case that the cardinality of this infinity, as the measured size of this set of possible universes, is dwarfed in size by the cardinality of the infinity measuring the set of possible universes in which one or more of these laws of physics differ in any mind-boggling number of possible ways (and each at perhaps an even more mind-boggling number of discrete temporal instants)? If it is the case, then it is certainly plausible that, relative to the cardinality of the latter infinity, the former infinity would be incredibly small such that the likelihood of stable constancy in an ontology of hyperchaotic being is itself incredibly small. In this case, the problem of frequentialism is just as, if not more, problematic after the replacement of pre-Cantorian chance with post-Cantorian contingency. Ironically, Cantor's discovery of a limitless multitude of incommensurable infinite cardinalities, a discovery to which Meillassoux appeals, makes Meillassoux's frequentialism problem more, not less, glaringly visible.

Meillassoux, in "Potentiality and Virtuality," contends that "*Hume's problem becomes the problem of the difference between chance and contingency.*"[65] Of course, Hume would not see it this way. For him, belief in the future enduring constancy of any cause-and-effect pattern is proportional to the past frequency with which this pattern regularly has unfolded for the mental observer—the greater the number of anomaly-free past instances of an observed causal sequence (i.e., "constant conjunction," in Hume's parlance),[66] the greater the strength of accustomed or habituated belief in the accuracy and validity of the idea of this causal association between spatially and temporally proximate (i.e., "contiguous") entities and events.[67] Therefore, in the Humean account of causality, there is no recourse, not even tacitly, to probabilistic aleatory reasoning as the vain effort imaginarily to catalog all of the possible variations on causal patterns in order to estimate the likelihood of a given idea of a particular cause-and-effect relation continuing to hold true. In his discussions of the belief in causality, Hume proportionally indexes the strength of belief (itself an unanalyzable elementary phenomenon) to the number of past experiences, free of the admixture of anomalous instances, of a given sequence of events involving given types of observed entities—and that is it.

This aside and returning to Meillassoux's philosophy, some additional remarks about the role and status of mathematics in the systems of both Badiou and Meillassoux merit mention. To be more precise, four points should be made here (I will not delve into the first three at any length since they have been elaborated upon extensively elsewhere). First, as both Brassier and I propose in other contexts, Badiou and Meillassoux excessively fetishize mathematics, thereby regrettably skewing and narrowing the picture of the empirical sciences.[68] Second, as Hallward succinctly and forcefully argues in his compact and effective review of *After Finitude,* speculative materialism sometimes conflates, without accompanying explicit justifications, the metaphysical-pure-logical-ontological and the physical-applied-empirical-ontic—at other times, speculative materialism insists upon the utter separateness of these dimensions—failing to explain and defend this conflation (one significant version of which is the juxtaposition of post-Cantorian trans-finite set theory, as pure mathematics, and the physical space-time mapped by the application of mathematical frameworks other than set theory).[69] As I claimed earlier, this criticism is readily applicable to Badiou too.

Third—the third and fourth points are closely connected—Meillassoux, in a brilliant essay critically analyzing the engagement with mathematics in *Being and Event,* describes how Badiou's distinction between being and event rests on a gamble betting that no unforeseeable future events in the formal science of mathematics will happen that overturn (if indeed any branch or sub-branch of mathematics can be said to be "overturned") the set theoretic basis for this distinction (something Badiou himself cannot entirely discount given his theory of events in philosophy's four "conditions" of art, love, politics, and science).[70] Although he does not acknowledge this, the same historical instability holds for the early modern Galilean-Cartesian distinction between primary (i.e., quantitative) and secondary (i.e., qualitative) properties, a distinction Meillassoux attempts to reactivate starting in the opening pages of *After Finitude* (see the sixth chapter above). Fourth, finally, and in relation to this previous point, the wager Meillassoux accurately identifies as lying at the very heart of Badiou's system as per *Being and Event* is symptomatic of what is one of the great virtues of Badiouian philosophical thought: its combination of a Pascalian-existentialist sensibility with rigorous systematicity. Summarizing too much too quickly, in delegating ontology to mathematics, Badiou makes a series of preliminary choices leading to his novel metaontology: a choice between all the different branches of pure mathematics; a choice between the different branches of pure mathematics that vie for the title of being the "foundational" branch of all other branches of mathematics (here, Badiou chooses set theory, despite its claim to foundational status, and even what such a claim by any branch or sub-branch of mathematics might mean, having become increasingly questionable during the past several decades); a choice between the different axiomatizations of set theory (here, Badiou chooses Zermelo-Fraenkel plus the axiom of choice [ZFC], even though there are other axiomatized versions of set theory, including versions allowing for the recognized existence of the Badiou-banished "One" of a set of all sets). And in the background motivating this chain of concatenated choices lurks Badiou's fundamental "decision" that, as he puts it in the first meditation of *Being and Event*, "the one *is not*."[71]

For Badiou, there are philosophically unavoidable ontological questions which can and must be answered with a pure decision (even Kant, whose transcendental idealist approach can be understood as limiting philosophy to epistemology and correlatively prohibiting the pursuit of an ontology, arguably cannot avoid tacitly reintroducing an implicit ontology into his critical system, an ontology consisting of answers to questions always-already posed). In other words, these questions can and must be answered without even the minimal assistance of (absent/lacking) guiding gut-level intuitions apparently favoring the decision to arrive at one answer rather than others. Badiou's choice of ZFC, itself one sub-branch of one branch among a large number of branches and sub-branches of mathematics, is comprehensible and defensible exclusively in light of this prime *Ur*-decision on the One's nonexistence in response to the inescapable Parmenidean-Platonic query "Being, One or Many?" As mentioned previously, Badiou, in an interview with Bosteels in which he reminisces about his intellectual youth, confesses that "I remember very clearly having raised the question, having formed the project of one day constructing something like a Sartrean thought of mathematics, or of science in general, which Sartre had left aside for the most part."[72] *Being and Event* fulfills this planned project of the young Badiou insofar as the mathematical ontology and parallel meta-ontology forming the basis of this magnum opus serving as the nucleus of his mature system initially stems from the first cause of the groundless ground of the freedom of a pure decision in response to one of several unavoidable questions of/about being, questions into which everyone is always-already thrown, whether they know and acknowledge it or not. The implications for Meillassoux's thought of Badiou's innovative combination of the nonfoundational foundation of the existentialist wager (as per Pascal and Sartre, among others) with the form of mathematical rationality à la philosophically systematic structures will be explored in what ensues very soon.

Returning one last time to the topic of Meillassoux's problematic relationship to the empirical sciences (before turning attention back to his startling proximity to strains of idealist religiosity despite his self-presentation as a heretical materialist), "Potentiality and Virtuality" contains a brief effort to apply the speculative materialist concept of hyper-Chaos to the field of biology, specifically, the enigma of the emergence of sentient life out of nonsentient physical matter (Meillassoux's version of "emergentism" will be front and center in the postface). As Meillassoux makes clear here, hyper-Chaos permits reviving the originally religious notion of creation ex nihilo (although, like Badiou with respect to the loaded idea-word "grace,"[73] he protests that this is a nonreligious version of the ex nihilo, a secular "miracle"—this protest will be addressed momentarily).[74] It permits this insofar as, at each discretely isolated and contingent temporal instant ungoverned by sufficient reason or causal necessity, anything could emerge for no reason whatsoever and out of no prior precedent as a preceding potential (i.e., out of nothing). With these theses in place, Meillassoux then has the luxury of being able effortlessly to dispatch with a riddle that has bedeviled the very best minds in the life sciences and those philosophers seriously contending with these sciences: the "hard problem" of how sentient life, as consciousness, arises out of nonconscious matter is not a problem at all—this genesis is simply an instance of the ex nihilo made possible by the time of hyperchaotic absolute contingency.[75] Abracadabra!

Hägglund quite appropriately submits Meillassoux's treatment of the problem of conscious life to pointed criticism as scientifically suspect.[76] I fully, albeit selectively, endorse Hägglund's employment specifically of his Derridean dynamic of "the becoming space of time" (as distinct from its flip side, "the becoming time of space") to complicate (in the name of, among other things, the life sciences) the speculative materialist mystifying obfuscation of this mystery of the emergence of sentience through appeals to a sovereign temporal power utterly independent of spatial materiality. In addition to Hägglund's objections, it ought to be underscored that not only does this application of hyper-Chaos to biology contradict Meillassoux's (and Brown's) insistence elsewhere (as remarked on above) that absolute contingency is postulated on a rational level separate and unrelated to the domains of the reasonable empirical sciences of nature—it illustrates a contention I advanced earlier here, namely, that the hyper-Chaos of Meillassouxian speculative materialism is stuck stranded between the Scylla and Charybdis of two undesirable options: either, one, it cannot or should not be applied to real scientific practices concerned with actual objects and occurrences (in which case, from the standpoint of my materialism, it is inconsequential and uninteresting); or, two, in being applied to the sciences, it licenses, without consistent intrasystemic means of preventing, the intellectual laziness of the cheap trick of transubstantiating ignorance into insight (i.e., the lack of a solid scientific solution to the "hard problem" of the emergence of sentient life is itself already a direct insight into a momentous moment of lawless, reasonless genesis out of thin air). Finally and in short, if emergence ex nihilo sparked by an omnipotent power is not a religious idea, then what is?

§4 Divine Retribution: A Wake-Up Call

The time has come to circle from science back to religion as regards Meillassoux's speculative materialism. Hallward perceptively draws readers' attention to the similarities between Meillassouxian hyper-Chaos, as per *After Finitude,* and the divinities of monotheistic religions.[77] Meillassoux furnishes Hallward with plenty of evidence for this comparison.[78] However, both Meillassoux and Brassier struggle to refute such a resemblance. The former, in, for example, "Deuil à venir, dieu à venir," contrasts his "contingent" and "unmasterable" God-to-come with the traditional God of pre-Kantian rationalist metaphysics (i.e., a necessary and rational supreme being eternally existent).[79] For Meillassoux, hyper-Chaos testifies to "the inexistence of the divine" to the extent that positing this absolute contingency correlatively entails denying the existence of the divinity of metaphysical theosophy (as though the signifier "God" can and does refer exclusively to this sort of divine as its invariant, one-and-only signified). Brassier adds that, because of the disturbing Otherness of its anarchic capriciousness, this omnipotent hyper-Chaos cannot be the object of fideistic adoration, respect, reverence, worship, and so on; in its unpredictable lawlessness, the alterity of this transcendent time of unlimited creative powers is unsuited to be the addressee of the aspirations and dreams of the religiously and spiritually inclined.[80] From a Lacanian standpoint, dark, inscrutable unpredictability, whether that of a god or an analyst, is a most powerful magnet for drawing out and attracting to itself various desires.[81] Furthermore, as the article "Deuil à venir, dieu à venir" shows, none of this stops Meillassoux himself from pinning his hopes on hyper-Chaos for the incalculably improbable springing to life of a God closely resembling that of established Christianity in every respect save for his speculated non-necessity (analogous to how perhaps the sole thing saving Kant from being Berkeley is the hypothesized noumenal *Ding an sich*).

When undergraduate students first are exposed to Leibniz's depiction of God in his rationalist ontology, many of them invariably express some version of a predictable reaction according to which this depiction illegitimately limits God's freedom to do as he pleases by restrictively

compelling him, through the principle of sufficient reason, to actual-
ize, out of the infinity of possible worlds of which he is omnisciently
cognizant, the single "best of all possible worlds." (Disarming this objection obviously begins with explaining how, in the history of Western philosophy going back to Plato's Socrates, acting under the commanding
governance of reason, on the one hand, and authentic autonomy, on
the other hand, are not opposed as mutually exclusive—doing what one
wants is not, for most philosophers, being truly free.) Although Meillassoux's hyper-Chaos differs from Leibniz's God in that the former, unlike
the latter, is liberated from the supposedly tyrannical yoke of the principle of sufficient reason—one additionally might mention here hyper-
Chaos's lack of intentional agency or will, although the God-to-come of
speculative divinology made possible by hyper-Chaos looks to be endowed
with these same subjective features and faculties exhibited by the Leibnizian God—this absolute contingency is very much like the God under-
graduates invoke against Leibniz's divinity metaphysically constrained by
his perfect moral and rational nature. Succinctly stated, Meillassoux's
hyper-Chaos resembles the God of "the spontaneous theosophy of non-/
not-yet-philosophers" (with reference to Althusser but not to François
Laruelle). While not a pre-Kantian metaphysical God, Meillassoux's
speculative hyper-Chaos, with its *Dieu á venir,* nonetheless is disturbingly
similar to this God of (post)modern non-/not-yet-philosophers. In fact,
Meillassoux splits up and distributes the bundle of features attributed
by pre-Kantian rationalist metaphysicians to God alone across these two
entities (i.e., hyper-Chaos and divinology's *Dieu á venir*).

What is more, Meillassoux's style of philosophizing is, in many ways,
Leibnizian, discounting the empirical, experiential, and experimental in
favor of the logical-rational and leading to the formulation of an entirely
unreasonable worldview that is both incontestable and yet counterintuitive, utterly at odds with what empirically informed reasoning tells investigators about the reality of the world. Sticking stubbornly to the logic
and rationality of the mathematics of his day alone, Leibniz is led to
deny the substantial real being not only of physical atoms, but of matter
in general; the result is a metaphysical monism of divinely harmonized
and orchestrated monads, as immaterial "formal atoms," that could not
be further from any and every materialism. As intellectually entertaining
as it might be to follow along with Leibniz's incredibly clever conceptual acrobatics and contortions, does one really want to go back to philosophizing in this pre-Kantian style, even if the philosophical content is
post-Kantian? Moreover, on the basis of pure reason alone, why should
one prefer Meillassouxian speculation over Leibnizian metaphysics? On
this basis, there is no reason. As Kant convincingly proves in the "Tran-

scendental Dialectic," the quarrels among the prior rationalist philosophers about being *an sich* are no more worth taking philosophically seriously than silly squabbles between sci-fi writers about whose concocted fantasy-world is truer or somehow more "superior" than the others; such quarrels are nothing more than fruitless comparisons between equally hallucinatory apples and oranges, again resembling the sad spectacle of a bunch of pulp fiction novelists bickering over the correctness-without-criteria of each others' fabricated imaginings and illusions. Discarding everything in Kant apart from his critical destruction of metaphysical absolutes, as does Meillassouxian speculative materialism, is tantamount to lifting the lid containing the swirling maelstrom of the specters of all other logically possible philosophies of pure reason (i.e., other than Meillassouxian speculative materialism). Only if one takes into account reasonable empirical considerations rooted in an experiential or experimental ground (as per, for example, Hume and his problem of induction) does Meillassoux's system appear relatively more preferable, if at all, to the innumerable other rationalisms licensed by mere logical possibility. But, as I stated previously, as soon as reasonable empirical considerations are (re)admitted, hyper-Chaos is immediately in trouble again. Such considerations are a bind for Meillassoux as conditions both for (as necessary for the Humean problem motivating the project of *After Finitude* as well as for the scientific arche-fossil hurled at correlationism) and simultaneously against (as unanimously testifying on behalf of alternate explanations different from those offered in *After Finitude*) his speculative philosophy with its absolute contingency.

Referring again to Žižekian philosophy is requisite at this stage. Speaking in a political register, Žižek insists that "true materialism" is inextricably intertwined with the matter of the chancy contingency of risk.[82] The same should be asserted apropos theoretical (in addition to practical-political) materialism. But what would this entail for Meillassoux and his speculative materialism? To begin with, and once more invoking Hallward, Meillassoux's "materialism" privileges "maybe" over "be," *peut-être* over *être*.[83] That is to say, speculative materialism, as the concluding pages of *After Finitude* corroborates, relies upon a presumed strict separation between, on the one hand, the physical-applied-empirical-ontic, and, on the other hand, the metaphysical-pure-logical-ontological[84] (and, as I maintained previously here, Brown's responses to Hallward's objections to the arguments of *After Finitude* seem to reinforce that this is indeed the case). Both Badiou and Meillassoux suffer from a Heideggerian hangover, specifically, an acceptance unacceptable for (dialectical) materialism of the veracity of ontological difference, of a clear-cut distinction between the ontological and the ontic. In this regard, one of the imperatives of a contemporary scientifically well-grounded materialism, a dialectical materialism, is the injunction "Forget Heidegger!" Genuine materialism, including theoretical materialist philosophy, is risky, messy business (something Brassier, for one, appreciates).[85] It does not grant anyone the low-effort luxury of fleeing into the uncluttered, fact-free ether of a "fundamental ontology" serenely separate from the historically shifting stakes of ontic disciplines. Although a materialist philosophy cannot be literally falsifiable as are Popperian sciences, it should be contestable as receptive, responsive, and responsible vis-à-vis the sciences.

Recalling the earlier discussion of the Pascalian-Sartrean wager of Badiou's equation of ontology with the ZFC axiomatization of set theory, this wager illustrates Badiou's conception of philosophy as a betting on the unforeseeable fortunes of the amorous, artistic, political, and scientific truths of its time—in this precise case, a wager on post-Cantorian trans-finite set theory as a scientific condition of Badiouian philosophy (as noted above, Meillassoux himself emphasizes that this is a gamble by Badiou, the leap into historical uncertainty of an existential choice or decision). This conception of philosophy, to be endorsed by a materialism of chancy contingency indebted to the dialectical materialist tradition, directly links philosophizing with the taking of risks with respect to its amorous, artistic, political, and scientific conditions.

Insofar as the arche-fossil he arbitrarily and selectively borrows from the physical sciences is merely a disposable propaedeutic on the way to the overcoming of correlationism, with this overcoming then resulting in a speculative materialist doctrine of hyper-Chaos (pretending to be) thereafter immune to science-based contestation, Meillassoux, unlike his teacher Badiou, avoids taking any real risks at the level of his philosophy's rapport with science. He clings to an unreasonable rationalism that appears reasonable solely when one disregards, on the questionable basis of an anti-immanentist appeal to a (too) neat-and-clean distinction between the physical-applied-empirical-ontic and the metaphysical-pure-logical-ontological, the actual practices of today's really existing sciences of material beings. This, combined with his related desire for absolute certainty, puts him in the company not only of pre-Kantian theosophical idealists—just as the one thing that saves Kant from being Berkeley is the thing-in-itself, the one thing that saves Meillassoux from being an early modern rationalist (i.e., a theosophical idealist) is his "intellectual intuition"[86] of the all-powerful (in)existent divine as capricious—but also of any number of outlandish and politically backward religious fideists and fanatics. Like solipsism, Pyrrhonic extreme/hyperbolic skepticism, religious dogmatism, and Berkeley's philosophy—if, as per Lenin and Meillassoux, one becomes prima facie absurd through being brought into uncomfortably close company with Berkeley, then Meillassoux should be worried given his desire for absolutely certain irrefutability—Meillassouxian speculative materialism poses as incontestable, as an easily defended but empty fortress. After relying on the realm of the reasonable, it tries to evade further critical evaluation at the level of the reasonable by attempting to escape into the confined enclosure of the strictly rational. It risks nothing, which is perhaps why, scientifically speaking, it says nothing (or, at least, nothing that should be taken seriously in empirical-material practice, unless one wishes to throw the door of the sciences wide open to transubstantiations of ignorance into insight, including ex nihilo creationist confabulations). Erroneously pointing out that this rational yet supposedly materialist philosophy is impervious to being delivered any scientifically backed death blows is already to deliver the coup de grâce.

The critique of Meillassoux laid out in the preceding actually is twofold. On the one hand, I charge that the vaguely Heideggerian version of ontological difference operative in Meillassoux's (and Badiou's) philosophy is inadmissible and invalid for a properly materialist philosophy. On the other hand, I issue the additional indictment that Meillassoux nonetheless does not invariably heed this stratified level-distinction between rational ontology and the reason(ableness) of ontic regions. At times and in an inconsistent fashion, he transgresses the line of ontological difference which his philosophy claims to maintain and respect.

Given Meillassoux's rationalist absolutism-without-an-absolute,[87] he is profoundly averse to skepticism. But this phobic aversion lulls him into overlooking a Badiouian manner of recuperating Humean attenuated skepticism so as riskily to wager on aspects of the contemporary sciences: just as there is no guarantee of future continued confirmation of any given scientific claim, so too is there no guarantee of future disconfirmation either (as Meillassoux would have to grant, considering both his glosses on Badiou's appropriation of mathematics as well as his explanations for why the concept of hyper-Chaos does not entail a Heraclitean flux doctrine).[88] Along these lines, Hume's skepticism is far from encouraging one to be hand-wringingly noncommittal vis-à-vis empirical scientific claims (all of which, according to Hume, are based on the ideational relation of cause and effect). Rather, Humean attenuated skepticism means one is aware that philosophically drawing upon the sciences is indeed far from being a "sure thing," amounting instead to risks, to bets or gambles that lack any promises or guarantees of final correctness in a future that can and will retroactively pass judgments on these present wagers. But, as with Pascal's wager, there is no honest and true way to avoid these risks. Or, as Meillassoux himself puts it, "As Sartre rightly insists, not choosing is still choosing."[89]

Moreover, a subtle but significant link connects Hume and historical/dialectical materialism à la Marx, Engels, Lenin, and Mao—and this despite Engels and Lenin associating Humean ontological agnosticism with idealism[90] (for Pascal, agnostically not choosing to believe in God is choosing not to believe in God, namely, choosing atheism; similarly, for Lenin, agnostically not choosing to be a committed materialist is choosing not to be a materialist, namely, choosing idealism, however overt or covert). Both Hume and historical/dialectical materialism in certain Marxist veins propose a nonabsolutist (as fallible) realism of revisable knowledge of the real world with the courage of conviction to wager on its own correctness in the absence of any absolute a priori assurances—and, in the process, also to risk being wrong in exposure both to theoretical contestation as well as to the danger of the falsification of the scientific materials upon which its wagers are placed. Incidentally, as regards the entire "speculative realism" movement largely inspired by Meillassoux's work, a warning is in order against the danger of getting stuck in endless philosophical tempests-in-teacups pitting realist materialism against idealist antimaterialism: even if the content of one's position is realist or materialist, conceding the form of an interminable and unwinnable epistemological debate is itself idealist. As others in the history of philosophy have observed, some problems are more effectively solved by being justly ignored, by not being dignified with any further engagement. There is a big difference between arguing for materialism/ realism versus actually pursuing the positive construction of materialist/ realist projects dirtying their hands with real empirical data.

Circumnavigating back to one of the initial points of reference for this intervention, a short, direct bridge connects Meillassoux's *After Finitude* with his "Deuil à venir, dieu à venir."[91] It is terribly tempting to indulge in a Dawkins-style move and joke about a "flying spaghetti monster *à venir*." Of all the incalculable contingent (im)possibilities permitted by Meillassoux's hyper-Chaos, he ends up speculating, in his article on a God-to-come, about the infinitely much less than one-in-a-trillion possibility of the arrival of a divinity resembling that mused about by the most traditional monotheistic religions and their old prophecies. This is telling. Should the detotalizing of probabilistic chance in favor of transfinite contingency not make this even less worth pondering, forcing its likelihood asymptotically but rapidly to approach zero?

Additionally, from this perspective, Meillassoux can be viewed as an inversion of Žižek, as an anti-Žižek: whereas Žižek tries to smuggle atheism into Christianity via the immanent critique of a Hegelian dialectical

interpretation of Christianity for the sake of a progressive radical leftist politics of Communism, Meillassoux, whether knowingly or unknow-
ingly, smuggles idealist religiosity back into materialist atheism via a nondialectical "materialism." Meillassoux's divinology and emergent life ex
nihilo are rigorously consequent extensions of the speculative materialism (with its central concept of hyper-Chaos) of *After Finitude*. These
very extensions arguably bear damning witness against the project of
this book—*After Finitude* has many striking virtues, especially in terms of
its crystalline clarity and ingenious creativeness, and deserves credit for
having played a role in inspiring some much-needed discussions in contemporary continental philosophy—at least for any atheist materialism
concerned with various modes of scientific and political praxis. Alert,
sober vigilance is called for against the danger of dozing off into a speculative, but no less dogmatic, slumber.

From Critique to Construction: Toward a Transcendental Materialism

In a newly published pair of exchanges, Élisabeth Roudinesco and Alain Badiou both provide a series of illuminating clarifications regarding Lacan's significance for psychoanalysis, philosophy, and a range of socio-political topics. Two of their observations in this context, one by Badiou and the other by Roudinesco, are relevant to my agenda here at the close of the first volume of *Prolegomena to Any Future Materialism*. First, affirming Roudinesco's comment that "Lacan turns his back to scientism, on the one hand, and to obscurantism on the other,"[1] Badiou energetically responds:

> Exactly. Today, these two dangers threaten more than ever! They form our conjuncture! Moreover, a secret alliance between the supposed adversaries which are narrow-minded scientism and superstitious obscurantism does not date from today. This is why we have so much need of Lacan. In any case, for my part, I am completely Lacanian on this question. In order to think that which is a truth, I need to find the point where the form of that which is and that which produces a rupture with this form are concomitant. My work is an investigation of formalism adequate for thinking the possibility of an effective cut in the context of forms. Neither determinism (current behaviorism is an avatar of this in the clinic) nor neo-religious horizon (in which a certain phenomenology inscribes itself today), but a radical materialism that grants the claims of the unpredictable real—what I call the event. With this ambition, I follow in my manner in the footsteps of Lacan.[2]

As I highlighted earlier (see the preface and chapter 1), Lacan's reflections on the defiant "triumph of religion" after Freud involve bringing to light the covert complicity between "narrow-minded scientism" and "superstitious obscurantism." For Lacan, this codependency amounts to scientisms provoking flights toward obscurantisms as themselves supplementary sources of meaningfulness, with these obscurantisms in turn making the nonsensical nihilism of scientisms tolerable and sustainable. Roudinesco and Badiou obviously endorse this diagnosis of the post-Enlightenment situation as regards science and religion in the twentieth and early-twenty-first centuries. I too agree that the contemporary "conjuncture" is, in certain crucial respects, structured by this self-reinforcing vicious circle, this "secret alliance" between apparent enemies that are, in reality, mutual supports of each other that form a seesawing balance. As Badiou declares in *Logics of Worlds*, "traversing Lacan's anti-philosophy remains an obligatory exercise today for those who wish to wrest themselves away from the reactive convergences of religion and scientism."[3]

Like Badiou and Roudinesco, I see Lacan as supplying the resources for steering between a scientistic Scylla and obscurantist Charybdis, a false dilemma that remains all too firmly in place up through the present. Rephrasing some of what Badiou articulates in the preceding block quotation in the language of Marx's 1845 "Theses on Feuerbach," a post-Lacanian materialist theory of subjectivity and corresponding ontology avoids falling back into a strictly "contemplative" materialism while nevertheless ruthlessly fighting off the embrace of the spiritualist irrationality of antimaterialist idealism; in Badiou's words, "a radical materialism that grants the claims of the unpredictable real" moves beyond the "determinism" of nondialectical as mechanistic, reductive, or eliminative materialisms without, for all that, taking flight toward any "neo-religious horizon." In the wake of Marx as well as Lacan, Badiou and I both are driven to pursue the construction of a properly dialectical materialism which, as such, does full justice to the contingent but still very real autonomy of subjects while not having to lapse regressively into the dualisms and distinctions of the subject-sustaining idealisms opposing subject-squelching pre-/nondialectical materialisms (as contemplative, deterministic, mechanistic, reductive, eliminative, etc.). In the combined shadows of Marx, Lacan, and Badiou (and Žižek as well), one can be a partisan of a really and indissolubly free subject while simultaneously and without incoherence or self-contradiction remaining entirely faithful to the uncompromising atheism and immanentism of the combative materialist tradition, making no concessions whatsoever thereby to the mysteries and transcendences of obfuscating obscurantist ideologies appealing to God, Nature, or whatever other big Other.[4]

Following the more structuralist side of Lacanian metapsychology, in the preceding block quotation Badiou again draws attention to the formalist nature of his Lacan-inspired philosophical endeavor to synthesize systematically the seeming opposites of a Sartrean-style theory of radically autonomous subjectivity and an Althusserian-type vision of individuals as the heteronomous puppets of sociostructural (over) determination. As already spelled out (see chapters 4 and 5), I think that Badiou's "formalism," resting on the foundations of his mathematical (meta-)ontology, fundamentally is incompatible with his avowed materialist commitments. Insofar as I share these same Marxist and Lacanian commitments, my criticisms of Badiou for his formalist philosophy constitute an immanent (rather than external) critique of his work. I am convinced that formalism alone cannot deliver a truly and robustly materialist materialism avoiding the twin pitfalls of the scientistic and the superstitious. However, I agree with Badiou that a materialist step beyond these two dead ends is urgently needed in a world ruled by the perverse diarchy of capitalism and fundamentalisms.

Later in their conversation, Roudinesco similarly praises Lacan's artful balancing acts along fine lines of tension. Speaking of Lacan, she remarks, "On the basis of his theory of the subject and the signifier (language, speech), he maintained a necessary gap between the human and the non-human, all the while remaining Darwinian properly speaking."[5] Of course, as observed (see chapter 4), the "necessary gap between the human and the non-human" is essential for Badiou as well.[6] Here, Roudinesco characterizes a delicately precise position Lacan only sometimes manages to maintain as if he solidly and unwaveringly sustains such a stance across the entire arc of his teachings. I have labored to show just how ambivalent and even inconsistent Lacan is apropos matters pertaining to the separation of the more-than-natural/denaturalized from the natural (see chapters 2 and 3). Similarly, ample evidence testifies to Lacan vacillating dramatically as regards the implications and consequences for psychoanalysis of post-Darwinian biology. As shown (see chapter 3), Lacan is at his least Darwinian (and his most Catholic) when speculating (or refusing to speculate) about the material-historical origins of linguistic humanity proper as the collectivities and generations of signifier-using-and-used *parlêtres* (speaking beings), origins forever after splitting off human creatures as markedly different from other animals. In short and contra Roudinesco, I suggest that Lacan does not formulate a consistent, rigorously materialist account of humanity's break with (its) animality carefully reconciled with Darwin's legacy as developed by the life sciences.

One of the advantages in this setting of Roudinesco's above-quoted remark is that her phrasing helps bring out the proximity of my transcendental materialism to specific facets of Lacan's theoretical edifice. For both Lacan and me, the dialectically entangled, reciprocally influencing dimensions of subjectivity and signifiers must be comprehended, rather than dismissed out of hand and explained away, on a monistic (i.e., nondualistic) basis that nonetheless is neither reductive nor eliminative. In other words, to be "Darwinian properly speaking," as Roudinesco puts it, is to be tethered voluntarily to the ground of an immanentist and materialist ontology in which lawless concatenations of accidental occurrences bringing into interaction contingently existing entities and events generate, through thoroughly bottom-up dynamics, law-like structures of varying complexity and longevity. Roudinesco's wording suggests that the chasm dividing unnatural humanity from natural animality is, in Lacan's thinking (as allegedly Darwinian), not a top-down imposition inexplicably descending from the enigmatic heights of an always-already there "Holy Spirit" (i.e., the big Other as symbolic order as per Lacan's fourth seminar[7]—see chapter 3), but, instead, a "gap" signaling a transcendence-in-immanence. That is to say, the Lacanian speaking subject is, in Hegelian parlance, an identity-in-difference irreducible to, and yet embedded in, the human animal as an animal. Despite Lacan's hesitations about whether or not a quasi-naturalist, scientifically backed conceptual framework can or should inquire into enigmas about the presupposed real genesis of such subjectivity, Lacan, at a minimum, rules out as illegitimate the pursuit of the sorts of phylogenetic investigations mandatory for a post-Darwinian materialism (see chapter 3). Without hesitation, I am invested in precisely these types of inquiries.

Transcendental materialism is "transcendental" insofar as, with Lacan, it affirms the immanence to material nature of subjects nonetheless irreducible to such natural materialities. In this sense, I deliberately play with the erroneous but oft-made equivocation between the transcendental and the transcendent; an aspect of what I aim to capture with the label for my philosophical position is this standing of the subject as transcendent-while-immanent vis-à-vis the sole, Otherless plane of lone physical being. Perhaps rewriting this label as "transcendent(al) materialism" might be more appropriate and accurate. That said, like Lacan and Žižek (or, at least, Žižek's Lacan), the picture of subjectivity at stake for me is drawn from Kantian transcendentalism and post-Kantian German idealism. Hence, this subject transcendent-while-immanent with respect to matter is also transcendental, namely, in fidelity to Kant, a network of conditions of possibility for what comes to be experienced as human reality.

Transcendental materialism is "materialist" insofar as, against Lacan (as well as both Kant and Badiou—see chapter 5), the dual phylo- and ontogenetic levels encompassed in my approach, levels linked to both psychoanalysis and the sciences, contain components of a meta-transcendental account of transcendental subjectivity. By contrast with Kant's transcendental idealism as well as Lacan's and Badiou's failures and refusals to extrapolate from evolutionary theory to phylogenetic analyses, as a post-Darwinian materialist I believe that thought is obligated to think the material conditions of possibility (i.e., the meta-transcendental real as substance) for subjectivity as itself a matrix of dematerialized conditions of possibility (i.e., the transcendental ideal as subject). Quite unlike the garden-variety scientisms rightly denounced by Lacan, Roudinesco, and Badiou, among others, this genetic meta-transcendentalism will not amount merely to compelling philosophy and psychoanalysis, in a lopsided, one-way movement, to adapt and conform to the current state of the empirical, experimental sciences, with the latter and their images of nature left unchanged in the bargain. Merging philosophy and psychoanalysis with the sciences promises to force profound changes, in a two-way movement, within the latter at least as much as within the former. Moreover, Roudinesco is correct that Lacan (periodically) expresses the desire to posit a split between the *parlêtre* and the rest of being (*être*) that would be both internal to being itself as well as of a piece with a materialist, realist, and science-friendly outlook. However, in my view, Lacan cannot be deemed to be "Darwinian" in the absence of a historical materialist narrative, informed by the sciences, of the immanent emergence of the worlds of human subjectivities out of the nonhuman material real (i.e., the genesis of the very "gap between the human and the non-human")—a narrative he tends to repudiate.

Yet even on its materialist side, transcendental materialism is positively indebted to Lacan. As the opening moments of this book reveal (see the preface, introduction, and chapter 1), not only does Lacan facilitate navigation out of the impasse represented by the pair scientism-obscurantism, as Badiou underscores—his register theory (i.e., the famous Real-Symbolic-Imaginary triad), particularly the later versions preoccupied with the Real, anticipates the types of ontologies advocated in different ways and guises by Badiou, Meillassoux, Žižek, and me (as well as a number of others). The late Lacan's rendition of material nature as a detotalized not-One/non-All, as a barred Real, provides a pivotal point of orientation for my Žižek-inspired transcendental materialism. I add two twists to this: one, the Lacanian barring of the natural-material Real provides a depiction of the ultimate, unsupported ground-zero of (in Badiouian locution) being qua being (*l'être en tant qu'être*); two, this ontology of a disunified, conflict-ridden physical universe (or, more accurately, universes) permits identifying the necessary (although not, by themselves, sufficient) metatranscendental conditions of possibility—these possibility conditions are themselves ontologically contingent and material—for the genesis of denaturalized, more-than-material subjectivity.

Transcendental materialism, in terms of its deeper historical sources of motivation, is a philosophical position arising from the speculative dialectics of Hegelianism and the historical materialism of Marx and his heirs—and this in addition to being profoundly and avowedly motivated by Freudian-Lacanian psychoanalysis, Badiouian-Žižekian philosophy, and the life sciences. However, whereas Hegelian-Marxian dialectical materialism favors emphasizing eventual unifying syntheses of such apparent splits as that between, simply put, mind and matter, transcendental materialism treats these splits as real and ineliminable (while at the same time depicting them as internally generated out of a single, sole plane of material being). As both Maoists and the young Badiou would put it, this is the distinction between the Two becoming One (dialectical materialism) and the One becoming Two (transcendental materialism). Or, with reference to emergentism as a grouping of theoretical scaffoldings in the life sciences, this is the difference between a somewhat weak and holistic/organicist emergentism versus a very strong and anti–holistic/organicist emergentism. Along these lines, I am tempted to characterize my transcendental materialism as an emergent dual-aspect monism, albeit with the significant qualification that these "aspects" and their ineradicable divisions (such as mind and matter, the asubjective and subjectivity, and the natural and the more-than-natural) enjoy the heft of actual existence (rather than being, as they are in Spinoza's dual-aspect monism, epiphenomena deprived of true ontological substantiality). One of the questions animating my philosophical program is: What sort of ontology of "first nature" (i.e., the one-and-only original real[ity] of material substances) allows for the genesis of a "second nature" (i.e., minded and like-minded autonomous subjects as epistemologically inexplicable and ontologically irreducible with reference to natural material substances alone)—a second nature immanently transcending first nature and requiring theorization in a manner that avoids the mirror-image dual traps of reductive/eliminative monisms and idealist/spiritualist dualisms?[8]

A recent collection of interviews with Badiou contains a perplexing moment. At one point during a discussion of philosophy's relations with the sciences, he enthusiastically refers to emergentism: "As regards what has to do with thought . . . I am a partisan of the doctrine of emergences. Life is a universe irreducible to matter, and thought is a universe irreducible to life. Thought is in every case a *sui generis* activity."[9] As exhibited (see chapter 4), Badiou is quite hostile to biology and its branches, the very fields in which emergentism features as a constellation of theoretical orientations. Thus, this self-identification as "a partisan of the doctrine of emergences" is somewhat odd. Given that there are many strains of emergentism, to which exact emergentist doctrine is Badiou committed?

A less charitable reading would suggest that Badiou's unspecified notion of emergence is taken from his student Meillassoux (particularly from the latter's unpublished thesis "Divine Inexistence" ["L'inexistence divine"], excerpts from which appeared in print only in 2011; the full text has not yet been published). But, before devoting attention to Meillassouxian "emergentism," some preliminary framing remarks are warranted. On a couple of recent occasions, Meillassoux explains that one of the manners in which he differs from his teacher is that Badiou is concerned with "the contingency of necessity" (simply put, the motif of contingent events giving rise to necessary truths),[10] whereas he, as the subtitle of *After Finitude* already announces, is focused on "the necessity of contingency."[11] The latter refers to Meillassoux's fundamental ontology of hyper-Chaos. In what follows, I will assume as established and familiar the criticisms of Meillassoux and of this ontology of his I already laid out above (see chapters 6 and 7).

Brassier's 2008 English translation of *Après la finitude* contains eight pages of material not included in the 2006 French original (running from pages eighteen to twenty-six in the English edition).[12] Therein, Meillassoux broaches much of what is central to talk about emergence and emergentism(s). Reminding readers of a distinction between the "ancient" and the "ancestral," he maintains:

> The ancestral does *not* designate an ancient event—it designates
> an event *anterior* to terrestrial life and *hence anterior to givenness itself.*
> Though ancestrality is a temporal notion, its definition does not invoke
> distance in time, but rather anteriority in time. This is why the arche-
> fossil does not merely refer to an un-witnessed occurrence, but to a
> non-given occurrence—ancestral reality does not refer to occurrences
> which a lacunary givenness cannot apprehend, but to occurrences
> which are not contemporaneous with any givenness, whether lacunary
> or not. Therein lies its singularity and its critical potency with regard to
> correlationism.[13]

That which is ancient (however old) falls within the time after the beginning of the existence of sentient or sapient life. By contrast, that which is ancestral (i.e., the conceptual figure of the arche-fossil) predates the very genesis of any and every living consciousness of whatever kind. As is evident, the matter of the emergence of living sentience is involved in Meillassoux's onslaught against correlationism.[14]

Meillassoux promptly proceeds to foreground the problem of emergence. He stipulates:

> One must concede that the ancestral poses a challenge to correlation-
> ism which is of an entirely different order than that of the unperceived,
> viz., *how to conceive of a time in which the given as such passes from non-being*

into being? Not a time which is given in a lacunary fashion, but a time wherein one passes from the lacuna of all givenness to the effectivity of a lacunary givenness.[15]

He immediately goes on to elaborate at length:

> Accordingly, there can be no question of resolving this problem by invoking a counterfactual, since this would presuppose precisely what is being called into question: if a consciousness had observed the emergence of terrestrial life, the time of the emergence *of* the given would have been a time of emergence *in* the given. But the time at issue here is the time wherein *consciousness* as well as *conscious time* have *themselves emerged in time.* For the problem of the arche-fossil is not the empirical problem of the birth of living organisms, but the ontological problem of the coming into being of givenness as such. More acutely, the problem consists in understanding how science is able to think—without any particular difficulty—the coming into being of consciousness and its spatio-temporal forms of givenness in the midst of a space and time which are supposed to pre-exist the latter. More particularly, one thereby begins to grasp that science thinks a time in which the passage from the non-being of givenness to its being has effectively occurred— hence *a time which, by definition, cannot be reduced to any givenness which preceded it and whose emergence it allows.* In other words, at issue here is not the time of consciousness but the time of science—the time which, in order to be apprehended, must be understood as harboring the capacity to engender not only physical things, but also correlations between given things and the giving of those things. Is this not precisely what science thinks? A time that is not only anterior to givenness, but essentially indifferent to the latter because givenness could just as well *never* have emerged if life had not arisen? Science reveals a time that not only does not need conscious time but that allows the latter to arise at a determinate point in its own flux. To think science is to think the status of a becoming which cannot be correlational because the correlate is in it, rather than it being in the correlate. So the challenge is therefore the following: to understand how *science can think a world wherein spatio-temporal givenness itself came into being within a time and a space which preceded every variety of givenness.*[16]

Apart from its further clarifications of the ancestral-ancient distinction, several other features of this passage call for commentary. First, Meillassoux himself emphasizes that it is science specifically (and not, for example, religion or even divinology as Meillassoux's religion-without-religion) that is capable of conceiving of the advent of life and, hence, of the surfacing of correlational consciousnesses to which things can be given as appearances, manifestations, phenomena, and so on. Moreover, this extended quotation exemplifies how Meillassoux employs the arche-fossil so as to push even the most sophisticated variants of correlationism (particularly Kantian transcendental idealism) toward either collapsing into the crudeness of Berkeley-style solipsism (i.e., absolutized subjective idealism) or abandoning any insistence on the strict ideality of space and time (in being compelled to admit the absolutely real as mind-independent status of space and time as scientifically knowable).

However, when Meillassoux portrays the sciences as able to think the emergences of life and consciousness out of non-living, non-conscious being *an sich* "without any particular difficulty," this is misleading. Admittedly, Meillassoux is perfectly correct in claiming that the spontaneous realist sensibilities of practicing scientists mean that they confidently assume, in an implicitly anticorrelationist fashion, both that life and consciousness must have emerged at some point in objectively real space-time as well as that these emergences arose from material substances preexisting sentient and sapient living beings. But these convictions are background presuppositions situated at the beginning of types of research programs still underway in the natural sciences, not the definitive end results of such programs as successfully completed. Starting assumptions are not final answers—especially not in empirical and experimental modern science.

As the subsequent critical examination of Meillassoux's "Divine Inexistence" will make evident shortly, Meillassoux almost certainly has his own doctrine of emergences in mind at this moment in *After Finitude*. Unlike the genetic "hard problems" involving life and consciousness exercising the minds of legions of scientists and (analytic) philosophers, the Meillassouxian idea of genesis ex nihilo licensed by the ontology of hyper-Chaos enables him to dress up a nonanswer as an answer. That is to say, once Meillassoux puts in place his portrayal of being as hyper-chaotic, he is free to assert that the problem of emergences is already its own solution. The apparently mysterious geneses of life and consciousness are just that, miraculous events surging up out of nowhere thanks to the incalculable capriciousness of hyper-Chaos, and, as such, both incapable and not in need of further explanation, scientific or otherwise. Hence, Meillassoux seems to believe that he can account for the rise of sentient and sapient life "without any particular difficulty." Other philosophers and scientists might not be so confident.

Just as I appreciate the appropriate polemics against "fideism" in *After Finitude,* so too am I sympathetic toward Meillassoux's insistence on squaring philosophical with scientific thinking. But, to resort to a cliché of biblical origin, the letter of Meillassoux's extrapolations of his system violate the spirit of his proscience, antireligion rhetoric. As regards religion and science, I see Meillassoux's oscillations between these poles as disappointing and unsatisfactory, much more so than what both Lacan and Badiou present along these lines. Meillassoux's arguments apropos transcendental subjectivity a few pages later in the addition to the English translation of *After Finitude* convince me more that my critiques of him are again immanent rather than external, as with those I direct against Lacan and Badiou. In other words, in addition to sharing some of Meillassoux's proscience/antireligion sentiments, I simultaneously accept his claims with respect to the transcendental subject (to be glossed momentarily) and contend that he falls short of the task he sets for himself through these very claims.

Assuming that given appearances/manifestations are experiences made possible by the structures and dynamics of a living mind (i.e., some version of transcendental consciousness), the validation of noncorrelationist scientific realism by the arche-fossil demands that the question of the transcendental subject's nonideal genesis be asked and answered. That is to say, the objective material spatiotemporal emergence of such subjects thereby becomes a legitimate and unavoidable topic. Meillassoux contends:

> Even if we concede that the transcendental subject does not exist in the way in which objects exist, one still has to say that *there is* a transcendental subject, rather than no subject. Moreover, nothing prevents us from reflecting in turn on the conditions under which there is a transcendental subject. And among these conditions we find that there can only be a transcendental subject on condition that such a subject *takes place*.[17]

The two italicized phrases in this passage ("*there is*" and "*takes place*") designate noncorrelational space and time. Meillassoux evinces an interest in investigating the asubjective possibility conditions for the subjective as a meshwork of second-order possibility conditions. To speculate regarding the real (or natural) conditions of possibility for the surfacing of ideal (or denaturalized/more-than-natural) transcendental subjectivity is to pursue metatranscendental reflections.

Meillassoux quickly infers that thinking the objective material spatiotemporal conditions of possibility for the transcendental subject entails tying this subject to a physical body. He states:

> The subject is transcendental only insofar as it is positioned *in* the world, of which it can only ever discover a finite aspect, and which it can never recollect in its totality. But if the transcendental subject is

localized among the finite objects of its world in this way, this means
that *it remains indissociable from its incarnation in a body;* in other words,
it is indissociable from a determinate object in the world. Granted,
the transcendental is the condition for knowledge of bodies, but it is
necessary to add that the body is also the condition for the taking place
of the transcendental. That the transcendental subject has *this* or that
body is an empirical matter, but that *it has* a body is a non-empirical
condition of its taking place—the body, one could say, is the "retro-
transcendental" condition for the subject of knowledge. We will invoke
an established distinction here and say that a subject is *instantiated*
rather than *exemplified* by a thinking body. An entity is said to be instantiated by an individual when that entity does not exist apart from its individuation; and it is said to be merely exemplified by an individual if one
assumes that the entity also exists apart from its individuation. Thus, in
Plato, the entity "man" is merely exemplified by the perceptible individual man since it also exists—and exists above all—as an Idea. By way
of contrast, for an empiricist, the species "man" is instantiated by individual men because this species does not exist apart from the individuals in which it is incarnated.[18]

Meillassoux's "retro-transcendental" and my "metatranscendental" are
roughly synonymous phrases, save for the difference that Meillassoux
privileges an emphasis on the ancestral past with his choice of "retro."
Furthermore, with the distinction between instantiation and exemplifi-
cation, Meillassoux indicates his preference for empiricist nominalism
(probably à la Hume, considering the importance of Humean empiricism for Meillassoux's project) over Platonic metaphysical realism, at
least in relation to his contemplation of the empirical spatiotemporal
emergence (i.e., the real genesis thinkable in and through the natural
sciences) of thereafter nonempirical as transcendental subjectivity (as
a "metaphysical" reality irreducible to the status of one empirical-ontic
entity or event among others studied through observation and experimentation). As a transcendental materialist, I too opt for conceiving
the transcendental subject, itself transcending the empirical, material,
and natural planes of existence, as immanently arising from these same
planes. In this, I concur wholeheartedly with Meillassoux.

Incidentally, in the preceding block quotation, Meillassoux strangely
seems to conflate empiricism, which is an epistemological position, with
nominalism, which is the ontological position diametrically opposed to
metaphysical realism. Of course, a glance at the history of early modern
philosophy reveals that empiricists tend to be nominalists and rationalists tend to be metaphysical realists. But these historical tendencies are

not ahistorical necessities, at least not in the case of the link between empiricism and nominalism. For instance, a Berkeleyian-style empiricist could conceptualize the mind (Berkeley's "spiritual substance") as a tabula rasa, some of the ideational contents of which are metaphysically real "ideas" (i.e., contra nominalism, notions not of or derived from unique concrete thises, thats, or others individuated in space and time) furnished by God over the course of that mind's lived existence. Alternately, Saul Kripke muses that "one might very well discover essence empirically."[19] In resonance with this Kripkean line, Andrew Cutrofello suggests that Lacanian theory introduces a fourth category missing in Kant's critical-theoretical philosophy, namely, the "analytic *aposteriori*."[20] Hallward accuses Meillassoux of carelessly lumping together epistemology and ontology in his assault on correlationism.[21] Meillassoux looks to be guilty of doing so in the above-quoted context as well.

One last stretch from the supplementary section of the English translation of *After Finitude* deserves examination before a turn to other texts by Meillassoux. In this section, he argues:

> When we raise the question of the emergence of thinking bodies in time we are also raising the question of *the temporality of the conditions of instantiation, and hence of the taking place of the transcendental as such.* Objective bodies may not be a sufficient condition for the taking place of the transcendental, but they are certainly a necessary condition for it. We thereby discover that the time of science temporalizes and spatializes the emergence of living bodies; that is to say, *the emergence of the conditions for the taking place of the transcendental.* What effectively emerged with living bodies were the instantiations of the subject, its character as point-of-view-on-the-world. The fact that subjects emerged here on this earth or existed elsewhere is a purely empirical matter. But the fact that subjects *appeared*—simply appeared—*in* time and space, instantiated by bodies, is a matter that pertains indissociably both to objective bodies and to transcendental subjects. And we realize that this problem simply cannot be thought from the transcendental viewpoint because it concerns the space-time in which transcendental subjects went from not-taking-place to taking-place—and hence concerns the space-time anterior to the spatio-temporal forms of representation. To think this ancestral space-time is thus to think the conditions of science and also to revoke the transcendental as essentially inadequate to this task.[22]

If any and every first-person transcendental subjectivity (i.e., "point-of-view-on-the-world") necessarily is embodied, as Meillassoux persuasively advocates just prior to this passage, then the natural scientific study and elucidation of the coming-to-be of such "thinking bodies" in and through the physical universe provides insight into the meta-/retrotranscendental conditions of possibility for such subjects. As is evident, when Meillassoux refers to "the transcendental" and "the spatio-temporal forms of representation," he clearly considers Kantian transcendental idealism, with its insistence on the exclusive ideality of space and time as the two "pure forms of intuition,"[23] as epitomizing the correlationist transcendentalism he targets.

As regards the first half of the last sentence of the prior quotation ("To think this ancestral space-time is thus to think the conditions of science"), Meillassoux's use of the definite article signals an oversimplified account of what makes science possible. However, aside from that reservation, I endorse much of the rest of what he advances in this passage. The Meillassoux of those select moments in *After Finitude* which, taken together, plead for an antifideistic and science-informed philosophical investigation into the real material conditions of possibility for the emergence of transcendental subjects is someone I recognize as a fellow traveler (along with the Badiou of *Logics of Worlds* who is dedicated to developing a materialist conception of the transcendental). My dismayed reaction to much of the rest of Meillassoux's output (in particular, his engagements with religion through both Stéphane Mallarmé and the God-to-come) is reinforced by this fraternal feeling of closeness to an intellectual neighbor occasionally quite proximate to transcendental materialism. Perhaps immanent critiques sometimes are more passionate than external ones in part due to the critic's disheartened reaction to the object of criticism selling itself short and betraying its own promises and potentials.

In the extended close reading of Mallarmé's poem "A Throw of the Dice Never Will Abolish Chance" that forms the content of the 2011 book *The Number and the Siren,* Meillassoux flirts with calling for a new religion-after-religion replete with its own special rituals and ceremonies sustaining a revivified atmosphere of high and holy sacredness through underscoring this poet's own project along these lines.[24] At this stage, there can be little doubt that Meillassoux considers his "divinology" of a *Dieu á venir* as fulfilling the Mallarméan prophecy he retells over the course of his meticulous unpacking of "A Throw of the Dice." This suspicion helps explain why Meillassoux publishes *The Number and the Siren* following *After Finitude* but preceding the yet-to-be-published "Divine Inexistence." The literary analysis situated between two very philosophical works is more than a mere tangent or non sequitur. Additionally, "Divine Inexistence," considering what has been made available from this manuscript, is glaringly and unapologetically centered on the attempt to plead for a novel theosophical framework that purports to break through to an unprecedented position that would be neither traditionally religious nor atheist.[25] Without getting bogged down in gilding the various quasi-theological niceties of "Divine Inexistence," I will remark that Meillassoux's divinology is quite literally post-secular.

"Divine Inexistence" directly addresses the notion of emergences, including those of life and thought, albeit explicitly within the fore-grounded parameters of the divinological ontology of hyper-Chaos visible to a slightly lesser degree in *After Finitude, The Number and the Siren,* and other texts (my critical interpretation of "Divine Inexistence" is based on the excerpts from it translated by Harman for his study on Meillassoux). Again, I worry that this is the version of "emergentism" Badiou has in mind when conversing with Tarby about the sciences. Apropos the issue of the real genesis in space and time (i.e., within the physical universe explored by the empirical and experimental natural sciences) of ideal dematerialized/more-than-material subjectivity (i.e., the living and thinking, sentient and sapient, transcendental subject), Meillassoux, in his thesis supervised by Badiou, puts forward some highly contentious claims. I intend to challenge these assertions in the name of transcendental materialism as an alternate philosophical position. Transcendental materialism, allied with the sciences and implacably opposed to both posturing scientisms and mystical obscurantisms, arguably accounts in a much more satisfactory and plausible manner than the speculative creed of the twin lords of hyper-Chaos and the God-to-come for what preoccupies both Meillassoux (at least occasionally) and me: the immanent natural emergence of that which is transcendent(al).

As stated, the Meillassoux of *After Finitude* demands that a realist and materialist genetic meta-/retrotranscendentalism be decisively shaped by the natural sciences of modernity. I would allege that the portions of "Divine Inexistence" he permitted Harman to include in the latter's book on his "philosophy in the making" violate this requirement of scientificity. In these selections, Meillassoux proposes, as though it were self-evident, that no materialist natural scientific account of the surfacing of sentient and sapient life out of nonliving matter is possible. He proposes this as an a priori explanatory constraint on the sciences.[26] However, at least for the historical time being, whether or not scientific solutions to emergence-type hard problems are a priori impossible looks to be itself an open a posteriori issue. In other words, Meillassoux declares this matter resolved while offering no assessment whatsoever of ongoing research programs directly addressing these topics in the life sciences and philosophy of mind. He totally ignores the past seven decades of biology, from the Miller-Urey experiment to Dolly the sheep and Craig Venter, when pronouncing on the topic of the emergence of life from matter. Rather than opening up his philosophy to scientific theories and evidence in thinking emergentist models of real material geneses playing meta-/retrotranscendental roles, he categorically excludes and dismisses out of hand the relevance of such resources in "Divine Inexistence."

More troublingly, Meillassoux holds up "advent *ex nihilo*" as the sole concept capable of doing justice to the emergences of life and thought in the wake of the purportedly preordained failures of the sciences to do so.[27] This conception of genesis is an intellectually permissible option for him on the basis of his hyperchaotic ontology as per *After Finitude*. How so? As noted, from Meillassoux's perspective, neither science nor any other sort of discipline, beginning with nothing more than nonliving material substances and the explanatory discourses appropriate to these kinds of beings, can explain adequately the arising of life and thought out of the spheres of nonliving matter. Sentience and sapience, as ostensibly different in kind from the non–sentient/sapient, are said to be not even dormant potentials latently dwelling within the physical world as it exists apart from any and every consciousness. There allegedly is nothing in the material that could give rise to the transcendent(al) as more-than-material (i.e., life and thought).

Where the materialist sciences and their philosophical comrades stumble, the divinological ontology of hyper-Chaos triumphantly strides forward as a savior. In the wake of ontologizing Hume's epistemological problem of induction and deriving "the necessity of contingency" from this gesture, "anything is possible" (to borrow a phrase from Hallward's critical assessment of Meillassoux) in Meillassoux's lawless acosmos. Within this anarchic expanse of being(s), entities and events always can occur that violate what, up until these occurrences transpire, seem to be the patterns and rules of cause-and-effect enchainments. Moreover, such violations of apparent "laws of nature" are not, according to Meillassoux, visible realizations of previously invisible possibilities eternally slumbering as potentialities hidden in the supposed subterranean entrails of reality.[28] Rather, new things are able suddenly to surface for no reason and out of nothing—as already observed, Meillassoux both suspends the principle of sufficient reason and stipulates that radically contingent newness springs up independently of prior causes and potentials—thanks to the hyperchaotic nature of being *an sich*. These reasonless, groundless emergences would be instances of advent ex nihilo.

Meillassoux proceeds to provide a more technical typology of emergences out of nothing as part of his divinological ontology of hyper-Chaos. He identifies *"matter, life, and thought"* as the "three *orders*" of advent ex nihilo testified to by what is found already to exist in extant reality.[29] In other words, Meillassoux's stance here is that the genesis of each of these dimensions of being (i.e., the coming-to-be of the material out of the immaterial, the living out of nonliving matter, and thinking out of nonthinking life) is inexplicable save for recourse to the concept of advent ex nihilo and its accompanying hyperchaotic ontological scaffolding. Related to this tripartite typology, Meillassoux distinguishes between "the world" (as post-Cantorian infinitely detotalized being in and of itself), "Worlds" (as the orders of matter, life, and thought), and the "intra-Worldly" (occurrences not of the advent ex nihilo of new orders, but happenings unfolding within an already existing order).[30] Divinology's *Dieu à venir*, were this divinity to erupt into existence out of nowhere unpredictably, would amount to a new World/order surging up out of the *Ur*-anarchy of the necessarily contingent and not-Whole world of hyper-Chaos.[31] This would be a fourth advent ex nihilo after the emergence of humans as thinking beings, rather than just another intra-Worldly event.

I am tempted to pause for a moment over the enigma of how Meillassoux reconciles his talk of emergence as real spatiotemporal genesis in *After Finitude* with his classification of matter as generated through advent ex nihilo in "Divine Inexistence." What, in Meillassoux's view, precedes the existence of matter? Is what presumably would be the pure nothingness of an immaterial void—Meillassoux lists no fourth order (other than the God-to-come showing up after thinking humans) as a World before the advent of matter—itself situated in a space and a time? Or does real space-time only come into being with the genesis of matter? Are these very questions to be resolved by philosophy, physics, both, or neither (or even, maybe, a postreligious quasi-religion)? What is accessible by Meillassoux in print at this date leaves these queries unanswered.

In "Divine Inexistence," Meillassoux observes that the notion of advent ex nihilo allows for solving the problems of the emergences of both life and thought.[32] In a certain sense, this is obvious. Once one erects a worldview in which levels and layers of reality randomly can pop into existence out of far less than thin air, one can wash one's hands of the difficulties animating not only debates within and between reductionists and emergentists in biology and philosophy, but the long-standing, deeply entrenched antagonism between idealism and materialism in the history of ideas across its vast sweep. I would suggest that Meillassoux offers not so much a solution to these problems as a refusal to acknowledge and treat them as problems (as is also indicated by his above-criticized dogmatism bluntly asserting their a priori insolubility for empirical, experimental science). Meillassoux sometimes self-identifies as a materialist, but only infidelity to materialism permits dismissing the challenges that confront all nonreductive materialisms relying upon the sciences (in particular, those materialisms faithful to the Darwin-event) and seeking to elucidate the immanent genesis of dematerialized, ideal, more-than-natural, transcendental subjectivity out of material, real, natural, meta-/retrotranscendental substance.

At the same point in "Divine Inexistence," Meillassoux character-izes advent ex nihilo as *"an irreligious notion of the origin of pure novelty."*[33] If this concept is not religious, then what concept is? Advent ex nihilo is an idea dependent on a vision of being incompatible with the sciences (assuming Meillassoux's approach to the hurdle of frequentialism falls flat, as I argue it does) and expressive of an ontology in which unanalyz-able and uncaused events akin to miracles are able spontaneously to hap-pen. I would tack on to this a reminder of something I drew attention to earlier: Meillassoux does not eradicate the bundle of attributes and properties said to belong to God particularly by pre-Kantian metaphy-sicians and theologians. Instead, whereas these predecessors assigned this set of features and predicates to a single entity (i.e., the one-and-only God), Meillassoux distributes them (and, hence, preserves them) across two entities (i.e., hyper-Chaos and the God-to-come). Duotheism still remains theism. Meillassoux's philosophy is, it seems, only debatably irreligious.

I have a few more criticisms of "Divine Inexistence" to voice before shifting away from Meillassoux and toward outlining how the subsequent two volumes of *Prolegomena to Any Future Materialism* will contribute to the construction of my own system, a defensible transcendental materialist position. First, Meillassoux's depictions of advent ex nihilo reveal a sig-nificant inconsistency in his conception of this load-bearing component of his ontology. Throughout "Divine Inexistence," he speaks of these emergences out of nothing as "effects." Again and again, Meillassoux stresses that there is more in the effect of an advent ex nihilo than in its cause; each World/order is an irreducible surplus of being in relation to the World(s)/order(s) preceding it (matter is in excess of whatever came before it, as is the case for life vis-à-vis matter and thought vis-à-vis life).[34] Yet, as a notion entirely consistent with and dependent upon Meil-lassoux's ontology of hyper-Chaos, advent ex nihilo cannot be under-stood along the lines of any cause-and-effect relation.

As I highlighted previously, Meillassoux stringently denies that the emergence of hyperchaotic newness (such as the geneses of his three Worlds/orders) can be traced back to implicit potentialities that merely are made into explicit actualities in advents. His notion of advent "ex nihilo" designates precisely this denial: nothing, in terms of underground possibilities already present but shrouded prior to a respective advent, preordains and produces such an advent. Moreover, in light of Meillassoux's reliance on Hume, the idea of causality operative in the speculative universe of hyper-Chaos, as itself the result of ontologizing Hume's problem of induction, would have to resemble the Humean empiricist one, with its three ingredients of spatiotemporal "contiguity" (a cause-and-effect relation involves entities and events proximate to each other in space and time), temporal "priority" (a cause-and-effect relation is consistently recognized as such only for as long as the chronological sequence of successive events remains the same in repeated experiences, with event A always preceding event B), and "constant conjunction" (the greater the number of iterations of a given pattern involving the first two ingredients of causality à la Hume, the more "accustomed" or "habituated" the mind will be to "believe" as anticipate and expect this pattern to continue to hold indefinitely off into the future).[35] As an empiricist, Hume ponders causality only insofar as this notion functions within the experienced world consisting of spatial and/or temporal contents accessible to consciousness. Thus, to word it in a contextually fitting fashion, Meillassoux "hypostatizes," in Kant's exact sense, the idea of causality upon which he relies when, in "Divine Inexistence," he renders advent ex nihilo as an effect (just as, for Kant, applying the concept of causality to the rapport between noumenal thing-in-itself and phenomenal object-as-appearance counts as an illegitimate extension of a concept of the understanding, itself legitimately employed within the limits of possible experience, beyond these same limits).[36] Put in the very language of "Divine Inexistence," a Hume-derived idea of causality always would have to be intra-Worldly (specifically, intramaterial and, as per Hume's Locke-inspired associationist psychology, intramental) and not inter-Worldly. But, of course, advent ex nihilo refers to the inter-Worldly, as the emergence of a new World instead of a happening internal to an old World, and not the intra-Worldly.

Therefore, within the constraints of his own system, Meillassoux cannot coherently characterize advent ex nihilo as a dynamic wherein an effect wholly irreducible to a prior cause explodes into existence— although this is what he does repeatedly in "Divine Inexistence." The World or Worlds preexisting a World that comes to be are not causes in any meaningful sense in that Meillassoux refuses to posit preceding potentials in old Worlds for new Worlds. In Meillassoux's Weltanschauung, if a relation between entities and events can be established as a connection in which one spatiotemporal entity/event appears to flow seamlessly within time from another spatiotemporal entity/event— this is integral to the Humean-style notion of causality appropriated by the author of *After Finitude*—then what this relation reflects is an intra-Worldly process instead of anything inter-Worldly (i.e., an advent ex nihilo). Or, again in the parlance of "Divine Inexistence," Meillassoux's casting of emergences out of nothing as effects is a hypostatization in which he conflates the causeless possibility of the disruption of all causes (i.e., the posited productive potency of the world as hyperchaotic) with the causalities at play within the already-here dimensions of acknowledged reality (i.e., any cause-and-effect relation as an intra-Worldly process internal to its corresponding enveloping World). As an instance of hyper-Chaos, an advent ex nihilo is an uncaused, lawless rupture with all preceding causal laws; if it can be said to be an effect, it is a paradoxical, oxymoronic "uncaused effect" with no relation whatsoever to what came before. Emergences of unprecedentedly novel Worlds, as precipitates of a hyperchaotic being devoid of sufficient reasons, are absolute discontinuities totally and completely without connection to anything prior.

This move of calling advents ex nihilo "effects" deceptively makes it seem as though they are elements of an account of causal structures and dynamics. In *After Finitude,* Meillassoux pledges to furnish a materialist philosophical clarification of the problem of irreducible emergences as this problem features in the natural sciences and closely associated disciplinary domains (modern scientific standpoints are unwilling and unable to dispense with the concept of causality, however broadly or narrowly construed). Instead, Meillassoux's divinological ontology as per "Divine Inexistence" simply explains (away) these geneses as inexplicable (through recourse to the unlimited capricious creativity of hyper-Chaos). It would be inaccurate to consider what Meillassoux proposes to be some sort of emergentist paradigm (as Badiou perhaps does) insofar as the very word "emergence" suggests one thing arising from another thing. The Meillassouxian idea of advent ex nihilo excludes the assertion of any link, including that of "arising from," between what was and is, on the one hand, and what comes to be "out of nothing," on the other hand. Recourse to the language of cause and effect is invalid by Meillassoux's own lights within the parameters of his philosophical discourse aiming at being *an sich.* Moreover, reliance on notions of causality surreptitiously supports an illusion of explanatory power, namely, the misleading appearance that the notion of hyperchaotic advent ex nihilo is in any way an answer to the types of questions bound up with scientific and materialist discussions concerning models of emergence (to which cause-and-effect relations are indispensable). The ontology of divinology is not so much a metatranscendentalism of real spatiotemporal geneses (foreshadowed in *After Finitude*) as a wholesale substitution of advent for genesis.

Elsewhere in "Divine Inexistence," Meillassoux undermines his materialist credentials even further. His speculations about the coming-into-being of life seem to emphasize my criticism that the ontology of hyper-Chaos does not truly qualify as an emergentist view:

> It could be that, like all radical novelty, the advent of life (the appear-ance of a hidden anatomical organization or cognitive activity) *is accom-panied by the simultaneous advent of material configurations that rupture with the physical laws in the midst of which they emerge.* Indeed, nothing forbids us from thinking that the advent of the qualitative universe of vital con-tents *should be one and the same as the advent of the material underpinning by which these contents are inscribed in the material Universe* that precedes them. In that case, the appearance of the material organization of life would have *no reason to obey the frequential constants of matter.* The configurations of life would break the laws of chance, because they would not at all be the possible cases *of* matter, but rather the correlate *within* matter of the appearance *ex nihilo* of vital contents.[37]

Meillassoux's use of the word "emerge" at the end of the first sentence has nothing to do with any variety of emergentism, serving instead as a synonym for advent ex nihilo. Furthermore, this passage makes evi-dent Meillassoux's advocacy of something incredibly close to outright ontological dualism—albeit in the form of the triad of the material, the living, and the thinking instead of the more traditional dyad of the physical (à la Cartesian *res extensa*) and the metaphysical (à la Cartesian *res cogitans*). Consistent with his distinction between the three orders of the Worlds of matter, life, and thought, life's "vital contents" are wholly and completely different in kind from the being of nonliving material "contents." For Meillassoux, and by sharp contrast with Darwin and his successors (including those of his offspring resisting reductionism), the vitalist "stuff" of living substances, whatever it consists of (awareness, drives, energies, forces, impulses, instincts, qualia, sentience . . . ?), is not generated out of matter and its regularities. Life's advent ex nihilo involves a "*rupture with . . . physical laws*"; "vital contents" are not "*of* mat-ter." Like all Meillassouxian advents, the (non-)emergence of life is not the immanent real, material, and spatiotemporal genesis of the there-after transcendent(al) as dematerialized/more-than-material. Rather, such an advent is the mysterious, incomprehensible surfacing of a new category of being utterly distinct from whatever else existed prior to this winking-into-existence.

Meillassoux's musings in the preceding block quotation may be motivated by the intention to head off mistaken impressions to the effect that hyperchaotic ontology's advent ex nihilo of life is in any manner compatible with the materialism of Darwinian evolutionary theories. In the latter, the immanent and contingent geneses of new physical configurations within material being gives rise to the possibility of properties associated with various kinds of life (and thought) emerging on the basis of these physical configurations. Meillassoux unambiguously demonstrates here that he washes his hands of even a nonreductionist version of this sort of biomaterial emergentism. The doctrines of his divinological "adventism" commit him to a strict ontological dualism of matter (i.e., nonvital material "contents") and life (i.e., "vital contents"), with the latter severed from any conceivable connection to the former.

Harman's study of Meillassoux contains an interview in addition to the translated excerpts from "Divine Inexistence." At one point, Harman asks Meillassoux:

> Although your book on the virtual God is not yet published, some critics are already attacking it in the same way that St Anselm's ontological proof has always been attacked. For example, "Why doesn't Meillassoux speak about a virtual unicorn that does not yet exist but might exist in the future?" Or, as Adrian Johnston puts it in a forthcoming critical article on your work, "a virtual flying spaghetti monster that does not yet exist but might exist in the future." What makes God so special out of all these virtual objects that might arise contingently without reason at any time in the future?[38]

Harman is referring to a remark I make in what appears in this book as the penultimate paragraph of the seventh chapter—this quip comes at the close of a more sustained critical assessment of the ontology of hyper-Chaos and its handling of the challenge of frequentialism. Meillassoux's answer to Harman's question is worth quoting in full:

> Everything is possible, as I have said. But it is senseless to believe in the rise of a virtual event (one that does not conform to the laws of our world) in the same fashion in which I await the rise of a potential event (one that does conform to the laws of our world). I can justifiably evaluate the probability that a comet will strike the earth and destroy every form of life: it is a potential event. On the other hand, a virtual event lies outside probability. And there we find its true strangeness: it is neither probable, nor improbable, nor impossible. If I have to determine my relationship with this type of possible, it would be in a very different fashion than in relation to a potentiality. The question becomes: of what absolutely remarkable event is virtual becoming capable, and how can this event modify my subjectivity once it is recognized as possible?

> And here it is not unicorns (or spaghetti monsters) that appear in
> the first rank. Instead, it is the end aimed at by all messianisms and all
> revolutionisms, though in a form that seems to me always defective. It
> is universal Justice, the equality of everyone, and even the equality of
> the living with the dead: Justice guaranteed as eternally possible by the
> absolute inexistence of God—that is to say, by the ultimate Non-sense
> of super-chaos. For if God does not exist, everything becomes fragile,
> even death. If God does not exist, things become capable of anything:
> whether of the absurd, or of reaching their highest state. Everything is
> irreversible, but nothing is definitive.[39]

Meillassoux does not employ the potentiality-virtuality distinction as a direct response to me. This indeed would be a false step since, as far as what present-best life science indicates, flying spaghetti monsters are not true potentialities (and, hence, could only be virtualities in Meillassoux's scheme). Furthermore, given the historicity of the sciences themselves (of which Meillassoux is well aware), the determination of the distinction between potentiality and virtuality always would have to be made from within the world of potentialities; expressed in Hegelian fashion, the difference between the potential and the virtual invariably is constrained to be a difference internal to the potential itself. That is to say, insofar as, one, a Meillassouxian "virtual event" (i.e., a hyperchaotic advent ex nihilo, such as the arrival of the God-to-come) is defined as something that "does not conform to the laws of our world" (as does a "potential event") and, two, scientific determination of these "laws" is subject to ongoing revisions and shifts of varying degrees of radicality (as any contemporary student of Humean empiricism not willing to make the philosophically and scientifically disastrous move of treating all these revisions and shifts as responses to hyperchaotic changes in real being is exquisitely conscious), the category of virtuality is a parasitic by-product in relation to the historically unstable and open-ended drawing and redrawing of the lines of the so-called laws of nature by the empirical, experimental sciences. Consequently, for the time being at least, the flying spaghetti monster-to-come must be classified as a "virtual object" à la Meillassoux. And, therefore, the potentiality-virtuality distinction contributes nothing here by way of a response to my critique.

The advents of both Meillassoux's God-to-come and my Dawkins-inspired flying spaghetti monster-to-come would have to qualify as Meillassouxian virtual events ex nihilo. In the lengthy quotation immediately above, Meillassoux appears to accept this. But if, as I argue, Meillassoux's recourse to trans-finite set theory in differentiating between chance and contingency (corresponding to potentiality and virtuality respectively) as a means of circumventing frequentialist difficulties backfires, then the above-alleged "true strangeness" of a virtual event as "neither probable, nor improbable, nor impossible" evaporates into thin air. In other words, if the post-Cantorian universe of infinite infinities actually renders any one virtual contingency even more unlikely than the most unlikely of potential chances, then, mathematically speaking, the likelihood of Meillassouxian advents ex nihilo is so incomprehensibly improbable (measured by the massive cardinalities of trans-finite set theory's limitless zoo of gargantuan infinities) as asymptotically to hurtle with infinite speed toward the point of being impossible. Hence, the God-to-come is no more and no less likely than the future materialization of a flying spaghetti monster. Neither deserves serious intellectual attention.

However, as the preceding quotation and "Divine Inexistence" both reveal, Meillassoux believes that the divinological God-to-come indeed merits being singled out for sustained philosophical consideration from among the immeasurably proliferating infinities of virtual possibilities. In the interview with Harman, he states, "It is not unicorns (or spaghetti monsters) that appear in the first rank." With both the God-to-come and the flying spaghetti monster in the same Meillassouxian ontological category (i.e., that of contingent virtual events as advents ex nihilo), Meillassoux abruptly switches to a poorly specified ethico-moral register in which possible contingent virtual events as advents ex nihilo are "ranked" in the order of which ones most deserve to be speculatively pondered based on human dreams and aspirations.

This sudden jump from the ontological to the ethico-moral is problematic for five reasons (at least). First, Meillassoux presumes, without supporting argumentation, that descriptions of *être* (being), when all is said and done, ought to be subordinated to prescriptions (stemming from human wants and worries) of *peut-être* (may-be[ing]). At a minimum, he owes his readers a substantial explicit justification for trying to situate a heterodox rendition of humanity's hopes at the grounding center of philosophy.

Second, Meillassoux's ranking of yet-to-be-realized virtual events tacitly relies on an undefended philosophical psychology/anthropology of human desiring vulnerable to contestation (especially on psychoanalytic grounds, but even at the level of current research in the very young field of "happiness studies"). This is an instance of superimposing the parameters of potentiality onto the dizzyingly greater-than-astronomical numbers of multiplicities of virtuality—more precisely, projecting the very limited range of humanity's already-extant and actual imaginings of certain possibilities (such as the possibility of a God who really exists in ways that would matter to humans as per certain established monotheistic doctrines) into the unimaginably sprawling vastness of everything possible in a hyperchaotic reality unchained from the principle of sufficient reason and obeying nothing more than the austere law of non-contradiction alone.

Related to this second point, in his atheist manifesto, 1927's *The Future of an Illusion*, Freud differentiates between an "illusion" (*Illusion*) in his precise sense and a simple "error" (*Irrtum*). Therein, he specifies:

> An illusion is not the same thing as an error; nor is it necessarily an error . . . What is characteristic of illusions is that they are derived from human wishes [*menschlichen Wünschen*]. In this respect, they come near to psychiatric delusions [*Wahnidee*]. But they differ from them, too, apart from the more complicated structure of delusions. In the case of delusions, we emphasize as essential their being in contradiction with reality [*Widerspruch gegen die Wirklichkeit*]. Illusions need not necessarily be false—that is to say, unrealizable or in contradiction to reality. For instance, a middle-class girl may have the illusion that a prince will come and marry her. This is possible; and a few such cases have occurred. That the Messiah will come and found a golden age is much less likely . . . Thus we call a belief an illusion when a wish-fulfilment [*Wunscherfüllung*] is a prominent factor in its motivation, and in doing so we disregard its relations to reality, just as the illusion itself sets no store by verification.[40]

Freud's mention of "the Messiah" as an example reveals that he recognizes unfalsifiable religious beliefs not to be mere errors as "in contradiction with reality." Freudian reality (*Wirklichkeit*), in this precise case, is implicitly defined in a minimal manner as what is "realizable" in terms of logical possibility alone, namely, what Meillassoux, after banishing the principle of sufficient reason as well as ontologizing the Humean problem of induction, reduces reality to being as hyperchaotic. Meillassoux's divinology of the God-to-come, like all previous religions, definitely would qualify for Freud as orbiting around an illusion. Pure, bare logical possibility by itself already admits as hypothetical eventualities an unimaginably large number of things—this number is even larger when logical possibility is decoupled from any other constraints, such as all reasons or causes—including a *Dieu à venir*. Narrowing down the vast universe of logical possibilities and the even vaster universe of hyperchaotic being to a single messianic visionary prediction requires assistance from currently influential wishes (*Wünschen*), as Freud observes and Meillassoux more or less concedes through his criteria for ranking the attention-worthiness of virtual events as future advents ex nihilo.

But this narrowing-down, despite its deceptive effects, adds nothing to the probability of its wishfully selected possibility. To paraphrase Freud, the dream of the salvation of all sentient beings living and deceased by a God-to-come is infinitely less likely than the fairy-tale fantasy of a working-class girl being rescued from her grinding existence by a gallant prince galloping by out of nowhere on his white horse. In fact, viewed from a psychoanalytic angle, any picture of reality that accords too closely with wishes is rightfully deserving of suspicion. Philosophical thought (along with psychoanalytic interpretation) should avoid being put in the position of being led around by the nose by wishful thinking.

An additional Freudian text is worth referring to in response to Meillassoux's divinology. Harman's selections from "Divine Inexistence" end with Meillassoux proposing a variant of Pascal's wager. The four possible options for wagering are: "1. *Not believing in God because he does not exist*" (i.e., atheism); "2. *Believing in God because he exists*" (i.e., theism); "3. *Not believing in God because he exists*" (i.e., Luciferian revolt); "4. *Believing in God because he does not exist*" (i.e., Meillassouxian divinology).[41] Meillassoux then closes with a Pascalian "One must choose."[42] He eliminates the first choice on emotional grounds—whether an ethical assessment of feeling-states can and should be decisive for ontological reflections is itself highly questionable—charging that atheism inevitably results in the "impasse" of "despair" as "sadness, tepidity, cynicism, and the disparagement of what makes us human."[43] Perusing Freud's succinct 1916 essay "On Transience" helps show just how contentious and far from apodictic are Meillassoux's assumptions about affective life. As a well-analyzed human being, Freud is willing and able to convert into positive sources of emotional sustenance and invigoration precisely what Meillassoux perceives in atheism as necessarily leading to a quagmire of negative affects.[44] If Meillassoux's process-of-elimination argumentative strategy here does not work, as psychoanalysis suggests, then another reason for preferring divinology falls away.

My related, third point involves the question Meillassoux poses so as to set the standard for his ethico-moral prioritization of divinology's *Dieu à venir* over the unlimited infinities of other possible advents ex nihilo allowed for in his ontology: "Of what absolutely remarkable event is virtual becoming capable, and how can this event modify my subjectivity once it is recognized as possible?" This query assumes that past and present (i.e., actual) expectations of what would count as "remarkable" and "subjectivity modifying" would be met in conformity with those same expectations by what Meillassoux himself casts as an irruption of overwhelmingly radical newness (i.e., the virtual as the advent ex nihilo of the God-to-come). It appears Meillassoux is not imaginative enough with respect to his abandonment of philosophizing to the whims and fancies of too much imagination.

Fourth, and following from the preceding third point, Meillassoux's divinology stealthily reintroduces continuity between the past and present of the actual and the potential (i.e., chance), on the one side, and the future of the virtual (i.e., contingency), on the other side. That is to say, the very sort of continuity disqualified by the idea of advents ex nihilo—according to Meillassoux, such hyperchaotic geneses are absolute ruptures in the order of being bearing no relation whatsoever to anything coming before their occurrences—returns in the guise of smooth, tight connections of resemblance between, on the one hand, select aspects of God as already described in specific religious discourses of the past and present and, on the other hand, the future God-to-come. As an apparent fulfillment of core components of various prophecies of old, divinology's supposedly virtual *Dieu à venir* is all too linked to the actual-potential couplet—and this in tension with the tenor of Meillassoux's insistence on the ontological surplus of total and complete discontinuity ostensibly ushered in with an advent ex nihilo.

Fifth, even accepting Meillassoux's gesture of elevating practical over theoretical philosophical concerns (in terms of selectively spotlighting certain ontological possibilities on the basis of ethico-moral aspirations), one should remember that practical philosophy includes the political in addition to the ethico-moral. Divinological ontology, from a Marxist perspective, is a recipe for religious-style quietism and *attentisme*. Kneeling down before the twin idols of hyper-Chaos and the God-to-come, patiently waiting for the former to deliver the latter so that He can save each wretched of the suffering earth who ever lived, holds the danger of all divine supplements (nontraditional or otherwise) of replacing activity with passivity. To resort to a cliché, the ethico-moral Perfect of the *Dieu à venir* risks becoming the enemy of the good of political action. To be more exact, Meillassoux's ideal Justice-with-a-capital-J (i.e., "universal Justice, the equality of everyone, and even the equality of the living with the dead: Justice guaranteed as eternally possible by the absolute inexistence of God—that is to say, by the ultimate Non-sense of super-chaos") threatens to sap motivational energies that might otherwise be directed toward real justice via interventions in the *hic et nunc.* Leftist politics has nothing to gain and only can lose from tolerating the overshadowing of its this-worldly revolutionary prophecies by this new theosophical messianism of the entirely otherworldly concept of the fourth World/order of the God-to-come. In this same vein, I cannot resist here quoting the young Maoist Badiou of 1975's *Theory of Contradiction:* "There is the radically New only because there are corpses that no trumpet of Judgment will ever reawaken."[45]

Later on in the segments from "Divine Inexistence" translated and published by Harman, Meillassoux comments, "Even today, the great philosophers are treated as sophists by the priests, and as priests by the sophists."[46] He may feel himself to be one of the "great philosophers" in jeopardy of being misrecognized in light of his divinology of the *Dieu à venir*. However, I view his attempts to circumnavigate around the deadlock between sophistry and religiosity as resulting not in an overcoming of this impasse through the founding of a neither-sophistical-nor-religious stance, but, instead, as combining the worst of both (one ought to hear an echo of the Leninist "Both are worse!" here). Much more so than in the case of Badiou (and even Lacan himself), Meillassoux's ostensibly materialist speculative philosophy is yet another symptom of the lack of a still-to-be-consolidated materialism that would be fully secularized so as to be stringently atheistic to its very core.

In *After Finitude*, Meillassoux briefly discusses Jean-René Vernes's *Critique of Aleatory Reason, or Descartes Contra Kant* (1982). Meillassoux's 2006 debut book closely resembles this compact treatise at the levels of both argumentative style and philosophical content, as Meillassoux himself readily admits.[47] Several similarities merit being highlighted in the course of a succinct summary of Vernes's position. Vernes maintains that "the problem of the existence of matter logically precedes that of the constancy of laws."[48] In the same vein, he emphatically claims, "*One cannot prove the constancy of laws if one does not first prove the existence of matter beforehand.*"[49] Although Meillassoux undermines causal patterns as constants, he certainly agrees with Vernes that a philosophical justification and defense of realism (in this context, the mind-independent existence of objective matter in and of itself as taken for granted by the default worldview of the natural sciences) is of the highest priority. Furthermore, both authors stress that reasserting a realist philosophy requires undoing the critical turn of Kantian transcendental idealism. Vernes presents this as a choice between Descartes or Kant,[50] just as Meillassoux appeals to the Galilean-Cartesian distinction between primary and secondary qualities at the start of his endeavor in *After Finitude*.

For Vernes, "science is Cartesian and certainly not Kantian."[51] In the fourth and sixth of his *Meditations on First Philosophy*, Descartes tries rationally to prove the existence of extended substances over and above thinking substances, namely, spatial entities really separate in their being from mental entities.[52] In other words, he offers a philosophical demonstration purporting to provide the simultaneously epistemological and ontological (i.e., metaphysical as first-philosophical) foundations for each and every branch of knowledge grounded thereby, including the then newborn sciences of modernity. *Critique of Aleatory Reason* and *After Finitude* both set out to accomplish a post-Kantian repetition, each via its own distinct means, of the Cartesian effort to establish through philo-sophical reason a firm basis for realism in the dual registers of ontology and epistemology.

Apropos the relations between philosophy and science, Vernes strikes a fine balance between the extremes of philosophical hubris and humility. On the one hand, he assigns to philosophy, and not science, the power to determine and declare when the ultimate demands of reason have been satisfied.[53] His prime illustration is the question of realism. Unlike philosophical reasoning, scientific observation and experimenta-tion are constitutively incapable, on their own, of demonstrating or prov-ing the ontologically real as mind-independent status of their results. For Vernes, philosophers are charged with proving the axiomatic intui-tions and assumptions of the scientists that the scientists themselves can-not prove, left to their own properly specific disciplinary devices. On the other hand, the kind of contributions philosophy thereby makes to knowledge are very modest ones.[54] Philosophy establishes the sheer, mere existence of real things apart from consciousness, whereas the sciences yield specifications regarding the essences and natures of these things.[55] Put differently, only philosophy can show that reality exists separately from sentient and sapient subjectivity. However, the nature of this reality can be delineated solely by the empirical and experimental sciences (I am quite receptive to this proposed division of labor between philos-ophy and science). Meillassoux sometimes, but far from always, exhibits a Vernesian balance between philosophical ambition and restraint.

How, exactly, does Vernes argue for a robust realism? Like Meil-lassoux after him, his case makes reference to the modalities of con-tingency and necessity. More precisely, Vernes recommends reversing the standard associations of the rational a priori and the experiential a posteriori with the necessary and the contingent respectively.[56] In assert-ing that "the idea of chance [*hasard*] logically precedes that of deter-minism,"[57] he means that pure reason, prior to particular empirical observations through experience (i.e., reason as a priori rather than a posteriori), is capable of representing to itself an indefinite number of possible ways in which the experienced world hypothetically could be (with allegedly only the unthinkable being truly impossible).[58] As Hume already suggests, a priori reasoning, without the constraints imposed by a posteriori experiencing, is at liberty to imagine countless possibilities for how entities, events, and states of affairs in empirically observable reality might be arranged and function. The structures and dynamics most proper to the mind, namely, those belonging to the activities of nonempirical reason, testify to an infinite number of contingent pos-sibilities and not to the single necessary actuality passively registered by empirical experience (i.e., a one-and-only world apparently governed by constant causal laws). Vernes declares that this situation cries out for a satisfactory account.[59] He insists, *"we have need of an explanation when the laws of nature appear contrary to the laws of thought."*[60]

From Vernes's standpoint, the sole viable explanation for this discrepancy between "the laws of nature" (corresponding to the experiential a posteriori) and "the laws of thought" (corresponding to the rational a priori) amounts to an affirmation of realism. He proposes that the incredibly circumscribed range of observed causal patterns and rules as compared with the virtually boundless expanse of rationally conceivable causal patterns and rules—experience reveals one actual necessity whereas reason discloses many possible contingencies—bears witness to the existence of a nonsubjective real(ity) impinging upon knowing subjectivity.[61] The sapient mind tames and domesticates the spiraling abyss of its own inner infinity exclusively through having empirical experiences impressed upon it, which serve to discount the proliferating surpluses of pure reason (in the form of the excess of contingent possibilities) through thrusting forward a tightly bounded bandwidth of necessary actualities. A radical Other, in the guise of realism's mind-independent objective being *an sich* of the material universe, is identified as the imposing source of these impressions. Obviously, Vernes relies on the traditional realist appeal to the passivity and receptivity of sensory-perceptual experience as evidence of an extramental Outside responsible for slapping external constraints on the otherwise free play of imagination and reason. Moreover, he remarks that his arguments in *Critique of Aleatory Reason* show how a careful consideration of the "calculus of probabilities" transforms chance from a sign of irrationality into a keystone supporting a rational and realist philosophical edifice.[62]

Interestingly, Meillassoux, despite being sympathetic to Vernes's endeavor on several counts, uses *Critique of Aleatory Reason* primarily as an excuse to reiterate the critique of probabilistic reasoning crucial to the handling of the problem of frequentialism in *After Finitude*. Specifically, Vernes is charged with continuing to adhere to a pre-Cantorian reckoning of probabilities according to which continual recurrences of experientially observed causal sequences are explicable solely through positing the real-world absoluteness of these causal sequences as ostensibly unbreakable laws of nature. At root, Meillassoux takes issue with Vernes's insistence on confining contingency to the "laws of thought" and placing realism under the authority of the modality of necessity.[63]

I mention Vernes, and Meillassoux's employment of him, in order to bring this postface to a close through presenting the transcendental materialist framework I will develop in the sequel two volumes of this *Pro-*

legomena to Any Future Materialism trilogy. As, in part, an *Aufhebung* of my immanent critiques of Lacan, Badiou, and Meillassoux, transcendental materialism preserves the merits of their stances while, at the same time, surmounting their difficulties and weaknesses as I have laid them out in this first volume. As I signposted in the preface, the second and third volumes (*A Weak Nature Alone* and *Substance Also as Subject*) will delineate the necessary/metatranscendental and sufficient/transcendental conditions respectively for an uncompromisingly materialist but vehemently antireductive (as well as antimechanical and antieliminative) theory of dematerialized subjectivity as thoroughly internal to material being in and of itself. In the largest philosophical scheme of things, this requires formulating a materialist ontology allowing for the real intramaterial genesis of more-than-material subjects who thereafter achieve independence from those aspects of material being that engendered them in the first place, consistent with an extremely strong version of nonreductive emergentism. Following Hegel and Žižek, among others, I am preoccupied with constructing an ontology of freedom, namely, an account of what metatranscendental substance must be (and has been) in the aftermath of the decision to affirm as an axiomatic intuition that desubstantialized transcendental subjects exist, albeit in modes nonetheless fully immanent to this same substantial being.[64]

The subsequent second volume of the trilogy, *A Weak Nature Alone,* focuses mainly on elaborating the fundamental ontological features of, to paraphrase Hegel's *Phenomenology of Spirit,* the substance behind, beneath, and beyond the subject (a subject that any thinking of substance must think as inhering within substance itself). With Badiou and Meillassoux, I reject the article of faith according to which philosophy can and should limit itself to a deontologized epistemology with nothing more than, at best, a complex conception of the cognizing mental apparatus. For a host of reasons, I concur with them that thought cannot indefinitely defer fulfilling its duty to build a realist and materialist ontology.[65] In particular, a theory of the autonomous negativity of self-relating subjectivity always is accompanied, at a minimum implicitly, by the shadow of a picture of being (as the ground of such subjectivity) that must be made explicit sooner or later.

A Weak Nature Alone spells out the metatranscendental necessary conditions for the spatiotemporal emergence of transcendental subjectivity from natural material substance. These ontological (pre)conditions for the real geneses of subjects are contingent (i.e., no eternally inherent teleology necessitates such geneses) as well as not sufficient (i.e., by themselves, the necessary conditions for the genesis of subjectivity do not provide an exhaustive account of what thereby is allowed to emerge out of them as more than what they are on their own). Despite my disagreements with these thinkers even with respect to the details of these very aspects of their bodies of thought, the three related ontological images of, one, the late Lacan's barring of the ground-zero Real as shot through with conflicts and gaps; two, Badiou's trans-finite detotalization of being qua being as a not-Whole non-One/All; and three, Meillassoux's science-inspired realism of contingency each contain components integral to the theory of being articulated in the next volume of *Prolegomena to Any Future Materialism.*

However, what about the preceding critical evaluation of Meillassoux culminating with the synopsis of Vernes and Meillassoux's objections to him? The comparison and contrast between Vernes and Meillassoux furnishes a means whereby to conclude this first volume of the trilogy with some foreshadowing of the transcendental materialist ontology to be constructed in the second volume. I agree with both Vernes and Meillassoux that thoroughgoing antirealist stances are unable to account in a satisfactorily plausible manner for a range of matters demanding to be acknowledged and explained; I share their realist instincts. Furthermore, I concur with Meillassoux that Vernes uncritically presupposes that cause-and-effect relations are necessarily stable constants, namely, purported laws of nature in the strongest sense of this phrase.

But I consider Meillassoux's alternative ontology of hyper-Chaos to fail judged by its own standards (for instance, in the face of the obstacle of frequentialism) and to reduce itself to the absurd (with divinology and its advents appearing to amount to Meillassoux performing a reductio ad absurdum on himself). Moreover, I am convinced that one can accept a realist ontologization of the Humean problem of induction without forcing oneself into the impasse of the arguably spurious either/or choice between the two extremes of Vernesian absolute necessity and Meillassouxian absolute contingency. That is to say, I embrace essential facets of the move of transforming Hume's epistemology into an ontology. Yet, unlike Meillassoux, I do not think that this entails being committed to a doctrine of the necessity of contingency in which (again to cite Hallward) anything is possible. More precisely, ontologically undoing the timeless necessity of causal connections does not automatically and immediately entail positing the supreme sovereign power of hyper-Chaos and everything this brings with it: especially the problem of frequentialism, the hypothesis of virtual events as advents ex nihilo, and faith in the logically possible future arrival of a God-to-come. As the concluding section of *A Weak Nature Alone* will demonstrate through recourse to the work of philosopher of science Nancy Cartwright, nature as spatiotemporal material being(s) can be and fundamentally is contingent on a plurality of irreducible levels without, for all that, being hyperchaotic à la Meillassoux.[66] I am confident in being able to take on the challenge of Hume's empiricist analyses of causality as a realist and a materialist (something Meillassoux maintains is mandatory) without either courting the deadly perils of frequentialism or giving rise to divinological spiritualism. In short and contra Meillassoux, the choice between necessity and hyper-Chaos is a false dilemma.

Additionally, as observed previously, Meillassoux thus far lacks a well-developed theory of the subject. The one he preliminarily outlines in the supplement to Brassier's English translation of *After Finitude* (i.e., a genetic, science-informed metatranscendentalism of the real spatio-temporal emergence of ideal transcendental subjectivity) is not delivered on as promised by the rest of his currently extant system. The above-mentioned closing part of *A Weak Nature Alone* ("Second Natures in Dappled Worlds") is crafted as a hinge between an ontology of meta-transcendental substance and a theory of transcendental subjectivity. It therefore outlines, in anticipation of *Substance Also as Subject* (the third and final volume of *Prolegomena to Any Future Materialism*), how the "weakening" of nature (via reconceptualizing it in the spirit of Lacan's barred Real and Badiou's not-Whole non-One/All) as contingent but not hyperchaotic permits constructing, at the intersections of philosophy, science, and psychoanalysis, a quasi-naturalist and entirely materialist conception of autonomous, self-reflexive/reflective subjects as denaturalized, more-than-material transcendences-in-immanence.

In the context of this concluding discussion of Meillassoux, Hume's reflections on "liberty and necessity" in both *A Treatise of Human Nature* and *An Enquiry Concerning Human Understanding* are useful given my purposes. With respect to the perennial philosophical debates between opposed partisans of freedom and determinism, one might be tempted to identify Hume as a compatibilist. However, insofar as he utilizes his empiricist epistemological analyses of causality to dismantle and liquidate the very distinction between liberty and necessity serving as the shared basis for the parties to this traditional dispute, he does not exactly make freedom and determinism "compatible" with each other. Instead, Hume essentially purports to show that problems of compatibility, along with the freedom/liberty–determinism/necessity distinction open to either compatibilist or noncompatibilist approaches, are pseudoproblems.

In a nutshell, Hume indicts advocates of both freedom and determinism for jointly assuming that nature, as the spatiotemporal entities and events manifest through sensory-perceptual experience, shows itself to human knowledge as a realm ruled by inviolably necessary, forever valid laws as enchainments of causes and effects. Put differently, the standard version of the old liberty-versus-necessity controversy is organized around the presumption that the kingdoms of natural matter are governed by exhaustively determining forces always and everywhere operative. Proponents of determinism maintain that there is nothing over and above these necessities, while proponents of freedom plead that a human liberty transcending the deterministic necessitation of material nature really exists too, in the form of a "free will" as an individual's power to be an uncaused self-cause of his or her thoughts and actions.

Of course, Hume's empiricist recasting of cause-and-effect relations has, as one of several significant upshots, the consequence of rendering null and void the assumption of natural necessity tacitly agreed upon by otherwise antagonistic partisans of freedom and determinism. In terms of the (post-Lockean, pre-Kantian) limits of the knowable, Humean empiricism seeks to illustrate the impossibility of one ever knowing a causal sequence as a "necessary connection" (i.e., an eternally holding, set-in-stone "law of nature"). As based in its initial origins on sensory-perceptual observations, the most of which empirical knowledge can be certain is that past and present experiences display certain patterned regularities involving the "constant conjunction" (i.e., repeated re-instantiation) of spatio-temporally contiguous objects and processes sequenced in the same order of temporal succession, in which one set type of occurrences are prior to another set type of occurrences. Hence, coupled with the problem of induction, the knowing mind is never actually supported in concluding that it has achieved a conceptual apprehension of real necessities (as causal determinations) within the natural world.

As regards liberty in addition to necessity, Hume executes a parallel maneuver in tandem with his dilution of the strength of claims apropos nature's deterministic character. Under the influence of associationist psychologies, he basically asserts that, through the effort of unbiased first-person introspection as well as honest examination of human social interactions, one will discern as much (or as little) patterned regularity at the level of humanity as at that of nature. In other words, Hume weakens the appearance of humans as free, as capriciously spontaneous, in conjunction with and to the same degree as he weakens the appearance of nature as determined, as ruled without exception or remainder by unbreakable bonds of causal necessitation. In short, Hume's conclusion is that, within the epistemological constraints of the humanly knowable, neither is nature as deterministic nor are humans as free as previously believed by participants in the traditional liberty-versus-necessity debate.[67]

In line with Meillassoux's ontologization of Hume's epistemology, I weaken not so much human knowledge of natural necessity, but natural necessity in and of itself. That is to say, I reject the supposition that necessities really exist in nature despite humanity's constitutive inability to know them (or, at least, know them as the necessities they actually are *an sich*). Instead, along with Meillassoux, I construe the problem of induction (plus problems of reduction in relation to the multiple branches and strata of the natural sciences) as signaling that the real spatiotemporal physical universe is permeated right down to the ground of its minimal, bare-bones being by factical contingencies (as well as ineliminable conflicts too). Nevertheless, as stated already and in sharp contrast to Meillassoux, I deny that this construal leads to the necessity of embracing hyper-Chaos and, in so doing, coming face-to-face with the daunting, formidable challenge of frequentialism.

Reconnecting with Hume on freedom and determinism, I consider his post-Lockean associationist model of the mental apparatus to be unsatisfactory. Yet I take from his handling of the opposition between liberty and necessity the intuition that human autonomy is, in select ways, not mysteriously different in kind from the rest of reality. Running with such an inspiration, I propose that this subjective power usually called "willing" (bearing in mind Hegel's insistence that cognitive, theoretical thinking and motivational, practical willing are inextricably intertwined)[68] is immanently anchored in (although not reducible to) the same lone ontological plane as other structures and phenomena. As seen, Hume dissolves the divide between free humanity and determined nature by watering down both the freedom of the former and the determinism of the latter. In related but importantly different fashions, like Meillassoux, I transform Hume's epistemological dilution of natural determinism into a load-bearing constituent of a new ontological apparatus.

A further step taken by my transcendental materialist theory of subjectivity is the systematic placement of this novel ontology as the substantial metatranscendental basis—this (baseless) base amounts to an ensemble of necessary-but-not-sufficient conditions making possible, again to put it in familiar Hegelese, substance becoming subject—for the accidental coming-to-be of emergent sapient subjects who, after their emergences, achieve a henceforward irreducible self-relating transcendence-in-immanence with respect to the rest of material being(s). Hume perceives the epistemological weakening (as denecessitation) of nature as closing within thought the gap between a no-longer-automatistic nature and a no-longer-spontaneous humanity. By contrast, Meillassoux holds open such gaps while de facto refusing to explain them insofar as he offers merely the implausible pseudo-explanatory device of appeal to virtual events of hyperchaotic advents ex nihilo. In a mirroring inversion of Hume, I perceive the ontological weakening of nature as opening within being qua being *an sich* the possibility of a gap between, on the one hand, a detotalized, disunified plethora of material substances riddled with contingencies and conflicts and, on the other hand, the bottom-up surfacing out of these substances of the recursive, self-relating structural dynamics of cognitive, affective, and motivational subjectivity—a subjectivity fully within but nonetheless free at certain levels from material nature. I wager that the genesis of this very gap can and should be explained in precise detail through a transcendental materialism drawing extensively upon Freudian-Lacanian psychoanalysis and the life sciences in addition to philosophy past and present (especially German idealism, Marxism, and Anglo-American analytic philosophy). This is the road to be paved in the subsequent two volumes of *Prolegomena to Any Future Materialism.*

Notes

There are two sets of abbreviations I use when citing certain works. All citations of Freud, in reference to the *Standard Edition,* are formatted as *SE,* followed by the volume number and the page number (e.g., *SE* 21: 154). The abbreviation system for Lacan's seminars is a little more complicated. All seminars are abbreviated *S,* followed by the Roman numeral of the volume number. For those seminars available in English (seminars 1, 2, 3, 7, 11, 17, and 20), I simply give the page numbers of the volumes as published by W. W. Norton and Company (e.g., Lacan, *SXI* 256). In a few instances, I refer to the original French editions of these translated seminars; when I do so, I indicate this in brackets as [Fr.]. For those seminars published in French in book form but not translated into English (seminars 4, 5, 8, 10, 16, 18, and 23), the listed page numbers refer to the French editions published by Éditions du Seuil (e.g., Lacan, *SX* 52). As for the rest of the seminars, the dates of the seminar sessions (month/day/year) are listed in place of page numbers (e.g., Lacan, *SXV* 12/6/67).

Preface

1. Johnston 2007a, 3–20; Johnston 2010b, 1–10; Johnston 2010d, 76–100; Johnston 2013c; Johnston 2012b; Johnston 2013a.
2. Johnston 2008b, 269–87.
3. Lacan 2005e, 67–102.
4. Johnston 2008a, 67–68; Johnston 2009c, 147–48, 178–81.
5. Johnston 2012b; Johnston 2014.

Introduction

1. Johnston 2010c, 157.
2. Lacan *SXIX,* 5/17/72.
3. Johnston 2008b, 189, 208, 286–87; Johnston 2009a, 41, 135; Johnston 2013c.
4. Badiou 1999a, 81–84; Badiou 2009a, 23–26.
5. Badiou 1999a, 28.
6. Ibid., 84.
7. Badiou 2011a, 36–37, 39; Badiou 2011d, 149.

212

8. Badiou 1982, 150.
9. Ibid.
10. Badiou 2008b, 14.
11. Marx 1976, 103; Badiou, Bellassen, and Mossot 2011, 62–63, 80–81.
12. Johnston 2008b, 85–90; Johnston 2009a, 119–24.
13. Johnston 2011a, 163–68.
14. Ibid., 161, 170.
15. Ibid., 162–70.
16. Badiou 2006g, 9–18.
17. Braver 2007, 3–11, 33–58, 497–514.

Chapter 1

1. Badiou 1982, 202.
2. Lucretius 1951, 92–93, 175–77; La Mettrie 1993, 85, 93, 117, 128, 133, 148–49.
3. Engels 1941, 31.
4. Kierkegaard 2004, 163.
5. Pascal 1966, 155.
6. Lenin 1972, 22–23, 33–34, 95, 106, 128–29, 140–42, 145, 167, 188–89, 191, 232, 321, 344, 407–13, 416–17, 431, 434.
7. Lacan *SXV*, 11/22/67; Lacan *SXVI*, 41; Lacan *SXXIII*, 72.
8. Lacan *SXVII*, 66.
9. Lacan *SXX*, 68, 70.
10. Lacan *SVII*, 213–14.
11. Sade 1968, 769–70, 772–73.
12. Lacan *SXVII*, 66.
13. Lucretius 1951, 41–44.
14. Lacan *SVII*, 261, 295; Lacan 2006j, 654–55.
15. Lacan *SVII*, 4; Lacan *SX*, 193–94; Lacan 2006j, 652–53, 667.
16. *SE* 13: 143.
17. Lacan *SXXIV*, 5/17/77.
18. Lacan *SII*, 31–32.
19. Varela, Thompson, and Rosch 1991, 37.
20. Lacan *SII*, 119, 168–69, 175, 304–5.
21. La Mettrie 1993, 97, 128, 132, 135, 143–44.
22. Lacan *SIV*, 31–32.
23. Diderot 1994, 242, 245–47.
24. Lacan *SIV*, 32–33.
25. Badiou 1982, 204; Johnston 2009a, 120–24.
26. La Mettrie 1993, 117.
27. Ibid., 133.
28. Spinoza 1949, Part I, Proposition 14 (51–52), Part I, Proposition 15 (52), Part II, Proposition 7 (83–84).

29. La Mettrie 1993, 147.
30. Ibid., 148.
31. Lenin 1972, 290.
32. Ibid., 292–93, 391–93.
33. Badiou 1982, 206, 208–9.
34. Hofstadter 2007, 357, 360–61.
35. Diderot 1966, 181.
36. Ibid., 230.
37. Ibid., 202.
38. Ibid., 203.
39. Johnston 2007a, 4; Johnston 2008b, 241.
40. Diderot 1966, 157–58.
41. Ibid., 158.
42. Diderot 1994, 484.
43. Diderot 1966, 159.
44. Lacan *SXI*, 197; Lacan 2006l, 717–18.
45. Chiesa and Toscano 2005, 10.
46. Lacan *SVII*, 213.
47. Ibid., 261.
48. Lacan *SX*, 357.
49. Ibid., 357.
50. Ibid., 357.
51. Ibid., 357.
52. Ibid., 357–58.
53. Ibid., 358.
54. Lacan *SXVI*, 280–81.
55. Ibid., 281.
56. Lacan *SXVII*, 119.
57. Johnston 2009c, 178–80.
58. Johnston 2008b, 189, 208; Johnston 2009a, 41, 88, 135; Johnston 2013c.
59. *SE* 21: 38, 49–50, 54–56; *SE* 22: 34, 160–61, 167–69, 172–74.
60. Lacan 2006m, 740–41, 744; Lacan *SXIII*, 3/23/66.
61. Lacan 2005e, 79–80.
62. Miller 2004b, 16–19.
63. Lacan *SXXV*, 12/20/77; Miller 1999, 89.
64. Lacan *SXI*, 265–66.
65. Lacan 2005e, 79.
66. *SE* 18: 52–53, 60–61; *SE* 19: 40–41, 59, 218, 239; *SE* 21: 118–19, 122, 141.
67. Johnston 2011a, 159–63.
68. *SE* 7: 215–16, 243; *SE* 13: 181–82; *SE* 14: 174–75; Kandel 2005b, 35–36.
69. Engels 1941, 25–27; Engels 1959, 515.
70. Mao 2007a, 92.
71. Engels 1959, 39–40.
72. Engels 1941, 59.
73. Johnston 2008b, 174–76.

74. Badiou 1975, 77–78.

75. Ibid., 61–62.

76. Mao 2007a, 78, 91, 98; Badiou 1975, 21, 36, 65.

77. Mao 2007a, 96; Badiou 1975, 43, 48, 78, 80.

78. Mao 2007a, 67, 72, 74, 75–76, 86.

79. Badiou 1982, 198.

80. Mao 2007a, 69.

81. Ibid., 69.

82. Ibid., 70.

83. Ibid., 71.

84. Badiou 1975, 41, 51–52.

85. Ibid., 32–33.

86. Changeux 2004, 210.

87. Tarby 2005b, 33–34.

88. Johnston 2006, 34–36; Johnston 2007a, 14, 17.

89. Malabou 2005b, 88–89, 94–95.

90. Malabou 2005a, 162–63; Malabou 2005b, 74.

91. Malabou 2005b, 72.

92. Ibid., 93.

93. Malabou 2005a, 192–93.

94. Malabou 2004, 161–63.

95. Malabou 2004, 27–28, 30–31, 156; Malabou 2005b, 19.

96. Dennett 2003, 90–91, 93; LeDoux 2002, 8–9; Ansermet 2002, 377–78, 383; Johnston 2007b; Johnston 2008b, 203–5, 277–78.

97. Malabou 2004, 21, 31–32; Malabou 2005b, 112.

98. Malabou 2004, 84–85.

99. Changeux 2004, 33.

100. Kandel 2005b, 47; Changeux 2004, 207–8; Solms and Turnbull 2002, 218; Rogers 2001, 20, 23–24.

101. Kandel 2005a, 23; Kandel 2005b, 39, 47–49.

102. Kandel 2005b, 41.

103. Libet 2004, 5.

104. LeDoux 2002, 20; Rogers 2001, 2–3, 68.

105. Rogers 2001, 5.

106. LeDoux 2002, 2–3.

107. Rogers 2001, 47–48.

108. LeDoux 2002, 66–67.

109. Changeux 2004, 152–53.

110. LeDoux 2002, 9, 91, 296; Solms and Turnbull 2002, 220; *SE* 11: 189; *SE* 19: 178; Moi 2000, 72–74.

111. Kandel 2005a, 21; Kandel 2005b, 42–43, 47; Damasio 2003, 162–64, 173–74.

112. Solms and Turnbull 2002, 221–22; Rogers 2001, 35.

113. Kandel 2005c, 94; Rogers 2001, 97–98.

114. Kandel 2005d, 150; Changeux 2004, 32.

115. Kandel 2005b, 39; Changeux 2004, 26, 28, 194–95; Rogers 2001, 105.

116. LeDoux 2002, 3, 5, 12, 66.

117. Ibid., 304.

118. Gould and Vrba 1982, 4, 6.

119. Malabou 2004, 147.

120. Ibid., 22, 81.

121. Malabou 2004, 15–17, 29–30, 40, 65–66, 145–46; Malabou 2005a, 8–9; Malabou 2005b, 25–26, 110–11.

122. Malabou 2004, 145; Malabou 2005b, 21.

123. Malabou 2004, 146.

124. Ibid., 159.

125. Johnston 2003, 60, 66, 71–73; Johnston 2004a, 228; Johnston 2004b, 232, 242–44, 247–51; Johnston 2005a, 122–25; Johnston 2006, 36–37, 51–53; Johnston 2008b, 269–87.

126. Malabou 2005b, 113–14.

127. Malabou 2004, 141.

128. Ibid., 164.

129. Lacan 2005e, 76–77.

130. Ibid., 81.

131. Ibid., 82, 87.

132. Ibid., 93.

133. Ibid., 89–91.

134. Ibid., 93.

135. Lacan *SXXIII*, 54–55, 94.

136. Johnston 2006, 34–36.

137. Lacan 2005e, 96.

138. Ibid., 96–97.

139. Badiou 1967, 443; Badiou 2005b, 140–41; Tarby 2005a, 21, 97–98; Tarby 2005b, 36–37, 76.

140. Johnston 2005b, xxxii–xxxiii, 229–30; Johnston 2008b, 128–29.

141. Lacan 2005e, 97–98.

142. Meillassoux 2008a, 61–62, 82–83, 93, 100–104.

143. Lacan 2005e, 79, 81–82.

144. Chiesa and Toscano 2007, 118.

145. Chiesa and Toscano 2005, 10.

146. Chiesa and Toscano 2007, 118.

147. Ibid., 118.

148. Chiesa and Toscano 2005, 10–11.

149. Ibid., 11.

150. Lacan *SXVII*, 33; Lacan *SXXIII*, 12; Lacan *SXXIV*, 5/17/77.

151. Copjec 2004, 6.

152. Ibid., 173.

153. Chiesa and Toscano 2005, 14.

154. Lacan 2005e, 70.

155. Badiou 2003a, 128–29; Badiou 2006g, 9–10, 12–13, 15; Badiou 2006h.

Chapter 2

1. Lacan 2001b, 187; Harari 2004, 19; Lemosof 2005, 105; Ansermet and Magistretti 2007, 11; Grigg 2008, 148, 181.

2. Johnston 2007a, 4; Johnston 2008b, 241.

3. Lacan *SXI*, 7.

4. Milner 1995, 104, 107, 109, 111, 121; Milner 2002, 145, 153–68.

5. Lacan 2006m, 726–27.

6. Fink 1995b, 58–59.

7. Lacan *SXXIV*, 1/11/77; Lacan *SXXV*, 11/15/77.

8. Lacan *SXII*, 12/9/64.

9. Leupin 2004, 52–53.

10. Nobus 2003, 59.

11. Lacan 2006m, 727.

12. Sipos 1994, 10–11.

13. Lacan 2006b, 161–75; Lacan 2006d, 237–38, 257; Johnston 2005b, 24–36, 42–44, 55–56, 75–76; Johnston 2008b, 242–68.

14. Miller 2002b, 94–115; Lacan *SXIII*, 4/20/66; Johnston 2005b, 110–17, 326.

15. Lacan 2006m, 728.

16. Ibid., 730.

17. Lacan 1990a, 114.

18. Lacan *SXVII*, 147.

19. Lacan *SXII*, 12/16/64, 6/9/65, 6/16/65; Lacan *SXV*, 3/6/68, 3/20/68; Lacan *SXVII*, 23; Lemosof 2005, 108.

20. Lacan 2006l, 712; Lacan *SXI*, 47, 231; Milner 1995, 39–42; Julien 1994, 109; Brousse 1996, 127; Vanier 2000, 38.

21. Koyré 1958, 99, 278; Lacan 2006d, 235–39; Lacan 2006e, 299–300; Lacan 2006i, 608; Lacan *SII*, 298–99; Lacan *SIII*, 238; Lacan *SXIII*, 12/8/65; Lacan *SXX*, 81–82; Miller 1996, 219; Miller 2002c, 152–53; Lee 1990, 187–93; Burgoyne 2003, 81; Grigg 2008, 141.

22. Lacan 2006m, 728.

23. Ibid., 728.

24. Ibid., 728.

25. Ibid., 727, 730–31.

26. Milner 1991, 29, 33; Johnston 2005b, 66.

27. Lacan *SXI* [Fr.], 239.

28. Lacan *SXIX*, 12/2/71; Lemosof 2005, 107.

29. Lacan 1990a, 109–10; Dolar 1998, 12.

30. Lacan 2006m, 728, 730, 737.

31. Miller 2002c, 155.

32. Leclaire 1996a, 106.

33. Miller 2004a, 33; Van Haute 2002, xxxiii; Burgoyne 2003, 83.

34. Lacan 2006c, 191–92; Lacan 2006d, 220–21; Lacan *SIII*, 236, 242; Lacan *SXV*, 5/15/68; Leupin 2004, 31–32, 59.

35. Lacan 2006h, 596; Lacan 2001f, 421–22, 429–30; Miller 2002c, 151, 155; Julien 1994, 109.

36. Lacan 2006k, 674; Miller 2004a, 33; Leupin 2004, 60–61.

37. Lacan 2006m, 730.

38. Lacan *SXIV*, 6/7/67; Fink 1995a, 139; Fink 1995b, 58–59, 63–64; Nobus 2002, 96.

39. Milner 1995, 92–95, 98; Milner 2000, 8.

40. Lacan 2006m, 730–31.

41. Fink 1995b, 64.

42. Fink 1995b, 64; Fink 2004, 127–28, 185; Johnston 2005b, 61–71.

43. Lacan 2006m, 727.

44. Ibid., 731.

45. Ibid.

46. Lacan 2006m, 726–27, 737; Balibar 1996, 23, 25; Lemosof 2005, 108–9.

47. Lemosof 2005, 111.

48. Miller 2002c, 161; Fink 1995a, 139; Nasio 1998, 138–40; Vanier 2000, 88; Cutrofello 2002, 155; Nobus 2002, 98; Grigg 2008, 145.

49. Lacan *SVII*, 139; Miller 1994, 75–77.

50. Lacan 2006f, 480; Lacan 2006m, 737–38, 742, 744–45; Lacan 2001e, 302; Lacan 2001f, 437; Lacan *SVII*, 130–31; Lacan *SXIII*, 12/15/65, 6/1/66; Lacan *SXVI*, 238–40; Lacan *SXVII*, 104–6; Lacan *SXXIV*, 5/17/77; Lacan *SXXV*, 12/20/77; Miller 2002a, 78–79; Miller 1999, 89; Miller 2002c, 161–62; Soler 2002, 48–49; Soler 2006, 142–43; Fink 1995a, 138–46; Lemosof 2005, 105, 115.

51. Lacan 2006m, 731; Lacan *SXIII*, 1/12/66, 4/20/66, 6/1/66; Fink 1995a, 139–41, 200.

52. Miller 2002a, 78.

53. Lacan 1990a, 114.

54. Lacan *SXXIII*, 36.

55. Lacan 2006m, 733–34; Fink 1995b, 64; Baas 1998, 53; Leupin 2004, 7.

56. Lacan 2006m, 733.

57. Lacan 2006k, 691; Lacan *SVI*, 11/12/58, 5/13/59, 5/20/59; Lacan *SIX*, 5/9/62, 5/23/62; Lacan *SXIII*, 5/11/66; Lacan *SXVI*, 23–24; Lacan *SXIX*, 6/21/72.

58. Lacan 2006j, 653; Lacan *SV*, 439; Lacan *SX*, 203–4; Baas 1992, 68–74.

59. Fink 1995a, 140; Fink 1995b, 64.

60. Fink 1995a, 140.

61. Lacan 2006m, 730.

62. Ibid., 732–33.

63. Lacan *SVI*, 4/15/59, 6/3/59, 6/10/59, 6/24/59; Lacan *SVII*, 99; Lacan *SVIII*, 424–25; Lacan *SIX*, 4/4/62; Lacan *SX*, 203–4; Lacan *SXIII*, 3/30/66; Lacan *SXIV*, 6/21/67; Chiesa 2007, 157.

64. Sipos 1994, 9; Le Gaufey 1996, 43, 48–49; Dolar 1998, 15; Johnston 2005b, 68–70.

65. Lacan 2006k, 671–76; Van Haute 2002, xxxiii–xliii; Leupin 2004, 31.

66. Johnston 2007a, 3–20; Johnston 2008b, 269–87; Johnston 2010a, 324–25, 333–35, 340–41; Johnston 2011a, 159–79; Johnston 2013b.

67. Soubbotnik 1996, 118; Nobus 2002, 108; Lemosof 2005, 116.

68. Lacan 2006m, 743.

69. Lacan 2006d, 248; Lacan 2006g, 496; Lacan 2001a, 137–38; Lacan 2001c, 199; Lacan 2001d, 224; Lacan 1970, 187; Lacan *SI*, 244; Lacan *SII*, 82; Lacan *SIII*, 32; Lacan *SIX*, 1/10/62; Lacan *SXIV*, 2/1/67, 5/10/67; Lacan *SXVI*, 88–90; Johnston 2008b, 87–89.

70. Lacan 1990a, 112.

71. Lacan 2006m, 743.

72. Metzinger 2009, 40, 215–16.

73. Johnston 2007a, 4; Johnston 2008b, 200–201, 240–41.

74. Ansermet and Magistretti 2007, 10–11.

75. Lacan 1966, 875.

76. Johnston 2011a, 163–70.

77. Lacan 2006a, 77–78; Lacan *SXVII*, 33; Lacan *SXXI*, 5/21/74; Lacan *SXXIII*, 12; Lacan *SXXIV*, 4/19/77, 5/17/77; Johnston 2008b, 270–73.

78. Lacan 2006a, 78; Lacan 1953, 13; Lacan 2005b, 46.

79. Johnston 2011a, 164–65.

80. Nassif 1968, 148–49.

81. Ibid., 150.

82. Lacan *SXV*, 12/6/67, 1/17/68, 2/7/68; Lacan *SXXI*, 11/2/73; Lacan *SXXII*, 11/19/74.

83. Lacan 1995, 10–11; Lacan *SXV*, 11/29/67; Lacan *SXIX*, 6/1/72.

84. Lacan 1995, 10.

85. Lacan 1990b, 129–31.

86. Lacan 1990c, 133.

87. Ibid.

88. Ibid.

89. Jablonka and Lamb 2005, 1–2, 5–7, 58–60, 62–65, 67, 72–75, 77–78, 109–11, 144–45, 160–61, 166, 176, 189, 191, 193, 204–5, 220–23, 226, 238, 285–86, 319, 344, 372, 378–80.

90. Leclaire 1996b, 138.

91. Ibid., 125.

92. Johnston 2005b, 349–56.

93. Leclaire 1996b, 125.

94. *SE* 7: 168–69, 183–84, 232–33.

95. Leclaire 1996b, 126.

96. Ibid., 126.

97. Johnston 2011a, 160–61.

98. Badiou 1982, 204; Laplanche 1987, 134.

99. Meillassoux 2008a, 5–11, 35–39.

100. Leclaire 1996b, 127.

101. Ibid., 130.

102. Ansermet 2002, 382.

103. Ibid., 381.

104. Ibid., 382.
105. Johnston 2013b.
106. Lacan *SV,* 251.
107. Lacan *SXXI,* 11/20/73.
108. Lacan *SXX,* 117.

Chapter 3

1. *SE* 16: 371; *SE* 17: 97, 119–20; *SE* 23: 167, 188, 206–7.
2. *SE* 15: 199; *SE* 16: 354; *SE* 19: 174, 220–21; *SE* 23: 99.
3. Smail 2010.
4. Freud 1987, 5–20.
5. Grubrich-Simitis 1987, xvi.
6. *SE* 17: 97; Johnston 2005b, 220–21.
7. *SE* 17: 103.
8. *SE* 19: 37–38.
9. *SE* 23: 100.
10. Lacan 2005d, 32.
11. Lacan *SX,* 377.
12. Lacan 2005c, 117, 120–21; Lacan *SXVII,* 65; Johnston 2009a, 149–50.
13. Lacan *SXI,* 63–64.
14. Lacan *SXV,* 11/29/67.
15. Lacan *SXXV,* 12/20/77; Lacan 2006c, 194; Lacan 1990a, 112.
16. Johnston 2007a, 3–20; Johnston 2008b, 167–76, 203–9, 269–87; Johnston 2011a, 159–79; Johnston 2012b; Johnston 2013b.
17. Lacan *SIV,* 41–58; Johnston 2011a, 170–76.
18. Lacan *SIII,* 306.
19. Lacan *SIX,* 12/20/61.
20. Lacan 2001g, 480.
21. Lacan *SIII,* 147–49; Lacan *SVI,* 11/12/58.
22. Lacan *SIII,* 81.
23. Ibid., 120.
24. Lacan 2005b, 39.
25. Lacan *SV,* 307–11, 317; Johnston 2011a, 171–72.
26. Lacan 1990a, 114.
27. Balmès 1999, 3.
28. Lacan *SIII,* 148.
29. Lacan *SIII* [Fr.], 168.
30. Lacan 2007, 75.
31. Lacan *SVII,* 213–14; Lacan *SVIII,* 12; Lacan 2001a, 135; Lacan 2005e, 89–91; Lacan 2007, 60.
32. Lacan 2005e, 90.
33. Lacan *SIV,* 48; Johnston 2011a, 170–76.
34. Lacan *SXXIV,* 1/18/77.
35. Lacan *SV,* 329.

36. Lacan and Granoff 1956, 266.

37. Ibid., 266–67.

38. Lacan *SII*, 5.

39. Ibid., 5.

40. Lacan *SIV*, 50; Johnston 2011a, 170–76.

41. Lacan 2005a, 27.

42. Lacan *SXVII*, 19.

43. Lacan *SXVIII*, 61.

44. Lacan *SXIX*, 2/3/72.

45. Lacan *SII*, 189.

46. Lacan *SXVII*, 155.

47. Lacan 2005b, 46–47.

48. Lacan 2005e, 79, 81–82.

49. Chiesa and Toscano 2005, 10; Chiesa and Toscano 2007, 118.

50. Brassier 2007c, 49–94; Harman 2007b, 104–17; Hallward 2008, 51–57; Žižek 2009a, 214–30; Hägglund 2011, 114–29.

51. Meillassoux 2008a, 10–22, 26–28.

52. Ibid., 5–11, 14–21, 35–45.

53. Brassier 2007c, 228–30, 238.

54. Badiou 1982, 204; Laplanche 1987, 134; Johnston 2009a, 120–23.

55. Meillassoux 2008a, 10, 14, 16–18, 20–23, 26–27, 34.

56. Smail 2008, 33–34, 40–47, 50–52, 75.

57. Ibid., 2.

58. Ibid., 2–3.

59. Ibid., 9–10, 13–14.

60. Ibid., 1.

61. Mannoni 1969, 9–33.

62. Smail 2008, 3–4.

63. Ibid., 35.

64. Ibid., 39.

65. Lacan *SXI*, 59; Lacan *SXVII*, 119–20.

66. Johnston 2009c, 178–81.

67. Lacan *SX*, 357–58; Lacan *SXVI*, 280–81; Lacan *SXVII*, 119.

68. Smail 2008, 112.

69. Johnston 2007a, 3–20; Johnston 2008b, 167–76, 203–9, 269–87; Johnston 2011a, 159–79; Johnston 2012b; Johnston 2013b.

70. Smail 2008, 124.

71. Johnston 2011a, 170–76.

72. Smail 2008, 4–6, 49–50.

73. Ibid., 44.

74. Ibid., 5–6, 53–56.

75. Ibid., 6.

76. Ibid., 55.

77. Lacan 1990a, 112; Lacan *SXX*, 17; Lacan *SXXV*, 11/15/77; Miller 2001, 21.

78. Lacan *SXI*, 150–51.

79. Smail 2008, 114–19, 124–26, 130–31, 133, 136–38, 144, 154–55.
80. Johnston 2005b, 300–15.
81. Smail 2008, 201–02.
82. Smail 2008, 127–28, 157–89.
83. Johnston 2005b, 253–55, 328–32, 340–41.
84. Johnston 2009a, 98–101.
85. Johnston 2004a, 227–28; Johnston 2004b, 250–51; Johnston 2005b, xxxvii, 264, 266, 270, 341; Johnston 2006, 34–55; Johnston 2008b, xxiii, 60, 63, 65, 79–81, 113, 284, 286; Johnston 2009a, 79; Johnston 2012b; Chiesa 2007, 123, 183, 187.
86. Linden 2007, 2–3, 5–7, 21–24, 26, 245–46; Marcus 2008, 6–16, 161–63; Johnston 2012b; Johnston 2013b.
87. Lacan 2006e, 286.
88. Johnston 2012b.
89. Lacan *SI*, 128; Lacan *SII*, 24; Lacan *SVII*, 126–27, 213–14, 223–24; Lacan *SVIII*, 120–22; Lacan *SXII*, 12/16/64; Lacan *SXIII*, 1/19/66; Lacan *SXIX*, 11/4/71, 2/3/72.
90. Johnston 2007a, 3–20; Johnston 2008b, 269–87; Johnston 2012b.
91. Smail 2008, 79.
92. Ibid., 124.
93. Ibid., 125.
94. Lacan *SVII*, 213–14; Chiesa and Toscano 2005, 10–11, 14; Chiesa and Toscano 2007, 118.
95. Lacan *SXXV*, 11/15/77.
96. Ibid.
97. Engels 1940, 279–96; Levins and Lewontin 1985a, 1–5; Levins and Lewontin 1985b, 45–46; Levins and Lewontin 1985c, 69–70; Levins and Lewontin 1985d, 89, 99.
98. Smail 2008, 55.
99. Lacan 1973, 54.

Chapter 4

1. Badiou 1994a, 123.
2. Badiou 2005b, 6; Badiou 1990, 8; Badiou 2011e, 236–37.
3. Badiou 2005b, 28; Badiou 2006c, 36; Badiou 1998, 126; Hallward 1998, 89–90; Tarby 2005b, 45–46, 88, 90, 91–92.
4. Hallward 2003, 60, 174; Tarby 2005a, 136.
5. Badiou 2005b, 1.
6. Ibid., 2.
7. Badiou 1999a, 66–67, 74, 76.
8. Badiou 2005b, xiii–xiv.
9. Ibid., xiv.
10. Ibid., 7.
11. Varela, Thompson, and Rosch 1991, 150.

12. Johnston 2007a, 4.

13. Hallward 2003, 174; Osborne 2007, 24.

14. Bandres 2007, 51–52.

15. Badiou 1999a, 104; Badiou 2004c, 27–28; Badiou 2004d, 74.

16. Badiou 2006c, 90, 94; Badiou 1995b, 63.

17. Tarby 2005a, 84–85.

18. Ibid., 22.

19. Badiou 2006c, 64.

20. Ibid., 71.

21. Badiou 1994b, 55, 65; Brassier 2000, 212, 216.

22. Tarby 2005a, 38–39.

23. Brassier 2005, 140.

24. Badiou 2005b, 127; Hallward 2003, 104.

25. Badiou 2005b, 127–29, 136–37; Besana and Feltham 2007, 15–16.

26. Badiou 2005b, 136.

27. Tarby 2005b, 79; Besana 2007b, 125.

28. Badiou 2005b, 177.

29. Bandres 2007, 45–46; Brassier 2007b, 60.

30. Badiou 2005b, 23–24, 27–29, 44–45; Badiou 2006c, 35–37.

31. Badiou 2005b, 23.

32. Tarby 2005b, 36–37, 76; Tarby 2005a, 21, 97–98.

33. Badiou 1967, 443.

34. Badiou 2005b, 140–41.

35. Besana and Feltham 2007, 16.

36. Kandel 2005b, 47; Kandel 2005c, 94; Changeux 2004, 33, 207–8; LeDoux 2002, 2–3, 20, 66–67; Solms and Turnbull 2002, 218; Rogers 2001, 2–3, 5, 20, 23–24, 68, 97–98.

37. Hallward 2003, 58.

38. Tarby 2005a, 80.

39. Badiou 2005b, 7.

40. Badiou 1998, 128.

41. Badiou 2004g, 236.

42. Ibid., 234.

43. Badiou 2006g, 83–84.

44. Brassier 2005, 140.

45. Badiou 1994a, 123.

46. Badiou 1994a, 123.

47. Engels 1941, 31; Lenin 1972, 22–23, 33–34, 95, 106, 128–29, 140–42, 145, 167, 188–89, 191, 232, 321, 344, 407–13, 416–17, 431, 434.

48. Badiou 2003a, 128–29.

49. Badiou 2006g, 9.

50. Ibid., 12–13.

51. Ibid., 12.

52. Badiou 2006g, 12, 17–18; Badiou 2011f, 26–27, 56, 107.

53. Badiou 2006g, 10.

54. Badiou 2007a, 176.

55. Malabou 2004, 7–8, 14–17, 20–23, 31–32.
56. Dennett 2003, 90–91, 93; LeDoux 2002, 8–9; Ansermet 2002, 377–78, 383; Johnston 2008b, 201–09.
57. Badiou 2007a, 100.
58. Besana 2007b, 125.
59. Badiou 2006g, 505, 617; Badiou 2006a, 252.
60. Badiou 2006g, 76.
61. Ibid., 499–502.
62. Badiou 2003g, 1–3.
63. Badiou 2003g, 109; Badiou 2003f, 61; Badiou 1998, 124–25; Badiou 2006g, 534, 536.
64. *SE* 19: 235–36, 239.
65. Changeux 2004, 23, 28, 32–33, 36, 246–47.
66. Ibid., 2004, 8.
67. Ibid., 23, 25.
68. Ibid., 9.
69. Metzinger 2003, 51.
70. Badiou 2006g, 225.
71. Badiou 2006d, 18–19.
72. Ibid., 19.
73. Ibid., 20–21.
74. Ibid., 21.
75. Ibid., 19–20.
76. Badiou 2004b, 16–17.
77. Acotto 2007, 85.
78. Ibid., 96.
79. Badiou 2006d, 18.
80. Hofstadter 2007, 27.
81. LeDoux 2002, 3, 5, 12, 66.
82. Hofstadter 2007, 31; Metzinger 2003, 115; Solms and Turnbull 2002, 64, 244, 271–72.
83. Badiou 2006d, 20.
84. Ibid., 21.
85. Badiou 1982, 206, 208–9.
86. Badiou 2001, 41.
87. Badiou 1998, 128–29.
88. Badiou 2006g, 43.
89. Ibid., 58.
90. Johnston 2006, 36–37, 50; Johnston 2008b, 269–87.
91. Badiou 1994b, 65.
92. Ibid., 65.
93. Hallward 2003, 180.
94. Ibid., 180.
95. Ibid.
96. Tarby 2005a, 165.
97. Hallward 2003, 276–77.

98. Brassier 2005, 140.

99. Smith 2004, 93.

100. Badiou 2004c, 36; Badiou 1994a, 86; Badiou 2006c, 23, 29–30.

101. Badiou 2005b, 173; Badiou 2006a, 253.

102. Badiou 2006g, 473.

103. Ibid., 124.

104. Hebb 1949, 63, 70.

105. LeDoux 2002, 79.

106. Malabou 2005a, 8–9; Malabou 2004, 15–17, 29–30, 40, 65–66, 145–46; Malabou 2005b, 25–26, 110–11.

107. Hasker 1999, 190–91, 194–95; Ansermet 2002, 377; Johnston 2008b, 277–80.

108. Badiou 1995a, 7; Badiou 2005a, 242.

109. Sartre 1948, 27–28, 42–43.

110. Badiou 2007a, 174–75.

111. Ibid., 176–77.

112. Badiou 2005a, 242.

113. Badiou 1999a, 35–36; Badiou 1990, 7–8, 11–12; Badiou 2005c, 14; Badiou 2003c, 101.

114. Badiou 2005b, 3–4; Badiou 1999a, 37–39; Badiou 1990, 25–26; Badiou 2003d, 165; Badiou 2001, 28.

115. Badiou 2007d, 8.

116. Badiou 2005b, 13–14; Gillespie 2007, 72.

117. Badiou 2005b, 25–26; Badiou 2003a, 130; Badiou 2003e, 174; Badiou 2006g, 197–98, 597.

118. Badiou 1999a, 64–65.

119. Ibid., 61.

120. Ibid., 61.

121. Ibid., 62.

122. Badiou 2011f, 69, 119.

123. Badiou 2003e, 184.

124. Ibid., 185.

125. Johnston 2006, 36–37, 51–53; Johnston 2008b, 269–87.

Chapter 5

1. Badiou 1995a, 7.

2. Badiou 2005a, 242.

3. Badiou 2005b, 6.

4. Osborne 2007, 25.

5. Badiou 2006f, 57–58; Badiou and Roudinesco 2012, 22–23, 33.

6. Badiou 2003b, 56; Badiou 2006g, 56.

7. Ricoeur 2004, 50.

8. Deleuze 1977, 112.

9. Badiou 2004a, 79.

10. Badiou 2006g, 561.

11. Badiou 1999b, 123–24; Badiou 2006c, 30; Badiou 2006g, 283–84.

12. Badiou 1982, 136–37; Badiou 2006c, 133, 141, 163.

13. Badiou 2005b, 1–2.

14. Badiou 2006g, 561.

15. Ibid., 111.

16. Toscano 2004, 202; Tarby 2005a, 79; Hallward 2005, 12, 16; Brassier 2007b, 60; Osborne 2007, 24.

17. Badiou 2005b, 10, 24–25, 34, 52–53.

18. Badiou 2006g, 608.

19. Ibid., 612.

20. Ibid., 618.

21. Ibid., 112, 124, 536.

22. Kant 1965, Bxvi–xvii (22), Bxxii (25).

23. Badiou 2007c, 67.

24. Badiou 2011f, 49–50.

25. Badiou 2002, 11.

26. Badiou 2006e, 91–92.

27. Badiou 2006g, 254.

28. Ibid., 323–24.

29. Badiou 2006c, 162; Badiou 2004e, 184.

30. Badiou 2004e, 182.

31. Badiou 1985, 80.

32. Badiou 2005b, 504.

33. Hallward 2003, 61.

34. Badiou 2005b, 23–24, 93; Tarby 2005b, 72.

35. Tarby 2005b, 64.

36. Tarby 2005a, 86.

37. Badiou 2005b, 24–25.

38. Ibid., 25, 52.

39. Ibid., 28–29, 33.

40. Ibid., 58.

41. Hallward 2003, 63; Hallward 2005, 12.

42. Besana 2007a, 36.

43. Badiou 2006b, xii.

44. Besana 2007a, 38.

45. Badiou 2005b, 28.

46. Badiou 2005b, 25–27; Badiou 2003a, 130; Badiou 2003e, 174; Badiou 2004g, 233; Badiou 2006g, 197–98, 597.

47. Badiou 1988, 36.

48. Badiou 2006g, 608.

49. Badiou 2005b, 29.

50. Simont 2002, 463–65.

51. Badiou 2005b, 24; Hallward 2003, 63.

52. Badiou 2005b, 5, 7–8.

53. Tarby 2005a, 88.

54. Badiou 2005b, 30.
55. Ibid., 34.
56. Ibid.
57. Ibid., 35.
58. Ibid., 52.
59. Kant 1965, Bxxvi–xxvii (27).
60. Gillespie 2007, 77.
61. Ibid., 77–78.
62. Badiou 2005b, 83–84, 93–94, 96–97, 99, 103.
63. Gillespie 2007, 77–78.
64. Besana 2007b, 130.
65. Acotto 2007, 86.
66. Desanti 2004, 60.
67. Badiou 2006c, 134–35.
68. Johnston 2005a, 126.
69. Badiou 2011b, 66; Badiou 2011c, 131.
70. Badiou 2006c, 137–38, 141.
71. Badiou 2002, 11; Badiou 2004f, 201; Badiou 2006g, 111–12, 185–86, 207; Badiou 2007c, 64–65, 67.
72. Badiou 2004e, 182–83; Badiou 2004f, 199; Badiou 2006g, 130–31, 317–18.
73. Badiou 2006g, 251.
74. Badiou 2004e, 183; Badiou 2006g, 168, 171.
75. Toscano 2004, 215.
76. Ibid., 215.
77. Badiou 2006g, 603, 608.
78. Ibid., 248.
79. Badiou 2011f, 44, 46, 50.
80. Badiou 2006g, 127, 167–68.
81. Ibid., 48, 112.
82. Badiou 2002, 9, 11; Badiou 2006g, 104, 109, 127, 199, 611.
83. Hallward 2003, 296–97.
84. Badiou 2006a, 250.
85. Badiou 2006c, 162.
86. Badiou 2006g, 121–24.
87. Badiou 2006c, 162.
88. Ibid., 162.
89. Badiou 2006g, 245.
90. Ibid., 205, 245.
91. Ibid., 613.
92. Ibid., 231.
93. Ibid., 232.
94. Ibid., 265.
95. Ibid., 255.
96. Ibid., 233.

97. Badiou 2006g, 233–34; Badiou 2004e, 187.
98. Badiou 2006g, 248.
99. Ibid., 234.
100. Ibid., 603.
101. Ibid., 604.
102. Badiou 2005b, 26.
103. Badiou 2005b, 23–24, 29, 33.
104. Ibid., 34.
105. Badiou 2006g, 234–35, 239, 276–77, 300, 316, 598, 618.
106. Ibid., 234.
107. Ibid., 235.
108. Ibid., 316.
109. Ibid., 240.
110. Ibid., 239–40.
111. Ibid., 245–46.
112. Ibid., 247–48.
113. Badiou 2006a, 253; Meillassoux 2011b, 17–18.
114. Badiou 2006g, 316–17, 326–27.
115. Ibid., 339–41.
116. Ibid., 246.
117. Ibid., 225.

Chapter 6

1. Badiou 2006g, 16.
2. Ibid., 16, 127, 167–68, 603, 608.
3. Badiou 2006c, 182; Badiou 2004e, 184; Badiou 2006g, 612, 618; Badiou 2008d, 119–21.
4. Badiou 2006c, 162; Badiou 2002, 9, 11; Badiou 2006g, 104, 109, 122–24, 127, 199, 611.
5. Badiou 2006c, 162; Badiou 2002, 11; Badiou 2004f, 201; Badiou 2006g, 111–12, 185–86, 205, 207, 245; Badiou 2007c, 64–65, 67; Badiou 2006a, 250; Hallward 2003, 296–97.
6. Badiou 2004f, 197–98; Badiou 2006g, 128–29.
7. Badiou 2006g, 205–6.
8. Engels 1941, 21–22; Lenin 1972, 9, 45–46, 100; Althusser 2001a, 2, 6; Althusser 2001b, 12–13, 16–18, 21.
9. Meillassoux 2008a, 34; Meillassoux 2006b, 115; Brassier 2007c, 63, 231.
10. Meillassoux 2008b.
11. Harman 2007b, 104.
12. Meillassoux 2008b.
13. Badiou 2006g, 316–17, 326–27.
14. Meillassoux 2008a, 5–6.
15. Ibid., 6–7.

16. Ibid., 37–38.

17. Badiou 1985, 80; Badiou 2004e, 182.

18. Meillassoux 2008a, 42, 132.

19. Ibid., 44.

20. Brassier 2007c, 52–53, 254.

21. Meillassoux 2008a, 9–10.

22. Ibid., 13–14.

23. Lenin 1972, 18–19, 38, 45–46, 68–69, 95, 139, 142–45, 152–53, 177–78, 195, 203, 205, 216, 305, 310–14, 420, 426.

24. Brassier 2007c, 246–47.

25. Ibid., 54–55.

26. Meillassoux 2008a, 13–14.

27. Ibid., 16.

28. Ibid., 14.

29. Brassier 2007c, 111; Acotto 2007, 86; Besana 2007b, 130.

30. Badiou 2006g, 225; Badiou 2006d, 19–21.

31. Brassier 2007c, 57–58, 143, 161.

32. Meillassoux 2008a, 16.

33. Ibid., 17.

34. Ibid., 17.

35. Lenin 1972, 95, 188–89, 344, 407–10, 412–13, 431, 434.

36. Boghossian 2006, 26–27, 38.

37. Meillassoux 2008a, 17–18.

38. Ibid., 17–18.

39. Ibid., 26.

40. Ibid., 37.

41. Meillassoux 2008a, 26; Brassier 2007c, 85, 223.

42. Meillassoux 2008a, 27.

43. Ibid., 27.

44. Ibid., 28.

45. Ibid., 128.

46. Ibid., 1.

47. Galileo 1957, 274–78; Meillassoux 2008a, 1–2.

48. Meillassoux 2008a, 2.

49. Ibid., 71.

50. Ibid., 3.

51. Meillassoux 2008a, 112–13; Brassier 2007c, 54–55.

52. Meillassoux 2008a, 112–13.

53. Ibid., 114.

54. Badiou 2006d, 21.

55. Meillassoux 2008a, 115.

56. Ibid., 115–16.

57. Ibid., 136.

58. Ibid., 117.

59. Ibid., 102–7.

60. Badiou 2008a, 211.
61. Meillassoux 2008a, 127–28.
62. Badiou 2005b, 7; Badiou 1998, 128; Badiou 2004g, 236; Meillassoux 2008b.
63. Badiou 2005b, 5, 7–8, 24; Badiou 2007b, 27–28; Badiou 2008c, 63; Hallward 2003, 63; Brassier 2007c, 86–88.
64. Badiou 2005b, 23–24, 29, 93, 504; Tarby 2005b, 72.
65. Badiou 2005b, 25, 28–30, 33–35, 52; Simont 2002, 463–65; Tarby 2005a, 88.
66. Badiou 2005b, 25–28; Badiou 2003a, 130; Badiou 2003e, 174; Badiou 2004g, 233; Badiou 2006g, 197–98, 597; Brassier 2007c, 98–99.
67. Harman 2007b, 111.
68. Harman 2007a, 382.
69. Brassier 2005, 140; Brassier 2007c, 102, 113–14, 116, 250; Brassier 2007a, 319–21.
70. Badiou 2004g, 235.
71. Badiou 2006g, 169, 194; Brassier 2007a, 331–32.
72. Badiou 2004g, 234; Badiou 2006g, 83–84.
73. Badiou 2006g, 233–34, 239–40, 248; Badiou 2004e, 187.
74. Badiou 2008a, 212; Badiou 2007d, 8.
75. Badiou 2005b, 3–4, 13–14; Badiou 1999a, 35–39; Badiou 1990, 7–8, 11–12, 25–26; Badiou 2005c, 14; Badiou 2003c, 101; Badiou 2003d, 165; Badiou 2003e, 184–85; Badiou 2001, 28; Badiou 2007b, 36; Gillespie 2007, 72.
76. Meillassoux 2002, 44.
77. Meillassoux 2002, 39–40, 57; Meillassoux 2008b.
78. Bosteels 2004a, 103; Bosteels 2004b, 153–54.
79. Meillassoux 2002, 41, 50–54.
80. Brassier 2007c, 109.
81. Berkeley 1982, 26–27.
82. Meillassoux 2007b, 449.
83. Brassier 2007c, 116–17, 250; Brassier 2007a, 333.

Chapter 7

1. Mao 2007a, 81, 87–89, 91–93.
2. Engels 1941, 20–21; Lenin 1972, 1, 22–23, 33–34, 106, 410, 431, 434.
3. Mao 2007a, 99–101; Mao 2007b, 131–33, 137–39, 153–54.
4. Badiou 1982, 202.
5. Meillassoux 2008b.
6. Meillassoux 2008a, 13, 26–27, 36–38, 113, 121.
7. Ibid., 45.
8. Ibid., 44–49.
9. Meillassoux 2006b, 110.
10. Ibid., 115.

11. Meillassoux 2006b, 110; Meillassoux 2008a, 33–34, 60, 71, 124–25; Meillassoux 2007a, 59–61.

12. Meillassoux 2006b, 110–12.

13. Ibid., 115.

14. Ibid., 110.

15. Ibid., 105–09.

16. Brassier 2007c, 49–94; Harman 2007b, 104–17; Hallward 2008, 51–57.

17. Meillassoux 2008a, 53, 91–92; Meillassoux 2006b, 112–15; Meillassoux 2007b, 433–34, 441–42; Harman 2007b, 109; Harman 2007a, 385.

18. Johnston 2008b, 12–13, 15, 128–33, 165–66, 172, 240–41.

19. Hallward 2008, 55, 57.

20. Lenin 1972, 18–19, 38, 45–46, 68–69, 95, 139, 142–45, 152–53, 177–78, 195, 203, 205, 216, 305, 310–14, 420, 426.

21. Althusser 2001b, 16–18, 31–34, 37–38, 40–42.

22. Meillassoux 2008a, 17–18.

23. Brassier 2007c, 246–47; Žižek 2009a, 214.

24. Žižek 2009a, 214.

25. Žižek 2000, 179–80; Žižek 2002b, 178–81; Žižek and Daly 2004, 96–97; Žižek 2006, 168; Žižek 2009b, 97, 100.

26. Meillassoux 2008a, 1–3, 8, 13.

27. Chalmers 1997, xii–xiii.

28. Brassier 2007c, 88–89.

29. Brassier 2007c, 3–31, 245; Johnston 2009b, 107–9; Johnston 2008b, 203–9, 241, 269–87; Johnston 2007a, 3–20.

30. Hägglund 2011, 121–22.

31. Žižek and Daly 2004, 96–97.

32. Meillassoux 2008a, 64; Brassier 2007c, 67–68.

33. Meillassoux 2007a, 58.

34. Meillassoux 2008a, 52–53, 62, 91–92.

35. Ibid., 32–34, 49.

36. Meillassoux 2011d, 168–69.

37. Meillassoux 2008a, 53, 57–60, 63–64, 73–75, 79–80, 82–83; Meillassoux 2007a, 59–60, 72, 75; Meillassoux 2007b, 428–29, 432; Brassier 2007c, 70–71.

38. Pascal 1966, 83–87, 149–55.

39. Hume 1993, 103–7, 109–13.

40. Meillassoux 2008a, 10–11, 35, 37–38, 48; Brassier 2007c, 64–65.

41. Meillassoux 2007a, 67–68.

42. Hume 1993, 30–32.

43. Ibid., 35–37, 70–72.

44. Ibid., 76.

45. Ibid., 75, 77–79, 81, 87–88.

46. Ibid., 77.

47. Meillassoux 2007a, 75.

48. Meillassoux 2008a, 1–3, 12–13.

49. Ibid., 10, 14, 16–18, 20–23, 26–27, 34.
50. Ibid., 12, 26–27, 113, 115–16, 118, 120.
51. Ibid., 85.
52. Berkeley 1982, 35–38, 42–43.
53. Meillassoux 2011e, 178.
54. Brown 2008.
55. Hodges 2010.
56. Meillassoux 2008a, 91–92; Harman 2007b, 112–13.
57. Brassier 2007c, 82; Harman 2007b, 114.
58. Meillassoux 2008a, 93.
59. Meillassoux 2008a, 93–94; Brassier 2007c, 78–79.
60. Meillassoux 2008b.
61. Badiou 2005b, 140–41, 273, 277; Badiou 2006c, 29–31.
62. Meillassoux 2008a, 103–7.
63. Ibid., 103.
64. Ibid., 100–107.
65. Meillassoux 2007a, 64.
66. Hume 1993, 46, 49–50, 52.
67. Ibid., 39.
68. Brassier 2007a, 331–33.
69. Hallward 2008, 55–56; Meillassoux 2007a, 65–67.
70. Meillassoux 2002, 39–41, 50–54; Brassier 2007c, 109.
71. Badiou 2005b, 23.
72. Badiou 2005a, 242.
73. Badiou 2003g, 71; Badiou 2006g, 534, 536.
74. Meillassoux 2007a, 72, 75.
75. Ibid., 73, 79–80.
76. Hägglund 2011, 121–22.
77. Hallward 2008, 55–56.
78. Meillassoux 2008a, 61–62, 64–66; Meillassoux 2007a, 59, 72, 75.
79. Meillassoux 2006b, 112.
80. Brassier 2007c, 71.
81. Lacan *SV*, 499; Lacan *SVI*, 4/15/59; Lacan *SVII*, 67; Lacan *SX*, 320–21;
Lacan 2006k, 690.
82. Žižek 2002a, lii.
83. Hallward 2008, 51.
84. Meillassoux 2008a, 127–28.
85. Brassier 2007c, 63.
86. Meillassoux 2008a, 82.
87. Ibid., 33–34.
88. Meillassoux 2007a, 58–59.
89. Meillassoux 2011c, 128.
90. Engels 1941, 22–23; Lenin 1972, 1, 22–23, 61, 65, 109–11, 127–29, 142,
152–53, 177–78, 188–89, 191, 241, 284, 312–13.
91. Meillassoux 2008a, 64–66.

Postface

1. Badiou and Roudinesco 2012, 34.
2. Ibid., 34.
3. Badiou 2009b, 523.
4. Badiou 2010, 144, 146–48.
5. Badiou and Roudinesco 2012, 50.
6. Badiou 2011b, 68; Badiou 2011f, 105; Badiou 2010, 45.
7. Johnston 2011a, 170–75.
8. Johnston 2008b, 269–87; Johnston 2007a, 3–20; Johnston 2014.
9. Badiou 2010, 119.
10. Badiou 1995b, 79–80.
11. Meillassoux 2011d, 169; Meillassoux 2011a, 123–24.
12. Harman 2011, 40.
13. Meillassoux 2008a, 20.
14. Ibid., 21.
15. Ibid.
16. Ibid., 21–22.
17. Ibid., 24.
18. Ibid., 25.
19. Kripke 1972, 110.
20. Cutrofello 1997, 13, 18–20, 24, 27, 32–33, 41; Johnston 2005b, 43–44, 80–82, 107–8.
21. Hallward 2011, 137–38.
22. Meillassoux 2008a, 25–26.
23. Kant 1965, A27–28/B43–44 (72), A35–36/B52–53 (78), A507/B535 (449).
24. Meillassoux 2011c, 103–8, 116–21, 205–6.
25. Meillassoux 2011e, 225–31, 233–37.
26. Ibid., 180–81.
27. Ibid., 180–81, 183–84.
28. Meillassoux 2007a, 71–72, 74–75, 80.
29. Meillassoux 2011e, 187.
30. Ibid., 189.
31. Ibid., 190.
32. Ibid., 178.
33. Ibid., 179.
34. Ibid., 190, 210–12.
35. Hume 1969, 124–26; Hume 1993, 21–22, 27–28, 30.
36. Kant 1965, A384 (355), A386 (355–56), A392 (359), A395 (361), B608 (493).
37. Meillassoux 2011e, 183–84.
38. Meillassoux 2011d, 171.
39. Ibid., 171–72.
40. *SE* 21: 30–31.
41. Meillassoux 2011e, 237–38.

42. Ibid., 238.
43. Ibid., 237.
44. *SE* 14: 305–7; Meillassoux 2011e, 225–28; Johnston 2009c, 154–56.
45. Badiou 1975, 86.
46. Meillassoux 2011e, 199.
47. Meillassoux 2008a, 95.
48. Vernes 1982, 23.
49. Ibid., 37.
50. Ibid., 26–27, 35.
51. Ibid., 49.
52. Descartes 1993, 39–42, 51–52.
53. Vernes 1982, 72.
54. Ibid., 109–10.
55. Ibid., 49.
56. Ibid., 40.
57. Ibid., 107.
58. Ibid., 108.
59. Ibid., 64–65.
60. Ibid., 59.
61. Vernes 1982, 45–47, 58; Meillassoux 2008a, 95–96.
62. Vernes 1982, 101, 104.
63. Meillassoux 2008a, 95–98.
64. Johnston 2012a.
65. Johnston 2011b, 153–56.
66. Johnston 2011c, 71–91.
67. Hume 1969, 447–55; Hume 1993, 53–64.
68. Hegel 1971, §443–45 (185–90); Hegel 1991, §4–5 (35–39).

Works Cited

Acotto, Edoardo. 2007. "Alain Badiou et l'ontologie du monde perdu." In *Écrits autour de la pensée d'Alain Badiou,* edited by Bruno Besana and Oliver Feltham, 83–100. Paris: L'Harmattan.

Althusser, Louis. 2001a. "Philosophy as a Revolutionary Weapon: Interview Conducted by Maria Antonietta Macciocchi." In *Lenin and Philosophy and Other Essays,* translated by Ben Brewster, 1–9. New York: Monthly Review.

———. 2001b. "Lenin and Philosophy." In *Lenin and Philosophy and Other Essays,* translated by Ben Brewster, 11–43. New York: Monthly Review.

Ansermet, François. 2002. "Des neurosciences aux logosciences." In *Qui sont vos psychanalystes?* edited by Nathalie Georges, Jacques-Alain Miller, and Nathalie Marchaison, 376–84. Paris: Éditions du Seuil.

Ansermet, François, and Pierre Magistretti. 2007. *Biology of Freedom: Neural Plasticity, Experience, and the Unconscious.* Translated by Susan Fairfield. New York: Other.

Baas, Bernard. 1992. *Le désir pur: Parcours philosophiques dans les parages de J. Lacan.* Leuven: Peeters.

———. 1998. *De la chose à l'objet: Jacques Lacan et la traversée de la phénoménologie.* Leuven: Peeters.

Badiou, Alain. 1967. "Le (re)commencement du matérialisme dialectique." *Critique* 240 (May): 438–67.

———. 1975. *Théorie de la contradiction.* Paris: François Maspero.

———. 1982. *Théorie du sujet.* Paris: Éditions du Seuil.

———. 1985. *Peut-on penser la politique?* Paris: Éditions du Seuil.

———. 1988. *L'être et l'événement.* Paris: Éditions du Seuil.

———. 1990. "L'entretien de Bruxelles." *Les temps moderne* 526: 1–26.

———. 1994a. "Being by Numbers: Lauren Sedofsky Talks with Alain Badiou." *Artforum International* 33, no. 2 (October): 84–87, 118, 123–24.

———. 1994b. "Gilles Deleuze, The Fold: Leibniz and the Baroque." Translated by Thelma Sowley. In *Gilles Deleuze: The Theatre of Philosophy,* edited by Constantin Boundas and Dorothea Olkowski, 51–69. New York: Columbia University Press.

———. 1995a. *Beckett: L'increvable désir.* Paris: Hachette.

———. 1995b. "Platon et/ou Aristote-Leibniz: Théorie des ensembles et théorie des topos sous l'oeil du philosophe." In *L'objectivité mathématique: Platonismes et structures formelles,* edited by Marco Panza and Jean-Michel Salanskis, 61–83. Paris: Masson.

―――. 1998. "Politics and Philosophy: An Interview with Alain Badiou (with Peter Hallward)." *Angelaki: Journal of the Theoretical Humanities* 3, no. 3: 113–33.

―――. 1999a. *Manifesto for Philosophy*. Translated by Norman Madarasz. Albany: State University of New York Press.

―――. 1999b. "The (Re)turn of Philosophy Itself." In *Manifesto for Philosophy*, translated by Norman Madarasz, 111–38. Albany: State University of New York Press.

―――. 2001. *Ethics: An Essay on the Understanding of Evil*. Translated by Peter Hallward. London: Verso.

―――. 2002. "L'investigation transcendentale." In *Alain Badiou: Penser le multiple—Actes du Colloque de Bordeaux, 21–23 octobre 1999*, edited by Charles Ramond, 7–18. Paris: L'Harmattan.

―――. 2003a. "Beyond Formalisation: An Interview (with Bruno Bosteels and Peter Hallward)." Translated by Bruno Bosteels and Alberto Toscano. *Angelaki: Journal of the Theoretical Humanities* 8, no. 2 (August): 111–36.

―――. 2003b. "Philosophy and Desire." In *Infinite Thought: Truth and the Return of Philosophy*, edited and translated by Oliver Feltham and Justin Clemens, 39–57. London: Continuum.

―――. 2003c. "Philosophy and Art." In *Infinite Thought: Truth and the Return of Philosophy*, edited and translated by Oliver Feltham and Justin Clemens, 91–108. London: Continuum.

―――. 2003d. "The Definition of Philosophy." In *Infinite Thought: Truth and the Return of Philosophy*, edited and translated by Oliver Feltham and Justin Clemens, 165–68. London: Continuum.

―――. 2003e. "Ontology and Politics: An Interview with Alain Badiou." In *Infinite Thought: Truth and the Return of Philosophy*, edited and translated by Oliver Feltham and Justin Clemens, 169–93. London: Continuum.

―――. 2003f. "Of an Obscure Disaster: On the End of the Truth of State." Translated by Barbara P. Fulks. *Lacanian Ink* 22 (Fall): 58–89.

―――. 2003g. *Saint Paul: The Foundation of Universalism*. Translated by Ray Brassier. Stanford, Calif.: Stanford University Press.

―――. 2004a. "The Flux and the Party: In the Margins of Anti-Oedipus." Translated by Laura Balladur and Simon Krysl. *Polygraph: An International Journal of Culture & Politics* 15/16: 75–92.

―――. 2004b. "Mathematics and Philosophy: The Grand Style and the Little Style." In *Theoretical Writings*, edited and translated by Ray Brassier and Alberto Toscano, 3–20. London: Continuum.

―――. 2004c. "Philosophy and Mathematics: Infinity and the End of Romanticism." In *Theoretical Writings*, edited and translated by Ray Brassier and Alberto Toscano, 21–38. London: Continuum.

―――. 2004d. "One, Multiple, Multiplicities." In *Theoretical Writings*, edited and translated by Ray Brassier and Alberto Toscano, 67–80. London: Continuum.

―――. 2004e. "Notes Toward a Thinking of Appearance." In *Theoretical Writings*, edited and translated by Ray Brassier and Alberto Toscano, 177–87. London: Continuum.

———. 2004f. "The Transcendental." In *Theoretical Writings*, edited and translated by Ray Brassier and Alberto Toscano, 189–219. London: Continuum.

———. 2004g. "Afterword: Some Replies to a Demanding Friend." Translated by Alberto Toscano. In *Think Again: Alain Badiou and the Future of Philosophy*, edited by Peter Hallward, 232–37. London: Continuum.

———. 2005a. "Can Change Be Thought?: A Dialogue with Alain Badiou (with Bruno Bosteels)." In *Alain Badiou: Philosophy and Its Conditions*, edited by Gabriel Riera, 237–61. Albany: State University of New York Press.

———. 2005b. *Being and Event*. Translated by Oliver Feltham. London: Continuum.

———. 2005c. *Handbook of Inaesthetics*. Translated by Alberto Toscano. Stanford, Calif.: Stanford University Press.

———. 2006a. "Matters of Appearance: An Interview with Alain Badiou (with Lauren Sedofsky)." *Artforum International* 45, no. 3 (November): 246–53, 322.

———. 2006b. "Preface to the English-Language Edition." In *Briefings on Existence: A Short Treatise on Transitory Ontology*, translated by Norman Madarasz, ix–xii. Albany: State University of New York Press.

———. 2006c. *Briefings on Existence: A Short Treatise on Transitory Ontology*. Translated by Norman Madarasz. Albany: State University of New York Press.

———. 2006d. "Philosophy, Sciences, Mathematics: Interview with Alain Badiou." Translated by Robin Mackay and Ray Brassier. *Collapse: Philosophical Research and Development* 1 (September): 11–26.

———. 2006e. "The Formulas of *L'étourdit*." Translated by Scott Savaiano. *Lacanian Ink* 27 (Spring): 80–95.

———. 2006f. "The Question of Democracy: Analía Hounie Interviews Alain Badiou." *Lacanian Ink* 28 (Autumn): 54–59.

———. 2006g. *Logiques des mondes: L'être et l'événement, 2.* Paris: Éditions du Seuil.

———. 2006h. "The Truth Procedure in Politics." Miguel Abreu Gallery, New York City, November 18, 2006. http://www.lacan.com/blog/files/archive-1.html.

———. 2007a. *The Century*. Translated by Alberto Toscano. Cambridge, Eng.: Polity.

———. 2007b. "Préface de la nouvelle édition." In *Le concept de modèle: Introduction à une épistémologie matérialiste des mathématiques—Nouvelle édition augmentée d'une préface inédite*, 7–37. Paris: Librairie Arthème Fayard.

———. 2007c. "Towards a New Concept of Existence." *Lacanian Ink* 29 (Spring): 63–72.

———. 2007d. "New Horizons in Mathematics as a Philosophical Condition: An Interview with Alain Badiou (with Tzuchien Tho)." Translated by Tzuchien Tho. *Parrhesia* 3: 1–11.

———. 2008a. *Number and Numbers*. Translated by Robin Mackay. Cambridge, Eng.: Polity.

———. 2008b. "Jacques Lacan (1901–1981)." In *Petit panthéon portatif*, 12–15. Paris: La Fabrique Éditions.

———. 2008c. "Louis Althusser (1918–1990)." In *Petit panthéon portatif*, 57–87. Paris: La Fabrique Éditions.

———. 2008d. "Jacques Derrida (1930–2004)." In *Petit panthéon portatif*, 117–33. Paris: La Fabrique Éditions.

———. 2009a. *Éloge de l'amour (avec Nicolas Truong)*. Paris: Flammarion.

———. 2009b. *Logics of Worlds: Being and Event, 2*. Translated by Alberto Toscano. London: Continuum.

———. 2010. *La philosophie et l'événement: Alain Badiou avec Fabien Tarby*. Paris: Éditions Germina.

———. 2011a. "Renaissance de la philosophie: Théorie du sujet (1) (avec Natacha Michel)." In *Entretiens 1: 1981–1996*, 35–44. Paris: Nous.

———. 2011b. "Dix-neuf réponses à beaucoup plus d'objections: Jacques Rancière, Jean-François Lyotard, Philippe Lacoue-Labarthe." In *Entretiens 1: 1981–1996*, 59–79. Paris: Nous.

———. 2011c. "Philosophie & politique (avec Ata Hoodashtian)." In *Entretiens 1: 1981–1996*, 125–39. Paris: Nous.

———. 2011d. "Les lieux de la vérité (avec Jacques Henric)." In *Entretiens 1: 1981–1996*, 141–55. Paris: Nous.

———. 2011e. "De quoi nous sommes l'avant (avec Benoît Casas)." In *Entretiens 1: 1981–1996*, 223–47. Paris: Nous.

———. 2011f. *Second Manifesto for Philosophy*. Translated by Louise Burchill. Cambridge, Eng.: Polity.

Badiou, Alain, Joël Bellassen, and Louis Mossot. 2011. *The Rational Kernel of the Hegelian Dialectic: Translations, Introductions and Commentary on a Text by Zhang Shiying*. Translated by Tzuchien Tho. Melbourne: Re.press.

Badiou, Alain, and Élisabeth Roudinesco. 2012. *Jacques Lacan, passé présent: Dialogue*. Paris: Éditions du Seuil.

Balibar, Françoise. 1996. "*À propos du 'sujet de la science.'* " In *Le moment cartésien de la psychanalyse: Lacan, Descartes, le sujet*, edited by Erik Porge and Antonia Soulez, 21–28. Paris: Éditions Arcanes.

Balmès, François. 1999. *Ce que Lacan dit de l'être (1953–1960)*. Paris: Presses Universitaires de France.

Bandres, Lenin. 2007. "Badiou et l'atomisme ancien." In *Écrits autour de la pensée d'Alain Badiou*, edited by Bruno Besana and Oliver Feltham, 41–52. Paris: L'Harmattan.

Berkeley, George. 1982. *A Treatise Concerning the Principles of Human Knowledge*. Edited by Kenneth Winkler. Indianapolis, Ind.: Hackett.

Besana, Bruno. 2007a. "Quel multiple?: Les conditions ontologiques du concept d'événement chez Badiou et Deleuze." In *Écrits autour de la pensée d'Alain Badiou*, edited by Bruno Besana and Oliver Feltham, 23–40. Paris: L'Harmattan.

———. 2007b. "L'événement de l'être: Une proposition de lecture, en forçage aux textes de Badiou, du rapport entre événement et situations." In *Écrits autour de la pensée d'Alain Badiou*, edited by Bruno Besana and Oliver Feltham, 125–30. Paris: L'Harmattan.

Besana, Bruno, and Oliver Feltham. 2007. "Préface des editeurs." In *Écrits autour de la pensée d'Alain Badiou*, edited by Bruno Besana and Oliver Feltham, 9–19. Paris: L'Harmattan.

Boghossian, Paul. 2006. *Fear of Knowledge: Against Relativism and Constructivism.* Oxford: Oxford University Press.

Bosteels, Bruno. 2004a. "Logics of Antagonism: In the Margins of Alain Badiou's 'The Flux and the Party.' " *Polygraph: An International Journal of Culture & Politics* 15/16: 93–107.

———. 2004b. "On the Subject of the Dialectic." In *Think Again: Alain Badiou and the Future of Philosophy,* edited by Peter Hallward, 150–64. London: Continuum.

Brassier, Ray. 2000. "Stellar Void or Cosmic Animal?: Badiou and Deleuze on the Dice-Throw." *Pli: The Warwick Journal of Philosophy* 10: 200–217.

———. 2005. "Badiou's Materialist Epistemology of Mathematics." *Angelaki: Journal of the Theoretical Humanities* 10, no. 2 (August): 135–50.

———. 2007a. "Speculative Realism: Presentation by Ray Brassier." *Collapse: Philosophical Research and Development* 3 (November): 308–33.

———. 2007b. "L'anti-phénomène—Présentation et disparaître." In *Écrits autour de la pensée d'Alain Badiou,* edited by Bruno Besana and Oliver Feltham, 55–64. Paris: L'Harmattan.

———. 2007c. *Nihil Unbound: Enlightenment and Extinction.* Basingstoke, Eng.: Palgrave Macmillan.

Braver, Lee. 2007. *A Thing of This World: A History of Continental Anti-Realism.* Evanston, Ill.: Northwestern University Press.

Brousse, Marie-Hélène. 1996. "Language, Speech, and Discourse." In *Reading Seminars I and II: Lacan's Return to Freud,* edited by Richard Feldstein, Bruce Fink, and Maire Jaanus, 123–29. Albany: State University of New York Press.

Brown, Nathan. 2008. "On *After Finitude:* A Response to Peter Hallward." http://nsrnicek.googlepages.com/Response_to_Hallward_on_Meillassoux.pdf.

Burgoyne, Bernard. 2003. "From the Letter to the Matheme: Lacan's Scientific Methods." In *The Cambridge Companion to Lacan,* edited by Jean-Michel Rabaté, 69–85. Cambridge, Eng.: Cambridge University Press.

Chalmers, David J. 1997. *The Conscious Mind: In Search of a Fundamental Theory.* Oxford: Oxford University Press.

Changeux, Jean-Pierre. 2004. *The Physiology of Truth: Neuroscience and Human Knowledge.* Translated by M. B. DeBevoise. Cambridge, Mass.: Harvard University Press.

Chiesa, Lorenzo. 2007. *Subjectivity and Otherness: A Philosophical Reading of Lacan.* Cambridge, Mass.: MIT Press.

Chiesa, Lorenzo, and Alberto Toscano. 2005. "Ethics and Capital, *Ex Nihilo.*" In *Umbr(a): A Journal of the Unconscious—The Dark God,* edited by Andrew Skomra, 9–25. Buffalo: Center for the Study of Psychoanalysis and Culture, State University of New York at Buffalo.

———. 2007. "*Agape* and the Anonymous Religion of Atheism." *Angelaki: Journal of the Theoretical Humanities* 12, no. 1 (April): 113–25.

Copjec, Joan. 2004. *Imagine There's No Woman: Ethics and Sublimation.* Cambridge, Mass.: MIT Press.

Cutrofello, Andrew. 1997. *Imagining Otherwise: Metapsychology and the Analytic A Posteriori.* Evanston, Ill.: Northwestern University Press.

———. 2002. "The Ontological Status of Lacan's Mathematical Paradigms." In *Reading Seminar XX: Lacan's Major Work on Love, Knowledge, and Feminine Sexuality,* edited by Suzanne Barnard and Bruce Fink, 141–70. Albany: State University of New York Press.

Damasio, Antonio. 2003. *Looking for Spinoza: Joy, Sorrow and the Feeling Brain.* New York: Harcourt.

Deleuze, Gilles. 1977. "I Have Nothing to Admit." Translated by Janis Forman. *Semiotext(e)* 2, no. 3: 110–16.

Dennett, Daniel C. 2003. *Freedom Evolves.* New York: Viking.

Desanti, Jean-Toussaint. 2004. "Some Remarks on the Intrinsic Ontology of Alain Badiou." In *Think Again: Alain Badiou and the Future of Philosophy,* edited by Peter Hallward, 59–66. London: Continuum.

Descartes, René. 1993. *Meditations on First Philosophy.* Translated by Donald A. Cress. 3rd edition. Indianapolis, Ind.: Hackett.

Diderot, Denis. 1966. *D'Alembert's Dream.* In *Rameau's Nephew/D'Alembert's Dream,* translated by Leonard Tancock. New York: Penguin Books.

———. 1994. *Encyclopédie.* In *Diderot, Oeuvres, Tome I: Philosophie,* edited by Laurent Versini. Paris: Éditions Robert Laffont.

Dolar, Mladen. 1998. "Cogito as the Subject of the Unconscious." In *Cogito and the Unconscious,* edited by Slavoj Žižek, 11–40. Durham, N.C.: Duke University Press.

Engels, Friedrich. 1940. *Dialectics of Nature.* Translated by C. P. Dutt. New York: International.

———. 1941. *Ludwig Feuerbach and the Outcome of Classical German Philosophy.* New York: International.

———. 1959. *Anti-Dühring: Herr Eugen Dühring's Revolution in Science.* Moscow: Foreign Languages Publishing House.

Fink, Bruce. 1995a. *The Lacanian Subject: Between Language and Jouissance.* Princeton, N.J.: Princeton University Press.

———. 1995b. "Science and Psychoanalysis." In *Reading Seminar XI: Lacan's Four Fundamental Concepts of Psychoanalysis,* edited by Richard Feldstein, Bruce Fink, and Maire Jaanus, 55–64. Albany: State University of New York Press.

———. 2004. *Lacan to the Letter: Reading "Écrits" Closely.* Minneapolis: University of Minnesota Press.

Freud, Sigmund. *The Standard Edition of the Complete Psychological Works of Sigmund Freud.* 24 volumes. Edited and translated by James Strachey, in collaboration with Anna Freud, assisted by Alix Strachey and Alan Tyson. London: Hogarth Press and the Institute of Psycho-Analysis, 1953–74.

———. *Three Essays on the Theory of Sexuality. SE* 7: 123–245.

———. "On the Universal Tendency to Debasement in the Sphere of Love (Contributions to the Psychology of Love II)." *SE* 11: 177–90.

———. *Totem and Taboo. SE* 13: 1–161.

———. "The Claims of Psycho-Analysis to Scientific Interest." *SE* 13: 163–90.

———. "The Unconscious." *SE* 14: 159–215.

———. "On Transience." *SE* 14: 303–7.

———. *Introductory Lectures on Psycho-Analysis. SE* 15–16.

———. "From the History of an Infantile Neurosis." *SE* 17: 1–123.

———. *Beyond the Pleasure Principle. SE* 18: 1–64.

———. *The Ego and the Id. SE* 19: 1–59.

———. "The Dissolution of the Oedipus Complex." *SE* 19: 171–79.

———. "The Resistances to Psycho-Analysis." *SE* 19: 211–24.

———. "Negation." *SE* 19: 233–39.

———. *The Future of an Illusion. SE* 21: 1–56.

———. *Civilization and Its Discontents. SE* 21: 57–145.

———. *New Introductory Lectures on Psycho-Analysis. SE* 22: 1–182.

———. *Moses and Monotheism. SE* 23: 1–137.

———. *An Outline of Psycho-Analysis. SE* 23: 139–207.

———. 1987. "Overview of the Transference Neuroses." Translated by Axel Hoffer and Peter T. Hoffer. In *A Phylogenetic Fantasy: Overview of the Transference Neuroses,* edited by Ilse Grubrich-Simitis, 5–20. Cambridge, Mass.: Harvard University Press.

Galileo Galilei. 1957. "The Assayer." In *Discoveries and Opinions of Galileo,* translated by Stillman Drake, 229–80. New York: Anchor Books.

Gillespie, Sam. 2007. "L'être multiple présenté, représenté, rendu vrai." In *Écrits autour de la pensée d'Alain Badiou,* edited by Bruno Besana and Oliver Feltham, 71–82. Paris: L'Harmattan.

Gould, Stephen Jay, and Elisabeth S. Vrba. 1982. "Exaptation—A Missing Term in the Science of Form." *Paleobiology* 8, no. 1: 4–15.

Grigg, Russell. 2008. *Lacan, Language, and Philosophy.* Albany: State University of New York Press.

Grubrich-Simitis, Ilse. 1987. "Preface to the Original Edition." In Sigmund Freud, *A Phylogenetic Fantasy: Overview of the Transference Neuroses,* edited by Ilse Grubrich-Simitis, xv–xvii. Cambridge: Harvard University Press.

Hägglund, Martin. 2011. "Radical Atheist Materialism: A Critique of Meillassoux." In *The Speculative Turn: Continental Materialism and Realism,* edited by Levi Bryant, Graham Harman, and Nick Srnicek, 114–29. Melbourne: Re.press.

Hallward, Peter. 1998. "Generic Sovereignty: The Philosophy of Alain Badiou." *Angelaki: Journal of the Theoretical Humanities* 3, no. 3: 87–111.

———. 2003. *Badiou: A Subject to Truth.* Minneapolis: University of Minnesota Press.

———. 2005. "Depending on Inconsistency: Badiou's Answer to the 'Guiding Question of All Contemporary Philosophy.'" *Polygraph: An International Journal of Culture & Politics* 17: 11–25.

———. 2008. "Anything Is Possible." *Radical Philosophy* 152 (November/December): 51–57.

———. 2011. "Anything Is Possible: A Reading of Quentin Meillassoux's *After Finitude.*" In *The Speculative Turn: Continental Materialism and Realism,* edited by Levi Bryant, Nick Srnicek, and Graham Harman, 130–41. Melbourne: Re.press.

Harari, Roberto. 2004. *Lacan's Four Fundamental Concepts of Psychoanalysis: An Introduction.* Translated by Judith Filc. New York: Other.

Harman, Graham. 2007a. "Speculative Realism: Presentation by Graham Harman." *Collapse: Philosophical Research and Development* 3 (November): 367–407.

———. 2007b. "Quentin Meillassoux: A New French Philosopher." *Philosophy Today* 51, no. 1 (Spring): 104–17.

———. 2011. *Quentin Meillassoux: Philosophy in the Making.* Edinburgh: Edinburgh University Press.

Hasker, William. 1999. *The Emergent Self.* Ithaca, N.Y.: Cornell University Press.

Hebb, Donald O. 1949. *The Organization of Behavior: A Neuropsychological Theory.* New York: John Wiley and Sons.

Hegel, G. W. F. 1970. *Philosophy of Nature: Part Two of the Encyclopedia of the Philosophical Sciences.* Translated by A. V. Miller. Oxford: Oxford University Press.

———. 1971. *Philosophy of Mind: Part Three of the Encyclopedia of the Philosophical Sciences.* Translated by William Wallace. Oxford: Oxford University Press.

———. 1991. *Elements of the Philosophy of Right.* Edited by Allen W. Wood. Translated by H. B. Nisbet. Cambridge, Eng.: Cambridge University Press.

Hodges, Aaron F. 2010. Intervention at the Sixth Annual Interdisciplinary Spring Conference of the Theory Reading Group at Cornell University: "Form and Its Genesis." Cornell University, Ithaca, New York, April 24, 2010.

Hofstadter, Douglas. 2007. *I Am a Strange Loop.* New York: Basic Books.

Hume, David. 1969. *A Treatise of Human Nature.* Edited by Ernest C. Mossner. New York: Penguin Books.

———. 1993. *An Enquiry Concerning Human Understanding.* Edited by Eric Steinberg. 2nd edition. Indianapolis, Ind.: Hackett.

Jablonka, Eva, and Marion J. Lamb. 2005. *Evolution in Four Dimensions: Genetic, Epigenetic, Behavioral, and Symbolic Variation in the History of Life.* Cambridge, Mass.: MIT Press.

Johnston, Adrian. 2003. "The Genesis of the Transcendent: Kant, Schelling, and the Ground of Experience." *Idealistic Studies* 33, no. 1 (Spring): 57–81.

———. 2004a. "Revulsion Is Not Without Its Subject: Kant, Lacan, Žižek and the Symptom of Subjectivity." *Pli: The Warwick Journal of Philosophy* 15 (Spring): 199–228.

———. 2004b. "Against Embodiment: The Material Ground of the Immaterial Subject." *Journal for Lacanian Studies* 2, no. 2 (December): 230–54.

———. 2005a. "There Is Truth, and Then There Are Truths—or, Slavoj Žižek as a Reader of Alain Badiou." *(Re)-turn: A Journal of Lacanian Studies* 2 (Spring): 85–141.

———. 2005b. *Time Driven: Metapsychology and the Splitting of the Drive.* Evanston, Ill.: Northwestern University Press.

———. 2006. "Ghosts of Substance Past: Schelling, Lacan, and the Denaturalization of Nature." In *Lacan: The Silent Partners,* edited by Slavoj Žižek, 34–55. London: Verso.

———. 2007a. "Slavoj Žižek's Hegelian Reformation: Giving a Hearing to *The Parallax View.*" *Diacritics: A Review of Contemporary Criticism* 37, no. 1 (Spring): 3–20.

———. 2007b. "Lightening Ontology: Slavoj Žižek and the Unbearable Lightness of Being Free." *Lacanian Ink: The Symptom* 8 (Spring): http://www .lacan.com/symptom8_articles/johnston8.html.

———. 2008a. "A Blast from the Future: Freud, Lacan, Marcuse, and Snapping the Threads of the Past." *Umbr(a): A Journal of the Unconscious—Utopia,* edited by Ryan Anthony Hatch, 67–84. Buffalo: Center for the Study of Psychoanalysis and Culture, State University of New York at Buffalo.

———. 2008b. *Žižek's Ontology: A Transcendental Materialist Theory of Subjectivity.* Evanston, Ill.: Northwestern University Press.

———. 2009a. *Badiou, Žižek, and Political Transformations: The Cadence of Change.* Evanston, Ill.: Northwestern University Press.

———. 2009b. "The Emergence of Speculative Realism: A Review of Ray Brassier's *Nihil Unbound: Enlightenment and Extinction.*" *Journal of the British Society of Phenomenology* 40, no. 1 (January): 107–9.

———. 2009c. "Life Terminable and Interminable: The Undead and the Afterlife of the Afterlife—A Friendly Disagreement with Martin Hägglund." Special issue: "Living On: Of Martin Hägglund," edited by David E. Johnson, *New Centennial Review* 9, no. 1 (Spring): 147–89.

———. 2010a. "Freud and Continental Philosophy." In *The History of Continental Philosophy.* 8 volumes, edited by Alan D. Schrift. *Volume III: The New Century—Bergsonism, Phenomenology, and Responses to Modern Science,* edited by Keith Ansell-Pearson and Alan D. Schrift, 319–46. Durham, Eng.: Acumen.

———. 2010b. "A Letter to Žižek Regarding *In Defense of Lost Causes.*" *International Journal of Žižek Studies* 4, no. 2: 1–10.

———. 2010c. "This Philosophy Which Is Not One: Jean-Claude Milner, Alain Badiou, and Lacanian Antiphilosophy." Special issue: "On Jean-Claude Milner," edited by Justin Clemens and Sigi Jöttkandt, *S: Journal of the Jan Van Eyck Circle for Lacanian Ideology Critique* 3 (Spring): 137–58.

———. 2010d. "The Misfeeling of What Happens: Slavoj Žižek, Antonio Damasio, and a Materialist Account of Affects." Special issue: "Žižek and Political Subjectivity," edited by Derek Hook and Calum Neill, *Subjectivity* 3, no. 1 (April): 76–100.

———. 2011a. "The Weakness of Nature: Hegel, Freud, Lacan, and Negativity Materialized." In *Hegel and the Infinite: Religion, Politics, and Dialectic,* edited by Slavoj Žižek, Clayton Crockett, and Creston Davis, 159–79. New York: Columbia University Press.

———. 2011b. "Repeating Engels: Renewing the Cause of the Materialist Wager for the Twenty-First Century." *Theory @ Buffalo* 15: 141–82.

———. 2011c. "Second Natures in Dappled Worlds: John McDowell, Nancy Cartwright, and Hegelian-Lacanian Materialism." *Umbr(a): A Journal of the Unconscious—The Worst,* edited by Matthew Rigilano and Kyle Fetter, 71–91. Buffalo: Center for the Study of Psychoanalysis and Culture, State University of New York at Buffalo.

————. 2012a. "The Voiding of Weak Nature: The Transcendental Materialist Kernels of Hegel's *Naturphilosophie*." *Graduate Faculty Philosophy Journal* 33, no. 1 (Spring): 103–57.

————. 2012b. " 'Naturalism or Anti-Naturalism? No, Thanks—Both Are Worse!': Science, Materialism, and Slavoj Žižek." Special issue: "On Slavoj Žižek," *La revue internationale de philosophie* 261: 321–46.

————. 2013a. "A Critique of Natural Economy: Quantum Physics with Žižek." In *Žižek Now*, edited by Jamil Khader and Molly Rothernberg. Cambridge, Eng.: Polity. Forthcoming.

————. 2013b. "Misfelt Feelings: Unconscious Affect Between Psychoanalysis, Neuroscience, and Philosophy." In *Self and Emotional Life: Merging Philosophy, Psychoanalysis, and Neurobiology*, by Adrian Johnston and Catherine Malabou. New York: Columbia University Press. Forthcoming.

————. 2013c. "Slavoj Žižek." In *The Blackwell Companion to Continental Philosophy*, edited by William Schroeder, 2nd edition. Oxford: Blackwell. Forthcoming.

————. 2014. *Adventures in Transcendental Materialism: Dialogues with Contemporary Thinkers*. Edinburgh: Edinburgh University Press. Forthcoming.

Julien, Philippe. 1994. *Jacques Lacan's Return to Freud: The Real, the Symbolic, and the Imaginary*. Translated by Devra Beck Simiu. New York: New York University Press.

Kandel, Eric R. 2005a. "Psychotherapy and the Single Synapse: The Impact of Psychiatric Thought on Neurobiologic Research." In *Psychiatry, Psychoanalysis, and the New Biology of Mind*, 5–26. Washington, D.C.: American Psychiatric.

————. 2005b. "A New Intellectual Framework for Psychiatry." In *Psychiatry, Psychoanalysis, and the New Biology of Mind*, 33–58. Washington, D.C.: American Psychiatric.

————. 2005c. "Biology and the Future of Psychoanalysis: A New Intellectual Framework for Psychiatry Revisited." In *Psychiatry, Psychoanalysis, and the New Biology of Mind*, 63–106. Washington, D.C.: American Psychiatric.

————. 2005d. "From Metapsychology to Molecular Biology: Explorations into the Nature of Anxiety." In *Psychiatry, Psychoanalysis, and the New Biology of Mind*, 117–56. Washington, D.C.: American Psychiatric.

Kant, Immanuel. 1965. *Critique of Pure Reason*. Translated by Norman Kemp Smith. New York: Saint Martin's.

Kierkegaard, Søren. 2004. *The Sickness unto Death*. Translated by Alastair Hannay. New York: Penguin Books.

Koyré, Alexandre. 1958. *From the Closed World to the Infinite Universe*. New York: Harper Torchbooks.

Kripke, Saul A. 1972. *Naming and Necessity*. Cambridge, Mass.: Harvard University Press.

Lacan, Jacques. 1953. "Some Reflections on the Ego." *International Journal of Psycho-Analysis* 34: 11–17.

————. 1966. "La science et la vérité." In *Écrits*, 855–77. Paris: Éditions du Seuil.

————. 1970. "Of Structure as an Inmixing of an Otherness Prerequisite to Any Subject Whatever." In *The Structuralist Controversy: The Languages of Criticism and the Sciences of Man,* edited by Richard Macksey and Eugenio Donato, 186–200. Baltimore: Johns Hopkins University Press.

————. 1973. *Télévision.* Paris: Éditions du Seuil.

————. 1990a. "Responses to Students of Philosophy Concerning the Object of Psychoanalysis." Translated by Jeffrey Mehlman. In *Television/A Challenge to the Psychoanalytic Establishment,* edited by Joan Copjec, 107–14. New York: W.W. Norton.

————. 1990b. "Letter of Dissolution." Translated by Jeffrey Mehlman. In *Television/A Challenge to the Psychoanalytic Establishment,* edited by Joan Copjec, 129–31. New York: W.W. Norton.

————. 1990c. "The Other Is Missing." Translated by Jeffrey Mehlman. In *Television/A Challenge to the Psychoanalytic Establishment,* edited by Joan Copjec, 133–35. New York: W.W. Norton.

————. 1995. "Proposition of 9 October 1967 on the Psychoanalyst of the School." Translated by Russell Grigg. *Analysis* 6: 1–13.

————. 2001a. "Discours de Rome." In *Autres écrits,* edited by Jacques-Alain Miller, 133–64. Paris: Éditions du Seuil.

————. 2001b. "Les quatre concepts fondamentaux de la psychanalyse: Compte rendu du séminaire 1964." In *Autres écrits,* edited by Jacques-Alain Miller, 187–89. Paris: Éditions du Seuil.

————. 2001c. "Problèmes cruciaux pour la psychanalyse: Compte rendu du Séminaire 1964–1965." In *Autres écrits,* edited by Jacques-Alain Miller, 199–202. Paris: Éditions du Seuil.

————. 2001d. "Petit discours à l'ORTF." In *Autres écrits,* edited by Jacques-Alain Miller, 221–26. Paris: Éditions du Seuil.

————. 2001e. "Allocution sur l'enseignement." In *Autres écrits,* edited by Jacques-Alain Miller, 297–305. Paris: Éditions du Seuil.

————. 2001f. "Radiophonie." In *Autres écrits,* edited by Jacques-Alain Miller, 403–47. Paris: Éditions du Seuil.

————. 2001g. "L'étourdit." In *Autres écrits,* edited by Jacques-Alain Miller, 449–95. Paris: Éditions du Seuil.

————. 2005a. "Le symbolique, l'imaginaire et le réel." In *Des noms-du-père,* edited by Jacques-Alain Miller, 9–63. Paris: Éditions du Seuil.

————. 2005b. "Place, origine et fin de mon enseignement." In *Mon enseignement,* edited by Jacques-Alain Miller, 9–73. Paris: Éditions du Seuil.

————. 2005c. "Donc, vous aurez entendu Lacan." In *Mon enseignement,* edited by Jacques-Alain Miller, 113–38. Paris: Éditions du Seuil.

————. 2005d. "Discours aux catholiques." In *Le triomphe de la religion, précédé de Discours aux catholiques,* edited by Jacques-Alain Miller, 9–65. Paris: Éditions du Seuil.

————. 2005e. "Le triomphe de la religion." In *Le triomphe de la religion, précédé de Discours aux catholiques,* edited by Jacques-Alain Miller, 67–102. Paris: Éditions du Seuil.

———. 2006a. "The Mirror Stage as Formative of the *I* Function as Revealed in Psychoanalytic Experience." In *Écrits: The First Complete Edition in English*, translated by Bruce Fink, 75–81. New York: W.W. Norton.

———. 2006b. "Logical Time and the Assertion of Anticipated Certainty: A New Sophism." In *Écrits: The First Complete Edition in English*, translated by Bruce Fink, 161–75. New York: W.W. Norton.

———. 2006c. "On the Subject Who Is Finally in Question." In *Écrits: The First Complete Edition in English*, translated by Bruce Fink, 189–96. New York: W.W. Norton.

———. 2006d. "The Function and Field of Speech and Language in Psychoanalysis." In *Écrits: The First Complete Edition in English*, translated by Bruce Fink, 197–268. New York: W.W. Norton.

———. 2006e. "Variations on the Standard Treatment." In *Écrits: The First Complete Edition in English*, translated by Bruce Fink, 269–302. New York: W.W. Norton.

———. 2006f. "On a Question Prior to Any Possible Treatment of Psychosis." In *Écrits: The First Complete Edition in English*, translated by Bruce Fink, 445–88. New York: W.W. Norton.

———. 2006g. "The Direction of the Treatment and the Principles of Its Power." In *Écrits: The First Complete Edition in English*, translated by Bruce Fink, 489–542. New York: W.W. Norton.

———. 2006h. "In Memory of Ernest Jones: On His Theory of Symbolism." In *Écrits: The First Complete Edition in English*, translated by Bruce Fink, 585–601. New York: W.W. Norton.

———. 2006i. "On an Ex Post Facto Syllabary." In *Écrits: The First Complete Edition in English*, translated by Bruce Fink, 602–9. New York: W.W. Norton.

———. 2006j. "Kant with Sade." In *Écrits: The First Complete Edition in English*, translated by Bruce Fink, 645–68. New York: W.W. Norton.

———. 2006k. "The Subversion of the Subject and the Dialectic of Desire in the Freudian Unconscious." In *Écrits: The First Complete Edition in English*, translated by Bruce Fink, 671–702. New York: W.W. Norton.

———. 2006l. "Position of the Unconscious." In *Écrits: The First Complete Edition in English*, translated by Bruce Fink, 703–21. New York: W.W. Norton.

———. 2006m. "Science and Truth." In *Écrits: The First Complete Edition in English*, translated by Bruce Fink, 726–45. New York: W.W. Norton.

———. 2007. "Du symbole, et de sa fonction religieuse." In *Le mythe individuel du névrosé, ou poésie et vérité dans la névrose*, edited by Jacques-Alain Miller, 51–98. Paris: Éditions du Seuil.

Lacan, Jacques. The Seminars:

———. *The Seminar of Jacques Lacan, Book I: Freud's Papers on Technique, 1953–1954*. Edited by Jacques-Alain Miller. Translated by John Forrester. New York: W.W. Norton, 1988.

———. *The Seminar of Jacques Lacan, Book II: The Ego in Freud's Theory and in the Technique of Psychoanalysis, 1954–1955*. Edited by Jacques-Alain Miller. Translated by Sylvana Tomaselli. New York: W.W. Norton, 1988.

———. *Le Séminaire de Jacques Lacan, Livre III: Les psychoses, 1955–1956.* Edited by Jacques-Alain Miller. Paris: Éditions du Seuil, 1981.

———. *The Seminar of Jacques Lacan, Book III: The Psychoses, 1955–1956.* Edited by Jacques-Alain Miller. Translated by Russell Grigg. New York: W.W. Norton, 1993.

———. *Le Séminaire de Jacques Lacan, Livre IV: La relation d'objet, 1956–1957.* Edited by Jacques-Alain Miller. Paris: Éditions du Seuil, 1994.

———. *Le Séminaire de Jacques Lacan, Livre V: Les formations de l'inconscient, 1957–1958.* Edited by Jacques-Alain Miller. Paris: Éditions du Seuil, 1998.

———. "Le Séminaire de Jacques Lacan, Livre VI: Le désir et son interprétation, 1958–1959." Unpublished typescript.

———. *The Seminar of Jacques Lacan, Book VII: The Ethics of Psychoanalysis, 1959–1960.* Edited by Jacques-Alain Miller. Translated by Dennis Porter. New York: W.W. Norton, 1992.

———. *Le Séminaire de Jacques Lacan, Livre VIII: Le transfert, 1960–1961.* Edited by Jacques-Alain Miller. 2nd corrected edition. Paris: Éditions du Seuil, 2001.

———. "Le Séminaire de Jacques Lacan, Livre IX: L'identification, 1961–1962." Unpublished typescript.

———. *Le Séminaire de Jacques Lacan, Livre X: L'angoisse, 1962–1963.* Edited by Jacques-Alain Miller. Paris: Éditions du Seuil, 2004.

———. *Le Séminaire de Jacques Lacan, Livre XI: Les quatre concepts fondamentaux de la psychanalyse, 1964.* Edited by Jacques-Alain Miller. Paris: Éditions du Seuil, 1973.

———. *The Seminar of Jacques Lacan, Book XI: The Four Fundamental Concepts of Psycho-Analysis, 1964.* Edited by Jacques-Alain Miller. Translated by Alan Sheridan. New York: W.W. Norton, 1977.

———. "Le Séminaire de Jacques Lacan, Livre XII: Problèmes cruciaux pour la psychanalyse, 1964–1965." Unpublished typescript.

———. "Le Séminaire de Jacques Lacan, Livre XIII: L'objet de la psychanalyse, 1965–1966." Unpublished typescript.

———. "Le Séminaire de Jacques Lacan, Livre XIV: La logique du fantasme, 1966–1967." Unpublished typescript.

———. "Le Séminaire de Jacques Lacan, Livre XV: L'acte psychanalytique, 1967–1968." Unpublished typescript.

———. *Le Séminaire de Jacques Lacan, Livre XVI: D'un Autre à l'autre, 1968–1969.* Edited by Jacques-Alain Miller. Paris: Éditions du Seuil, 2006.

———. *The Seminar of Jacques Lacan, Book XVII: The Other Side of Psychoanalysis, 1969–1970.* Edited by Jacques-Alain Miller. Translated by Russell Grigg. New York: W.W. Norton, 2007.

———. *Le Séminaire de Jacques Lacan, Livre XVIII: D'un discours qui ne serait pas du semblant, 1971.* Edited by Jacques-Alain Miller. Paris: Éditions du Seuil, 2007.

———. "Le Séminaire de Jacques Lacan, Livre XIX: . . . ou pire, 1971–1972." Unpublished typescript.

———. "Le Séminaire de Jacques Lacan, Livre XIX: Le savoir du psychanalyste, 1971–1972." Unpublished typescript.

———. *The Seminar of Jacques Lacan, Book XX: Encore, 1972–1973.* Edited by Jacques-Alain Miller. Translated by Bruce Fink. New York: W.W. Norton, 1998.

———. "Le Séminaire de Jacques Lacan, Livre XXI: Les non-dupes errent, 1973–1974." Unpublished typescript.

———. *Le Séminaire de Jacques Lacan, Livre XXII: R.S.I., 1974–1975.* Edited by Jacques-Alain Miller. *Ornicar?* 2, 3, 4, 5 (1975).

———. *Le Séminaire de Jacques Lacan, Livre XXIII: Le sinthome, 1975–1976.* Edited by Jacques-Alain Miller. Paris: Éditions du Seuil, 2005.

———. *Le Séminaire de Jacques Lacan, Livre XXIV: L'insu que sait de l'une-bévue s'aile à mourre, 1976–1977.* Edited by Jacques-Alain Miller. *Ornicar?* 12/13, 14, 15, 16, 17/18 (1977–79).

———. "Le Séminaire de Jacques Lacan, Livre XXV: Le moment de conclure, 1977–1978." Unpublished typescript.

Lacan, Jacques, and Wladimir Granoff. 1956. "Fetishism: The Symbolic, the Imaginary and the Real." In *Perversions: Psychodynamics and Therapy,* edited by Sandor Lorand, 265–76. New York: Gramercy Books.

La Mettrie, Julien Offray de. 1993. *Man, a Machine.* Translated by Gertrude C. Bussey. Revised by M. W. Calkins. La Salle, Ill.: Open Court.

Laplanche, Jean. 1987. *Problématiques V: Le baquet—Transcendance du transfert.* Paris: Presses Universitaires de France.

Leclaire, Serge. 1996a. "Note sur l'objet de la psychanalyse: Séminaire à l'École Normale Supérieure, mars 1966." In *Écrits pour la psychanalyse, 1: Demeures de l'ailleurs, 1954–1993,* 105–15. Paris: Éditions du Seuil.

———. 1996b. "Le refoulement: Séminaire à l'École Normale Supérieure, novembre 1966–mars 1967." In *Écrits pour la psychanalyse, 1: Demeures de l'ailleurs, 1954–1993,* 117–38. Paris: Éditions du Seuil.

LeDoux, Joseph. 2002. *Synaptic Self: How Our Brains Become Who We Are.* New York: Penguin Books.

Lee, Jonathan Scott. 1990. *Jacques Lacan.* Amherst: University of Massachusetts Press.

Le Gaufey, Guy. 1996. *L'incomplétude du symbolique: De René Descartes à Jacques Lacan.* Paris: E.P.E.L.

Lemosof, Alain. 2005. "L'objet de la psychanalyse (1965–1966)." In *Lacaniana: Les séminaires de Jacques Lacan, 1964–1979,* edited by Moustapha Safouan, 105–37. Paris: Librairie Arthème Fayard.

Lenin, V. I. 1972. *Materialism and Empirio-Criticism.* Beijing: Foreign Languages.

Leupin, Alexandre. 2004. *Lacan Today: Psychoanalysis, Science, Religion.* New York: Other.

Levins, Richard, and Richard Lewontin. 1985a. "Introduction." In *The Dialectical Biologist,* 1–5. Cambridge, Mass.: Harvard University Press.

———. 1985b. "Evolution as Theory and Ideology." In *The Dialectical Biologist,* 9–64. Cambridge, Mass.: Harvard University Press.

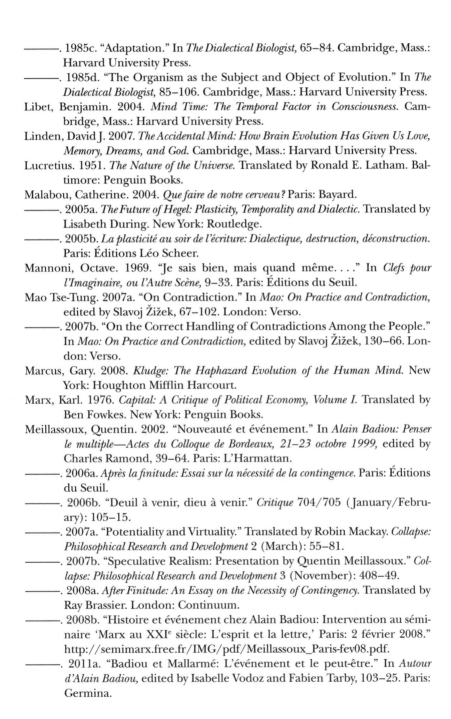

————. 1985c. "Adaptation." In *The Dialectical Biologist,* 65–84. Cambridge, Mass.: Harvard University Press.

————. 1985d. "The Organism as the Subject and Object of Evolution." In *The Dialectical Biologist,* 85–106. Cambridge, Mass.: Harvard University Press.

Libet, Benjamin. 2004. *Mind Time: The Temporal Factor in Consciousness.* Cambridge, Mass.: Harvard University Press.

Linden, David J. 2007. *The Accidental Mind: How Brain Evolution Has Given Us Love, Memory, Dreams, and God.* Cambridge, Mass.: Harvard University Press.

Lucretius. 1951. *The Nature of the Universe.* Translated by Ronald E. Latham. Baltimore: Penguin Books.

Malabou, Catherine. 2004. *Que faire de notre cerveau?* Paris: Bayard.

————. 2005a. *The Future of Hegel: Plasticity, Temporality and Dialectic.* Translated by Lisabeth During. New York: Routledge.

————. 2005b. *La plasticité au soir de l'écriture: Dialectique, destruction, déconstruction.* Paris: Éditions Léo Scheer.

Mannoni, Octave. 1969. "Je sais bien, mais quand même. . . ." In *Clefs pour l'Imaginaire, ou l'Autre Scène,* 9–33. Paris: Éditions du Seuil.

Mao Tse-Tung. 2007a. "On Contradiction." In *Mao: On Practice and Contradiction,* edited by Slavoj Žižek, 67–102. London: Verso.

————. 2007b. "On the Correct Handling of Contradictions Among the People." In *Mao: On Practice and Contradiction,* edited by Slavoj Žižek, 130–66. London: Verso.

Marcus, Gary. 2008. *Kludge: The Haphazard Evolution of the Human Mind.* New York: Houghton Mifflin Harcourt.

Marx, Karl. 1976. *Capital: A Critique of Political Economy, Volume I.* Translated by Ben Fowkes. New York: Penguin Books.

Meillassoux, Quentin. 2002. "Nouveauté et événement." In *Alain Badiou: Penser le multiple—Actes du Colloque de Bordeaux, 21–23 octobre 1999,* edited by Charles Ramond, 39–64. Paris: L'Harmattan.

————. 2006a. *Après la finitude: Essai sur la nécessité de la contingence.* Paris: Éditions du Seuil.

————. 2006b. "Deuil à venir, dieu à venir." *Critique* 704/705 (January/February): 105–15.

————. 2007a. "Potentiality and Virtuality." Translated by Robin Mackay. *Collapse: Philosophical Research and Development* 2 (March): 55–81.

————. 2007b. "Speculative Realism: Presentation by Quentin Meillassoux." *Collapse: Philosophical Research and Development* 3 (November): 408–49.

————. 2008a. *After Finitude: An Essay on the Necessity of Contingency.* Translated by Ray Brassier. London: Continuum.

————. 2008b. "Histoire et événement chez Alain Badiou: Intervention au séminaire 'Marx au XXIᵉ siècle: L'esprit et la lettre,' Paris: 2 février 2008." http://semimarx.free.fr/IMG/pdf/Meillassoux_Paris-fev08.pdf.

————. 2011a. "Badiou et Mallarmé: L'événement et le peut-être." In *Autour d'Alain Badiou,* edited by Isabelle Vodoz and Fabien Tarby, 103–25. Paris: Germina.

———. 2011b. "Destinations des corps subjectivés." In *Autour de "Logiques des mondes,"* edited by David Rabouin, Oliver Feltham, and Lissa Lincoln, 7–21. Paris: Éditions des Archives Contemporaines.

———. 2011c. *Le nombre et la sirène: Un déchiffrage du "Coup de dés" de Mallarmé.* Paris: Librairie Arthème Fayard.

———. 2011d. "Interview with Quentin Meillassoux (August 2010) (with Graham Harman)." Translated by Graham Harman. In *Quentin Meillassoux: Philosophy in the Making,* by Graham Harman, 159–74. Edinburgh: Edinburgh University Press.

———. 2011e. "Appendix: Excerpts from *L'inexistence divine.*" Translated by Graham Harman. In *Quentin Meillassoux: Philosophy in the Making,* by Graham Harman, 175–238. Edinburgh: Edinburgh University Press.

Metzinger, Thomas. 2003. *Being No One: The Self-Model Theory of Subjectivity.* Cambridge, Mass.: MIT Press.

———. 2009. *The Ego Tunnel: The Science of the Mind and the Myth of the Self.* New York: Basic Books.

Miller, Jacques-Alain. 1994. "Extimité." Edited by Elisabeth Doisneau. Translated by Françoise Massardier-Kenney. In *Lacanian Theory of Discourse: Subject, Structure, and Society,* edited by Mark Bracher, Marshall W. Alcorn Jr., Ronald J. Corthell, and Françoise Massardier-Kenney, 74–87. New York: New York University Press.

———. 1996. "A Discussion of Lacan's 'Kant with Sade.'" In *Reading Seminars I and II: Lacan's Return to Freud,* edited by Richard Feldstein, Bruce Fink, and Maire Jaanus, 212–37. Albany: State University of New York Press.

———. 1999. "Return from Granada: Knowledge and Satisfaction." Translated by Mischa Twitchin. *Psychoanalytic Notebooks of the London Circle: The Unconscious* 2 (Spring): 75–90.

———. 2001. "The Symptom and the Body Event." Translated by Barbara P. Fulks. *Lacanian Ink* 19 (Fall): 4–47.

———. 2002a. "Action de la structure." In *Un début dans la vie,* 57–85. Paris: Éditions Gallimard.

———. 2002b. "La suture: Éléments de la logique du signifiant." In *Un début dans la vie,* 94–115. Paris: Éditions Gallimard.

———. 2002c. "Elements of Epistemology." Translated by Leonardo S. Rodríguez. In *Lacan and Science,* edited by Jason Glynos and Yannis Stavrakakis, 147–65. London: Karnac Books.

———. 2004a. "Mathemes: Topology in the Teaching of Lacan." Translated by Mahlon Stoutz. In *Lacan: Topologically Speaking,* edited by Ellie Ragland and Dragan Milovanovic, 28–48. New York: Other.

———. 2004b. "Religion, Psychoanalysis." Translated by Barbara P. Fulks. *Lacanian Ink* 23 (Spring): 8–39.

Milner, Jean-Claude. 1991. "Lacan and the Ideal of Science." In *Lacan and the Human Sciences,* edited by Alexandre Leupin, 27–42. Lincoln: University of Nebraska Press.

———. 1995. *L'oeuvre claire: Lacan, la science, la philosophie.* Paris: Éditions du Seuil.

————. 2000. "De la linguistique à la linguisterie." In *Lacan, l'écrit, l'image,* edited by L'École de la Cause freudienne, 7–25. Paris: Flammarion.

————. 2002. *Le périple structural: Figures et paradigme.* Paris: Éditions du Seuil.

Moi, Toril. 2000. "Is Anatomy Destiny?: Freud and Biological Determinism." In *Whose Freud?: The Place of Psychoanalysis in Contemporary Culture,* edited by Peter Brooks and Alex Woloch, 70–92. New Haven, Conn.: Yale University Press.

Nasio, Juan-David. 1998. *Five Lessons on the Psychoanalytic Theory of Jacques Lacan.* Translated by David Pettigrew and François Raffoul. Albany: State University of New York Press.

Nassif, Jacques. 1968. "Freud et la science." *Cahiers pour l'Analyse: Généalogie des sciences* 9 (Summer): 147–67.

Nobus, Dany. 2002. "A Matter of Cause: Reflections on Lacan's 'Science and Truth.'" In *Lacan and Science,* edited by Jason Glynos and Yannis Stavrakakis, 89–118. London: Karnac Books.

————. 2003. "Lacan's Science of the Subject: Between Linguistics and Topology." In *The Cambridge Companion to Lacan,* edited by Jean-Michel Rabathé, 50–68. Cambridge, Eng.: Cambridge University Press.

Osborne, Peter. 2007. "Neo-Classic: Alain Badiou's *Being and Event.*" *Radical Philosophy* 142 (March/April): 19–29.

Pascal, Blaise. 1966. *Pensées.* Translated by A. J. Krailsheimer. New York: Penguin Books.

Ricoeur, Paul. 2004. "Structure and Hermeneutics." Translated by Kathleen McLaughlin. In *The Conflict of Interpretations,* edited by Don Ihde, 27–60. London: Continuum.

Rogers, Lesley. 2001. *Sexing the Brain.* New York: Columbia University Press.

Sade, Marquis de. 1968. *Juliette.* Translated by Austryn Wainhouse. New York: Grove.

Sartre, Jean-Paul. 1948. *Existentialism and Humanism.* Translated by Philip Mairet. London: Methuen.

Simont, Juliette. 2002. "Critique de la représentation et ontologie chez Deleuze et Badiou (Autour du 'virtuel')." In *Alain Badiou: Penser le multiple—Actes du Colloque de Bordeaux, 21–23 octobre 1999,* edited by Charles Ramond, 457–76. Paris: L'Harmattan.

Sipos, Joël. 1994. *Lacan et Descartes: La tentation métaphysique.* Paris: Presses Universitaires de France.

Smail, Daniel Lord. 2008. *On Deep History and the Brain.* Berkeley: University of California Press.

————. 2010. Personal communication with the author via e-mail. May 27, 2010.

Smith, Daniel W. 2004. "Badiou and Deleuze on the Ontology of Mathematics." In *Think Again: Alain Badiou and the Future of Philosophy,* edited by Peter Hallward, 77–93. London: Continuum.

Soler, Colette. 2002. "Hysteria in Scientific Discourse." Translated by François Raffoul and David Pettigrew. Revised and edited by Bruce Fink. In *Reading Seminar XX: Lacan's Major Work on Love, Knowledge, and Feminine Sexu-*

ality, edited by Suzanne Barnard and Bruce Fink, 47–55. Albany: State University of New York Press.

———. 2006. "Lacan en antiphilosophie." *Filozofski Vestnik: Philosophie, psychanalyse—alliance ou mésalliance?*, edited by Jelica Šumič-Riha, 27 no. 2: 121–44.

Solms, Mark, and Oliver Turnbull. 2002. *The Brain and the Inner World: An Introduction to the Neuroscience of Subjective Experience*. New York: Other.

Spinoza, Baruch. 1949. *Ethics*. Translated by William H. White. Revised by Amelia H. Stirling. New York: Hafner.

Soubbotnik, Michael. 1996. "Hobbes, Lacan, le cogito: Brèves remarques sur un théâtre d'opérations." In *Lacan, Descartes, le sujet*, edited by Erik Porge and Antonia Soulez, 107–18. Paris: Éditions Arcanes.

Tarby, Fabien. 2005a. *Matérialismes d'aujourd'hui: De Deleuze à Badiou*. Paris: L'Harmattan.

———. 2005b. *La philosophie d'Alain Badiou*. Paris: L'Harmattan.

Toscano, Alberto. 2004. "From the State to the World?: Badiou and Anti-Capitalism." *Communication & Cognition* 37, nos. 3 and 4 (2004): 199–223.

Van Haute, Philippe. 2002. *Against Adaptation: Lacan's "Subversion" of the Subject—A Close Reading*. Translated by Paul Crowe and Miranda Vankerk. New York: Other.

Vanier, Alain. 2000. *Lacan*. Translated by Susan Fairfield. New York: Other.

Varela, Francisco J., Evan Thompson, and Eleanor Rosch. 1991. *The Embodied Mind: Cognitive Science and Human Experience*. Cambridge, Mass.: MIT Press.

Vernes, Jean-René. 1982. *Critique de la raison aléatoire, ou Descartes contre Kant*. Paris: Éditions Aubier-Montaigne.

Žižek, Slavoj. 2000. "Postface: Georg Lukács as the Philosopher of Leninism." In Georg Lukács, *A Defense of "History and Class Consciousness": Tailism and the Dialectic*, translated by Esther Leslie, 151–82. London: Verso.

———. 2002a. "Foreword to the Second Edition: Enjoyment within the Limits of Reason Alone." In *For They Know Not What They Do: Enjoyment as a Political Factor*, xi–cvii. 2nd edition. London: Verso.

———. 2002b. "Afterword: Lenin's Choice." In V. I. Lenin, *Revolution at the Gates: Selected Writings of Lenin from 1917*, edited by Slavoj Žižek, 165–336. London: Verso.

———. 2006. *The Parallax View*. Cambridge, Mass.: MIT Press.

———. 2009a. "An Answer to Two Questions." In *Badiou, Žižek, and Political Transformations: The Cadence of Change*, by Adrian Johnston, 214–30. Evanston, Ill.: Northwestern University Press.

———. 2009b. "The Fear of Four Words: A Modest Plea for the Hegelian Reading of Christianity." In Slavoj Žižek and John Milbank, *The Monstrosity of Christ: Paradox or Dialectic?*, edited by Creston Davis, 24–109. Cambridge, Mass.: MIT Press.

Žižek, Slavoj, and Glyn Daly. 2004. *Conversations with Žižek*. Cambridge, Mass.: Polity.

Index